WITHDRAWN

WISDOM
⁓ FOR ⁓
EVERYDAY
LIVING

365 Daily Devotions from America's
Most Influential Christian Leaders

STEVE M. WOODS

Health Communications, Inc.
Deerfield Beach, Florida

www.hcibooks.com

242
Woods

Library of Congress Cataloging-in-Publication Data

Woods, Steve M.
  Wisdom for everyday living : 365 daily devotions from America's most influential Christian leaders / Steve M. Woods.
     p. cm.
  Includes bibliographical references and index.
  ISBN-13: 978-0-7573-1754-5 (hardback)
  ISBN-10: 0-7573-1754-5 (hardback)
  ISBN-13: 978-0-7563-1755-2 (ePub)
  ISBN-10: 0-7573-1755-3 (ePub)
  1. Christian life—Biblical teaching.   I. Title.
  BS680.C47W66 2013
  242'.2—dc23

                                               2013021763

Publisher: Health Communications, Inc.
       3201 S.W. 15th Street
       Deerfield Beach, FL 33442–8190

Cover image ©Fotolia.com
Cover and interior design by Lawna Patterson Oldfield
Inside formatting by Dawn Von Strolley Grove

Presented to:

_____

By:

_____

Contents

Acknowledgments

I want to say thank you to God for giving me the faith to believe that he would complete this devotional book, the contributors who donated their precious time to write these devotions, Nancy Jernigan and the staff at HCI Books for their pursuit of excellence with this book, and my family and friends who supported me in prayer and with their words of encouragement. This book was a vision that God gave me many years ago, and in his time it is now completed.

A true miracle from start to finish!

PLAY YOUR OWN GAME

*Then Saul dressed David in his own tunic. He put a coat of
armor on him and a bronze helmet on his head. David fastened
on his sword over the tunic and tried walking around, because
he was not used to them. "I cannot go in these," he said
to Saul, "because I am not used to them."
So he took them off.*

1 SAMUEL 17:38–39, NIV

We have all been equipped by God to do something in this world that no one else can do quite like us. Scripture from the Old Testament to the New Testament teaches that God knows us intimately and has a plan in place for each person. The writer of Hebrews put it this way: "And let us run with perseverance the race marked out for us" (Hebrews 12:1). David showed up at the battlefield to visit his brothers and found himself dressing to battle a trained nine-foot-tall warrior. However, David cannot go in Saul's armor; he had to "play his own game."

It is great to learn lessons from others, but it is important that we run the race God has given us to run. We spend a lot of time in life trying to be or live like someone else while missing what God has planned for us to do. David went out and fought Goliath the way that he had fought all of his other battles . . . with a slingshot, staff, and some smooth stones.

What has God gifted you to do? May you use your gifts each day to be the best that you can be to "serve your purpose in your generation" (Acts 13:36)!

Mike Linch
Senior Pastor, NorthStar Church, Kennesaw, GA

An Arm Around the Shoulder

Rejoice with those who rejoice.
Weep with those who weep.

ROMANS 12:15, NKJV

In 1947 Jackie Robinson was the first black man to play Major League Baseball. In his debut season with the Brooklyn Dodgers, Robinson experienced hatred nearly everywhere. Pitchers threw fastballs at his head. Runners spiked him on the bases. During one game, tension reached a peak. Robinson committed an error and stood at second base humiliated while the fans hurled insults at him. Dodger Pee Wee Reese, a man from the South, called time-out. Reese walked from his position at shortstop toward Robinson at second base. He put his arm around Robinson's shoulder. The fans grew quiet. Robinson later said that arm around his shoulder saved his career.

Encouragement can be an arm on a shoulder, a smile, or a simple compliment. Pray to the Lord to make you a friend. "A friend loveth at all times" (Proverbs 17:17, KJV).

Holy Father, help me today to speak a timely word to a weary soul. Help me to be a friend to encourage someone today in Jesus's name.

Dr. Roger Freeman
Senior Pastor (Retired), First Baptist Church, Clarksville, TN

START SOMEWHERE

All hard work brings a profit, but mere
talk leads only to poverty.

PROVERBS 14:23, NIV

Stonewall Jackson, a great military general known for his absolute, unswerving determination, once said, "You may be whatever you resolve to be." He was exactly right. The Word of God is filled with this truth. Personal resolve has the power to take you past intimidation to the dreams in your heart.

If you have a dream of becoming an artist, pick up a paintbrush and start creating. If you want to become the CEO of a large corporation, you need to do well in school, take extra classes, or get your MBA. Talk to people in your field of interest and see what steps they took to achieve success, and most important, pray about the direction to take. The anointing and power of God enables you to achieve the highest and best that God has for you, no matter the obstacles you may face. That power, though, is released only through your preparation and personal resolve.

Never get stuck at good intentions. Put action to your dreams today, and step by step, you'll see them become a reality.

Mac Hammond
Senior Pastor, Living Word Christian Center, Brooklyn Park, MN

CHOOSING JOY

Consider it pure joy, my brothers, whenever
you face trials of many kinds, because you know that
the testing of your faith develops perseverance.
Perseverance must finish its work so that you may be
mature and complete, not lacking anything.

JAMES 1:2–4, NIV

*O*ne Sunday I had preached about choosing joy when you encounter trials of every kind. But it was only a few days later, and I was frustrated and perturbed over a quickly fixed computer glitch. One of the staff greeted me during my computer malfunction and tried to fist-bump me hello. But I said, "I am not fist-bumping this morning," and I whined. Later that day, my staff member asked me graciously, "Did you listen to the message you preached on Sunday?"

Ouch. Double ouch. I felt really humbled and had nothing to say. I was guilty of doing the exact opposite of what I had preached about.

The Spirit of God used that friend to confront me. But instead of wallowing over the fact that I had blown it, the Spirit urged me to repent and choose to walk in a new direction (1 John 1:9). Maybe you are in the same place. You had every intention of walking in the Spirit this week . . . but then you blew it. Now you have a choice. You can either wallow in your blunder or you can put on joy. Choosing a new attitude does not guarantee your day will get easier. In fact, it may actually get harder! But remember, "The joy of the LORD is your strength" (Nehemiah 8:10)!

Mike Bickley
Senior Pastor, Olathe Bible Church, Olathe, KS

SONG IN THE NIGHT

I will remember my song in the night.

PSALM 77:6, NASB

orrie ten Boom was sent to a Nazi death camp during World War II. There she witnessed many people get murdered—and her own sister died from anemia. She, too, felt the sting of a whip against her back. But in her account of the terrible things that transpired all around her in that camp, she writes of the secret Bible study, hymn singing, and acts of compassion that were bringing light into the darkness of the camp.

Corrie penned these profound words in her journal: "However deep the pit, God's love is deeper still!" That's exactly what the psalmist discovered as well in his own time of darkness. The darker his night grew, the louder his song became.

Is that true for you as well? Are you able to see God's light shining in your own darkness? There's a choice you need to make in life. A lot of people in that Nazi death camp gave up on God. They let the darkness hide him . . . and overwhelm them. But not Corrie ten Boom. She chose to remember her song in the night.

Will you?

Dr. Stephen Davey
Senior Pastor, Colonial Baptist Church, Cary, NC

EMBRACE COMMUNITY

Let us not give up meeting together, as some are
in the habit of doing, but let us encourage one another—
and all the more as you see the day approaching.

People are pesky. They betray us. They hurt us. They trample our hearts. So why even try? Why not just give in to bitterness and isolate ourselves for the rest of our lives? Because we will never grow in life if we cut ourselves off from others.

"God's most beautiful jewels are often delivered in rough packages by very difficult people, but within the package we will find the very treasure of the king's palace and the bridegroom's love" (A. B. Simpson).

In short, we grow better together.

I've lamented this truth because it doesn't always make sense to me. If people hurt me, wouldn't it be wiser to steer clear of them? If I did that, I could prevent future bitterness and protect my heart from injury. Isn't an uninjured heart better?

Actually, no. It's the healed heart that dares to risk in relationship again that changes the world.

Here's a hard truth: When we're injured by others, God often asks us to reengage with a safe community to heal our hearts. Do you have a heart in need of healing? If so, may you find the loving embrace for your wounded heart in God's community.

Mary DeMuth
Speaker and Author, www.marydemuth.com

CATCHING EXCELLENCE

Whatever you do, work at it with all your heart,
as working for the Lord, not for men, since you know
that you will receive an inheritance from
the Lord as a reward. It is the Lord
Christ you are serving.

COLOSSIANS 3:23–24, NIV84

I love football. Growing up in the 1960s also made me a Green Bay Packer fan. Their legendary coach, Vince Lombardi, offered enough quotes to fill a book, but one stands out in my mind: "We're going to relentlessly chase perfection, knowing full well we will not catch it, because perfection is not attainable. But we are going to relentlessly chase it because in the process, we will catch excellence."

God demands our best in life: in worship, in the home, and at the workplace. We should strive for perfection in each of these areas, knowing we will fall miserably short on this side of heaven. But in seeking only the highest standard, we can attain a level of excellence in all we do or say. Our Heavenly Father deserves no less. Don't give a halfhearted effort in anything. God is watching. The bar is high; life is challenging. Always give him and those around you your very best!

David Welsh
Senior Pastor, Central Christian Church, Wichita, KS

GETTING UNSTUCK

I don't know about you, but from time to time I get stuck. The image I have in my head is that of a driver whose tire is stuck in a muddy hole. No matter how fast he spins the wheels, the car goes nowhere. The psychologists who are much smarter than I am might even have a word for it: depression. I'm not always sure just how I get to that place, but from time to time I get the blues. When my wheels are just spinning, I want to turn off the car and quit.

The psalmist has an interesting promise for those of us who might get depressed. He writes, "Those who sow in tears shall reap in joy. He who continually goes forth weeping, bearing seed for sowing, shall doubtless come again with rejoicing, bringing his sheaves with him" (Psalm 126:5–6, NKJV).

Pay attention to what is being said. The farmer isn't planting seeds made of tears. The farmer is planting seeds *despite* his tears. Sowing seed is simply what a farmer must do if he wants to have an actual harvest. The idea here is simply this: Don't stop. You may want to quit because of your tears, but you can't. The farmer can't stop sowing his seeds if he wants to put food on his table and provide for his family. If the farmer will sow his seed, even though he's weeping, there will be a day when he reaps his harvest, and the harvest will come with joy.

Feel like your wheels are spinning? You may need to get out of the car and start walking. Keep sowing. Don't stop.

Rich Cathers
Senior Pastor, Calvary Chapel, Fullerton, CA

ACCEPT RESPONSIBILITY

Be very careful, then, how you live—
not as unwise but as wise, making the most of every
opportunity, because the days are evil.

EPHESIANS 5:15–16, NIV84

*O*ne of the most important qualities of all successful people is that they are able to accept responsibility. You will grow in life when you see an opportunity, step out, and accept the responsibility involved. Look at each opportunity as a chance to learn something new and challenging. The popular phrase *"carpe diem"* [seize the day] should be your motto.

Own your actions and choices. Like everyone else, you make choices and take actions. When your actions have positive results, it is easy to take credit and compliments for what you've done. However, owning your choices and actions when circumstances do not go well is much harder (Proverbs 19:3, 8; 27:23–24).

Learn from failure. Hopefully your life will be full of many successes. But all of us have times when we fail. You may get discouraged or down on yourself, or even give up. But have faith and remember: These failures are often God's stepping-stones for future success.

Judy Douglass
Author, Campus Crusade for Christ

A Vibrant Faith

am not sure there is anything less useful than a flat tire. The same is true for a flat faith.

In Mark 9:21–24, we read about a boy afflicted with a demon and the intervention of Christ. Toward the end of the passage, after Christ tells the man, "Everything is possible for one who believes," the father responds, "I do believe; help me overcome my unbelief" (NIV). I think a lot of us could utter that same plea.

It has been a while since I sat in a science classroom, but I seem to recall that cold is not itself a property, only the absence of heat. The less heat, the colder we feel. Is unbelief, then, a property, or merely the absence of faith? Further, is it possible that we cannot really feel God's presence until we have experienced his absence? In the ebbs and flow of life, each of us has felt the cold of unbelief, followed by the warmth of our Father's embrace.

If one can live a life of faith without significant testing from time to time, then that is a wonderful thing . . . and rare. However, if one can know faith—work through personal challenge and uncertainty only to return—then I think that is a deeply blessed person, once described by William James as "twice born."

Andrew K. Benton
President and CEO, Pepperdine University, Malibu, CA

WORRY? SOME

Worry. It comes easily to most of us. In Matthew 6:25, Jesus is teaching in what we now know to be the Sermon on the Mount. Underlining the need to choose whether to serve God or something else with our lives, he warns, "Therefore I tell you, do not worry about your life, what you will eat or drink; or about your body, what you will wear" (NIV).

The word "worry" here literally means "to be drawn in a different direction." To worry is to be torn. When we react to stress with worry, it's like dividing ourselves in two. Half of us is focused on God and his power; the other half directed toward the eventuality we fear. Half toward hope, half toward disaster.

Some worry is inevitable as we face that which we can't humanly control. But when we give ourselves over to worry, we divide our attention and therefore our energy. We won't parent well while investing half of our efforts in worrying. We won't pay careful attention to the events of our world while our eyes are distracted by our fears.

Worry? Some. It's natural. It's normal. But remember that in the end, worry solves nothing. Put your energy—heart and head—into prayer instead.

"Do not be anxious about anything, but in everything, by prayer and petition, with thanksgiving, present your requests to God. And the peace of God, which transcends all understanding, will guard your hearts and your minds in Christ Jesus" (Philippians 4:6–7).

Elisa Morgan
Author, Speaker, Publisher, www.fullfill.org
President Emerita, MOPS International

PEOPLE OF VISION

Record the vision and inscribe it on tablets. . . .
Though it tarries, wait for it; for it
will certainly come, it will not delay.

HABAKKUK 2:2–3, NASB

*A*nything worth having takes time. "What we obtain too easily, we esteem too lightly," Thomas Paine wrote. But in addition to hard work and the occasional long wait or detour through the wilderness, the Bible says that a key ingredient is vision. Never underestimate the momentum that comes from having a goal or a dream.

Thousands have tried to conquer Mount Everest. Of those who make the attempt, only one in seven make it to the top. One of the greatest factors in success versus failure is the climbers' ability to see where they are headed. When storms blow in and obscure the top of the mountain, the climbers grow discouraged and despondent and consider retreat. But when storm air clears and the peak is again visible, the journey becomes easier, commitment renews, and faith is strengthened. Suddenly, getting there feels possible.

Setting your mind on something ahead and believing in it motivates, mobilizes, fuels, and inspires like nothing else. Ask God to give you a view of where you're heading with him. Fix your eyes on the "peak" and keep climbing.

Shawn Mitchell
Senior Pastor, New Venture Christian Fellowship, Oceanside, CA

YOUR LIFE MATTERS

*For we are His workmanship, created in Christ Jesus
for good works, which God prepared beforehand
so that we would walk in them.*

EPHESIANS 2:10, NASB

There have been times in my life when I have gazed up at the night sky and pondered the vastness of the universe, or looked at a globe and been overwhelmed by the sheer number of people living in every corner of the world. In those moments I wonder about my value when I am such a small part of such a big place. God has often used Ephesians 2:10 to encourage me in three specific ways.

1. *We have worth.* We are God's workmanship. We are not an accident, a worthless throwaway, or a random product of chance. Rather, we are a priceless work of art, a treasured creation handcrafted by the God of the universe.
2. *We have purpose.* We are created to do good works. We were made for a reason and have a heavenly responsibility to fulfill. Each of us has a calling, placed there by God himself. We were meant to make a lasting difference in this world. We were meant to matter.
3. *We have potential.* Our times and circumstances are not an accident. God prepared a plan for our lives long before we were ever born. As we partner with God, we unlock the hidden potential inside of us by discovering our role in redemptive history and by connecting others to God in a way no one else can.

Scott Chapman
*Senior Pastor and President, Christ Together
The Chapel, Northern Chicagoland, IL*

THE WIND/RUACH

Since we live by the Spirit, let us keep in step with the Spirit.

GALATIANS 5:25, NIV

The Hebrew word for wind is *ruach*, and the word even sounds like the wind rushing by. *Ruach* is also the word for the Spirit of God (*Ruach ha Kodesh*, "the Holy Wind"), and this is powerful. At first you might think it is easy to live against the Spirit and walk in sin (selfishness, greed, worldliness, lust, and so on). But think again. You're living against the *Ruach*. You're walking against the wind.

Have you ever walked against the wind? Life becomes difficult. Every action is harder. You get tired, weary, burdened . . . aerodynamically speaking it creates drag. Likewise when we live against the *Ruach*, we get tired and weary, and life becomes a drag. But God doesn't want our life to be a drag. That's why he calls us to walk by the Spirit in the way of love, faith, purity, dying to self, sacrifice, truth, giving no compromise, and doing what we know is right.

Do you think it's too hard to live God's way? It's just the opposite. Life is too hard not to walk by the Spirit. Remember, the Spirit is the *Ruach*. When you walk by the Spirit of God, the wind is at your back! So if your life has become a drag, God has something much better. Jesus said, "Come to Me all you who are weary and heavy-laden, and I will give you rest. . . . My yoke is easy and My burden is light" (Matthew 11:28, 30, NASB). You want life? The answer, my friend, is blowing in the wind. It's as simple as turning around! Walk by the *Ruach*, walk in the Spirit, and he will turn your drag into a breeze.

Jonathan Cahn
Author, The Harbinger, *Senior Pastor and Messianic Rabbi
the Jerusalem Center / Beth Israel, Wayne, NJ*

Our Refuge and Fortress

He who dwells in the shelter of the Most High will rest
in the shadow of the Almighty. I will say of the LORD,
"He is my refuge and my fortress, my God, in whom I trust."

PSALM 91:1–2, NIV

It's powerful to have faith in this simple truth: God is with us. Sometimes during life's challenges we may lose sight of this simple truth. We must not, as it could change everything.

During difficult times, some may even find themselves shipwrecked in their faith. I experienced this at seventeen years old when my father was killed in a car accident. Even though he was a man of faith, I lost my sight and my heart was wounded. For many years while entering into my adult life, I felt that I was letting go of God. I began to lead a life of superficial goals, comprehending only what was apparent, obvious, and shallow. Today, I know that God's love is everlasting and he promised never to leave me or forsake me. This became my "refuge and my fortress."

I learned that prayer is the key to finding God as my refuge and fortress. May you choose to go to God through prayer, practicing his presence, placing your trust and confidence in him and the promises in his Word. God will bring you the rest that is promised. You will find his loving guidance through grace in your daily tasks. Remember, those who put their hope in the Lord will renew their strength and find the grace and understanding they need.

Paige Junaeus
Founder, Paige Junaeus Ministries, International Speaker,
Columnist, and Creative, www.turn2paige.com

Keeping Him First

Trust in the LORD with all your heart
and lean not on your own understanding;
in all your ways acknowledge him,
and he will make your paths straight.

PROVERBS 3:5–6, NIV84

'm often asked, "What's the most difficult thing about being a pastor? Preaching? Counseling? Administration?" While any one of these tasks can be daunting and demanding on any given day, there is something even more difficult.

The greatest challenge pastors face is probably the very one that you face: maintaining a personal, growing relationship with Jesus. How do we keep him first? Our primary task as followers of Christ is to ensure that no relationship, career, duty, or possession replaces Jesus as the primary desire in our hearts. This remains the most difficult activity in our daily walk.

The early Christians in Ephesus knew the Word, served the Lord faithfully, and endured persecution patiently. Yet the Lord told them, "You have forsaken your first love" (Revelation 2:4). Service, stewardship, and study aren't enough. We just can't put spirituality on a checklist. That's because Christianity is not a religion; it is a relationship. The Lord is very concerned with the condition of our hearts toward him. So ask yourself, *Is Jesus first in my life?*

David Welsh
Senior Pastor, Central Christian Church, Wichita, KS

WORDS CREATE WORLDS

*A new commandment I give to you, that you love one
another; as I have loved you, that you also love one another.
By this all will know that you are my disciples,
if you have love for one another.*

JOHN 13:34–35, NKJV

*T*ry this thirty-second, simple, powerful, impacting exercise of love and affirmation. Look at your spouse, a youngster, or your grandchild right in the eyes and tell that person, "You know what I really love about you?"

- Your thoughtfulness, kindness, gentleness . . .
- How you share, serve, give . . .
- How you go to work or look for work . . .
- How you keep calm when I'm not . . .
- How you listen, smile, etc., etc. . . .

Then say, "The Lord bless you!" and "I love you!" Then give them a noogie on the head! (Okay, that last one is a joke.) Remember, Proverbs 18:21 states that our words have the "power of life and death" (NIV) in someone's life. I hope the words you speak to others will bring life. Remember, words create worlds in the lives of others.

Victor Marx
Founder and President, All Things Possible Ministries

Avoiding Aaron's Actions

The people gathered together to Aaron, and
said to him, "Come, make us gods."

EXODUS 32:1, NKJV

As Moses was leading the Israelites through the wilderness, God told Moses to meet with him atop Mount Sinai. So Moses left his brother, Aaron, in charge. After several days the people started getting restless. They questioned if Moses was coming back and put pressure on Aaron to come up with a new god to guide them.

That's exactly what Aaron did. The Bible tells us he gave in to the demands for a new god. He gathered together all of their gold jewelry and created a calf similar to the idols that were worshiped back in Egypt.

We've all experienced being in a position where people want us to do something that's wrong. But the pressure mounts, and we reach a place of just wanting to make them happy. We become people pleasers at the expense of pleasing God, which is always a mistake. Pleasing God is always the right choice . . . period!

If you sense people pressuring you to please them, stop and seek the Lord. Ask him what would please him—and do it with a clear conscience.

Bob Coy
Senior Pastor, Calvary Chapel, Fort Lauderdale, FL

SPAM FOLDER

With this in mind, we constantly pray for you,
that our God may make you worthy of his calling,
and that by his power he may bring to fruition
your every desire for goodness and your
every deed prompted by faith.

2 THESSALONIANS 1:11, NIV

*J*unk email—you know, spam. Thankfully we have computer programs to remove those pesky emails, and on most days they go into the spam folder without notice. But every now and then the program can't tell the difference between the emails we don't want and an email that is important or valuable. Have you ever wondered how many emails you've missed because they've been automatically discarded?

The National Science Foundation says that the average person will have 12,000 thoughts per day. No doubt some of these thoughts could be considered spam: random thoughts, maybe temptations that need to be immediately discarded. But some promptings are from God: "Help that person in need," "Express words of appreciation to that friend," "Share your testimony with that person." It's important that we don't let these promptings from God fall into our spam folders. Therefore, the next time you hear a message from God, don't ignore it like spam; act on it instead.

C. H. Dyer
President, Bright Hope, CHDyer.com

SUCCESSFUL IN PRAYER

👑 LUKE 1:1–24 (BIBLE READ)

There is surely a future hope for you, and
your hope will not be cut off.

PROVERBS 23:18, NIV

One of the best lessons on being successful in prayer can be found in John the Baptist's parents, Zacharias and Elizabeth. They prayed for years, and God always said "Wait" when it came to having a son. But they showed us how to be successful when God says "Wait."

First, Zacharias served God, even though his prayer wasn't answered. Second, Zacharias was ready to serve, so he got called in to burn the incense in the temple. That just happened to be the day the angel Gabriel appeared to him to tell him of his son to be, and all the great things he would do in the kingdom of God. This answer to prayer was far beyond any of his dreams about having a son some day. But he didn't just sit home wishing he could have a son; he was busy serving God in the temple when his miracle was delivered.

Let us go to God's house and serve him. Let's wait on our prayers together.

Steve Price
Senior Pastor, Calvary Chapel, Bear Creek, CA

STAND FIRM

*It is God who enables us, along with you,
to stand firm for Christ.*

2 CORINTHIANS 1:21, NLT

In years past, when shipbuilders were planning on making a great ship, they knew that the life of the crew and the safety of the cargo depended upon the ship's mainmast.

To make the mainmast, they would find a straight, tall tree on the top of a mountain near the coast. Then they would cut down all the other trees around it so that it would be exposed to the full force of the angry winds and mighty gusts that blew off the sea. After many years of exposure to such harshness, the tree would become stronger and stronger, its very fiber being strengthened by the intense buffeting it was experiencing day after day. Finally, after many testing storms alone on the mountaintop, the tree was ready to be trusted as the mainmast of a great ship.

Do you feel like that tree, singled out and everything around you cut away? Maybe you thought you were being picked on or judged by God. Instead, it might be that God has marked you out for a great purpose in his kingdom's plan.

Mark Martin
Senior Pastor, Calvary Community Church, Phoenix, AZ

An Example to Follow

You, however, know all about my teaching, my way of life,
my purpose, faith, patience, love, endurance, persecutions,
sufferings—what kinds of things happened to me in Antioch,
Iconium, and Lystra, the persecutions I endured.
Yet the Lord rescued me from all of them.

2 TIMOTHY 3:10–11, NIV

Ancient Christian writings state that the apostle Paul was "a man small of stature, with a bald head and crooked legs, in a good state of body, with eyebrows meeting and nose somewhat hooked." Timothy could have thought, "You know, I'd really rather have a mentor who was actually one of the twelve disciples of Jesus . . . and this guy Paul—actually, well, he's rockin' the unibrow—and personally I think I could mentor *him* in how to use some tweezers!" Obviously, Timothy didn't come to this conclusion.

In 2 Timothy 3:10, Paul is describing a long-term mentoring relationship that both he and Timothy were well acquainted with. Apparently Timothy did "know all about it," because he had paid attention to Paul's character, teaching, and suffering as the mentor God had provided for him.

For you to grow in wisdom through God's Word, you need a mentor too. Pay attention to the mentors God gives you. Today, ask yourself who the godly mentors are in your life. How can you be more deliberate about learning from them?

John V. Hansen
Lead Pastor, Centerpoint Church, Murrieta, CA

FINISH STRONG

Do you not know that in a race all the runners run,
but only one gets the prize? Run in such a way as to get the prize.
Everyone who competes in the games goes into strict training.
They do it to get a crown that will not last, but we do it
to get a crown that will last forever. Therefore I do not run
like someone running aimlessly; I do not fight like a boxer
beating the air. No, I strike a blow to my body and make
it my slave so that after I have preached to others,
I myself will not be disqualified for the prize.

1 CORINTHIANS 9:24–27, NIV

*L*ife with Christ is not a life for the weak or the faint of heart. It is demanding, requiring commitment, focus, and intentionality. As an athlete rigorously trains to win in his sport, so we as Christians are to wholeheartedly commit to following Christ and doing all that he requires of us that we might be effective for him.

God has given all of us specific talents and purposes in the body of Christ. We must identify our talents and purposes and strive to be the best at using our gifts and accomplishing our purposes for God's kingdom. Paul tells us not to get sidetracked because staying on task is vital to accomplishing our goals. When we stay focused on the work God has for us to do and we discipline ourselves to do his work well, our lives cannot be meaningless.

Let us not live wasted lives. Know your purpose. Aim for it. Pursue it with passion and excellence. Finish first and finish strong!

Chuck Booher
Senior Pastor, Crossroads Christian Church, Corona, CA

23

SILENCE

My soul, wait silently for God alone,
for my expectation is from Him. He only is my rock
and my salvation; He is my defense; I shall not be moved.

We live in such a fast-paced and noisy culture. We have the radio, television, computer, iPods, and other gadgets so that we can listen to people and music constantly. We seem to be afraid of silence—afraid to hear from God.

It is really important for us to listen when the Lord is speaking to our hearts. We should respond, but there is a time when we need to step back and be silent, so that we can hear what God has to say.

The best times for me to listen for the Lord are when I am completely by myself, and I can give myself fully and completely without any interruptions. Then I can hear from the Lord. It is a blessing for me. I get to pray for my wife, my family, and myself, and no one is talking to me. I get to talk to the Lord, and, more important, he talks to me. That is the conversation I want to have.

Take time daily, not just to pray and speak to God, but to be silent and wait for his response.

Raul Ries
Senior Pastor, Calvary Chapel Golden Springs, Diamond Bar, CA

His Garden

There are great stories of valor and triumph that come from World War II. When Japan invaded China, many people were assigned to concentration camps. These camps were brutal places of inhuman treatment, and many didn't survive the ordeal. Those who did were forever changed.

One man, a Christian pastor, was imprisoned in one of these horrible places. While there, his assignment was to clean out the cesspool. Every day he was to wade into the quagmire of human waste and unclog the drainage system. This task was vile and unthinkable, but this godly man embraced his lot in life with joy. How?

Upon his release he shared that he learned to love the cesspool. He learned to treat it as his private place to meet with God. While in the cesspool he could sing, pray, and quote Scripture without the harassment of the guards. He called the cesspool his garden.

I have learned that there are times you have to wade into the cesspool. I have also learned that the cesspool can become a place where you can meet God and grow to become more dependent on him and his Holy Spirit. There is an old hymn called "In the Garden"; every time I sing it, I think about the cesspool.

Scott Weatherford
Lead Pastor, First Alliance Church, Calgary, AB, Canada

A Sharp Knife

As iron sharpens iron, so one person sharpens another.

PROVERBS 27:17, NIV

Great chefs know that a dull blade renders a knife nearly useless in the kitchen. A sharp blade makes swift work at the cutting board and increases safety. Dull blades are not tolerated.

Proverbs 27:17 illustrates the importance of the people in our lives who are intentional with us so that we develop into useful and sharp tools for God's purposes. Through confession, accountability, truth telling, and instruction, the intentional acts of mentoring and discipleship prepare us to be used by God for his work in the world. Each of us, in our walk of faith, is called to be sharpened and to sharpen others.

Do you have a friend who speaks into your life with wisdom and discernment? Are you allowing the Holy Spirit to use you for accountability, confession, and truth telling in the life of a friend?

Father, give us the humility to accept correction and the courage to speak the truth in love. Please mold us into useful tools sharpened for your assignment. Amen.

Jon R. Wallace, DBA
President, Azusa Pacific University, Azusa, CA

LIVING LIKE AN UNDERCOVER BOSS

Sitting down, Jesus called the Twelve and said,
"If anyone wants to be first, he must be
the very last, and the servant of all."

MARK 9:35, NIV84

A television program, *Undercover Boss*, provides helpful insight on the kind of humble character Christ desires of his followers. The story line involves the CEO of a mid-sized company disguising himself or herself as a new, lower-level employee. Cameras discreetly follow the "worker" experiencing the rigors and challenges of the employees. At the conclusion of the show, the CEO (typically) weeps with humility at the epiphany of what life is like at the bottom of the food chain in his or her own company. By purposing to take a lower position, the boss learned a thing or two about true greatness.

In Luke 9:46, the disciples were arguing "as to which of them would be the greatest." Did you ever consider how incredibly presumptuous it was of them to assume that one of them deserved to be *greatest* in Christ's kingdom? Did you observe how a craving for personal greatness was so deeply embedded in their hearts that it drove them to an argument? In God's upside-down kingdom, the greatest person is not the person who is at the top. Rather, the greatest person is the one who is at the bottom. Jesus asks all believers to live a daily life of simplicity and humility, and to consider others better than ourselves. May we walk with grace and humility this day.

Gary Hoyt
Senior Pastor, Bellevue Christian Center, Bellevue, NE

GOD WILL BE WORSHIPED

👑 PSALM 99 (BIBLE READ)

Let everything that has breath praise the Lord. Praise the Lord!

PSALM 150:6, NKJV

What is going on in heaven right now? We can't fully answer this question, but the Bible contains occasional glimpses that do offer some insight. In Genesis 28, Jacob saw God stationed at the top of a ladder filled with angelic beings ascending and descending in constant motion. It was an unforgettable sight for this budding patriarch.

Isaiah saw God "high and lifted up, and the train of his robe filled the temple" (Isaiah 6:1). He also saw a myriad of heavenly beings moving about in God's presence, worshiping him.

What do we learn from stories like these? First, God is awesome! He is glorious. We are catching only a glimpse of the true nature of our God. Second, he is being worshiped. That's right. God is already being worshiped by his creation. Regardless of what you or I ever do, he *will* be worshiped.

Our God is glorious. Further, our God will be worshiped. Isn't it incredible that he has invited you to join your voice with the eternal heavenly chorus in worship?

Have you ever had an overwhelming sense of God's presence? When? Where?

Dennis R. Wiles, PhD
Senior Pastor, First Baptist Church, Arlington, TX

Do Sweat the Small Stuff

But David said to Saul, "Your servant has been
keeping his father's sheep. When a lion or a bear came and
carried off a sheep from the flock, I went after it . . .
Your servant has killed both the lion and the bear;
this uncircumcised Philistine will be like one of them,
because he has defied the armies of the living God."

1 SAMUEL 17:34, 36, NIV84

Everyone wants the big opportunities to come their way; how-ever, most people miss how the small things in life prepare them. The small things more often than not are done in private and are not noticed by anyone. It is easy to think of those things as wasted time spent in anonymity when, in reality, it is the quiet times spent in solitude that prepare us for the great things that God has in store.

God may have you in one of the quiet places right now. You may feel lonely or forgotten, or assume your time is being wasted some-how. However, it may be God's appointed obscurity that is preparing you for the big things that he has in store for you.

I remember a great Bible teacher named Ron Dunn who was famous for saying, "God never wastes time, and he never wastes our experiences."

Remember, your experiences are never wasted and God may be using some right now to get you ready for something great! Will you be ready?

Mike Linch
Senior Pastor, NorthStar Church, Kennesaw, GA

Seize the Day

For to me, to live is Christ
and to die is gain.

PHILIPPIANS 1:21, NASB

In the movie *Dead Poets Society*, Robin Williams plays a professor who teaches his class the Latin phrase *carpe diem*, which means "seize the day." Thus inspired, their adventure is exhilarating at first, but it soon takes a horrifying turn as one boy, seizing the day, commits suicide. What went so horribly wrong?

In Genesis 41:16, a young Joseph's life also begins full of enthusiasm but soon takes a horrific turn, and he, too, seizes the day. Pharaoh summons Joseph to interpret a dream, but Joseph boldly responds, "I cannot interpret your dream, but God can." And Joseph's adventure ends wonderfully.

What's the difference? The problem with *carpe diem* is that the unspoken suggestion is to seize the day for oneself, which inevitably puts one at odds with others who also are trying to do the same. The result is often disaster. Instead of *carpe diem*, Joseph practiced what might be called *carpe diem Deo*: seize the day for God! Joseph knew the secret: a life lived for God is the wisest and most exciting life of all.

Rick Stedman
Senior Pastor, Adventure Christian Church, Roseville, CA

THE PURPOSE OF
THE COMMANDMENT

Now the purpose of the commandment is love from
a pure heart, from a good conscience, and from sincere faith,
from which some, having strayed, have turned aside
to idle talk, desiring to be teachers of the law, understanding
neither what they say nor the things which they affirm.

1 TIMOTHY 1:5–7, NKJV

The commandment Paul refers to here was his commission to Timothy to remain in Ephesus and deal with false teachers. Both the motive and goal of all he did had to be love: love for God and his people.

False doctrine stokes pride and an arrogant self-righteousness that eclipses love. Show me a false teacher, and I'll show you someone who's superior and judgmental. Such people may appear at first to be humble, but spend a little time with them and the arrogance reveals itself. Find someone cleaving faithfully to the gospel of grace, and you'll discover a selfless love.

We live in an age that Jesus said in Matthew 24:4, 11, 23–25 would be marked by great deception—so deep, even the elect would be in peril of being led astray. An important test we can apply to what we hear is to ask, *Does this move me to a deeper love of God and others? Or does this appeal to my flesh? Is this about elevating* my *glory or* God's?

Lance E. Ralston
Senior Pastor, Calvary Chapel, Oxnard, CA

Turning Our
Problems into Prayer

Don't worry about anything; instead, pray about everything.
Tell God what you need, and thank him for all he has done. Then
you will experience God's peace, which exceeds anything
we can understand. His peace will guard your hearts
and minds as you live in Christ Jesus.

PHILIPPIANS 4:6–7, NLT

*H*ave you ever noticed that 95 percent of the things you spend so much time worrying about never happen? What a huge waste of time and emotional energy.

The Bible tells us that we can spare ourselves a whole lot of stress and honor God a lot more by turning our problems into prayers.

Obviously, God is big enough to handle our cares. He's much more experienced at solving problems than we are.

I read of a weary Christian who was lying awake one night trying to hold the world together by his worrying. Then he heard the Lord gently say to him, "Now you go to sleep, Jim, I'll sit up."

"Praise the Lord; praise God our savior! For each day he carries us in his arms" (Psalm 68:19).

Mark Martin
Senior Pastor, Calvary Community Church, Phoenix, AZ

WE ARE HIS SHEEP

*G*od often refers to his children as sheep. Psalm 95:7 reads, "For He is our God, and we are the people of His pasture, and the sheep of His hand (NASB)".

Sheep have several unique characteristics. First, they cannot protect themselves. They are defenseless animals. Second, they easily wander from the shepherd's path, so they must be watched over constantly. Third, they must be led to food and water. Unlike most animals, they have no natural sense of what is good or bad for them. Fourth, they must be constantly cleaned. Their skin is naturally greasy, which causes their wool to pick up everything in their environment, such as burrs, seeds, dirt, and bugs. Without constant tending, sheep make a mess of themselves. Fifth, because of their natural tendency to pick up all kinds of parasites and diseases, the shepherd must look over each of his sheep daily to make sure that none is infested.

When we mull it over, it seems as though God created sheep specifically to be a spiritual example for his people. How grateful we should be for his daily, watchful care. The old hymn by Joseph Hart, "How Good Is the God We Adore" is still true today: "How good is the God we adore, our faithful, unchangeable Friend! His love is as great as His power, and knows neither measure nor end!" Let's give thanks today for our Great Shepherd!

Ron Hindt
Senior Pastor, Calvary Chapel, Houston, TX

FINDING YOUR IDENTITY

As you know, we count as blessed those who have persevered.
You have heard of Job's perseverance and have seen what the LORD
finally brought about. The LORD is full of compassion and mercy.

I wonder what Job would say if he knew that his name was synonymous with suffering and loss. Would he agree with us that his life was defined by the things he lost? Or would he argue that his life was better depicted in his faithfulness through the trials and the blessings he received afterward? Job's response to his loss tells us where he found his identity.

Job was the richest man in the east, blessed beyond blessing, beyond proportion, beyond measure. He was the man with the Midas touch in his day. And not only that, but he had a great family, too. He lost all of that in literally one day. Everything came crashing down, and he was left with four servants who had nothing to do and a bitter wife who wanted him to die. Yet through it all, he never turned from God. He remained patient and faithful. And in the end, God gave him double what he had lost, including seven sons and three daughters. Job's faith, attitude, and will to honor God in his words sustained him through the loss and pain. Job's life was defined by God and not by his possessions, family, or anything else this world had to offer.

Are you grounded in a God-centered identity? If you are, then you can be remembered like Job, unshakable regardless the trial, faithful to the end, and rewarded of God.

Bob Botsford
Senior Pastor, Horizon Christian Fellowship North, Rancho Santa Fe, CA

By Faith

For we walk by faith, not by sight.

2 CORINTHIANS 5:7, NASB

It turns out that watching Christian television and sitting in church do not on their own lead to the abundant life promised by Jesus any more than watching exercise DVDs sheds unwanted pounds. The entertainment industry has spawned a generation of couch potatoes. More recently, computers have given us mouse potatoes—a growing horde of people who waste countless hours surfing the Internet. Now we have iPads and smartphones so that we can socially network without ever getting out of bed. Who needs to expend the energy to go to the couch?

The transition from watching life happen to actually living life can be described with two words: by faith. "For we walk by faith, not by sight" (2 Corinthians 5:7, NASB). Like a new credit card that does not work until activated by calling the toll-free number, the blessings of God lie around like unopened Christmas presents until activated by a faith that walks. Has the time come to stop sitting and observing and to start walking and experiencing God's best?

Dr. Jim Reeve
Senior Pastor, Faith Community Church, West Covina, CA

PATIENCE

Be completely humble and gentle; be patient,
bearing with one another in love.

*T*he noun "patience," though a significant ancient concept in Hebrews, is not found in the King James Version of the Old Testament. Instead we find it as the adjective "patient." The Hebrew word translated "long-suffering" is the one most commonly used in the Old Testament to indicate patience.

One of the most soul stirring of all passages using this human term for God's patience is found in 2 Peter 3:9: "The Lord is not slack concerning His promise, as some count slackness but is long-suffering [patient] toward us, not willing that any should perish but that all should come to repentance" (NKJV).

James the brother of Jesus also emphasized the hope in Christ that is the underpinning of our faith and the reason for our patience: "Be patient, brethren, until the coming of the Lord. See how the farmer waits for the precious fruit of the earth, waiting patiently for it until it receives the early and latter rain. You also be patient. Establish your hearts, for the coming of the Lord is at hand" (James 5:7–8).

Patience is not a desperate soul waiting in doubt, but a hopeful heart waiting in confidence.

Eugene Burrage
Senior Pastor, Original Greater Rock M.B. Church, Chicago, IL

UNTIE YOUR FAITH

Now faith is confidence in what we
hope for and assurance about what we do not see.
This is what the ancients were commended for.

HEBREWS 11:1–2, NIV

Have you seen what happens to a ship tied "permanently" to a dock? Or what a car up on blocks does to your property value? You need to give it wheels, hit the ignition, pull away from the curb. The same equation applies to our faith. We need to put it to action.

Faith isn't something someone hands you or you carry in your pocket. It's a verb—a thing you *do* . . . every day. In the battle between faith and works, faith wins. Both are important, but in God's Word, faith gets more screen time than works. It's the greatest thing you can offer God.

Hebrews 11 has traditionally been referred to as the "Faith Hall of Fame." Nineteen individuals are mentioned (with many more alluded to) who actively applied their faith by seeing the future in advance (believing before seeing), and working to bring that into their present situation. Those recognized in Hebrews—and the many today like them—put their faith to *work*. Will you be inducted into "Heaven's Hall of Faith"? If not, what key can you turn or rope can you untie to set your faith to action?

Shawn Mitchell
Senior Pastor, New Venture Christian Fellowship, Oceanside, CA

HOW TO BE A FRIEND

*The LORD does not look at the things people look at.
People look at the outward appearance,
but the LORD looks at the heart.*

1 SAMUEL 16:7, NIV

Some of the greatest men and women in the Bible were ordinary people. Others did not see their potential, but God saw their potential!

- King David started out as a despised shepherd boy.
- Joseph was hated by his brothers, became a prisoner for a crime he did not commit, and was finally elevated to the position of second in command of Egypt under Pharaoh.
- The apostle Paul was a murderer before he met Jesus.
- Rahab, a prostitute, earned unique praise for her faith and a place in the lineage of Christ.
- Gideon was an unsure, insecure, and fearful man who became a mighty victorious warrior for God.

One of the greatest gifts we can give is looking at others with the eyes of Jesus. Be careful in assigning value by the appearance of what people can do or have accomplished, without an honest look at who their character declares they truly are. The friends you make can be the kind who will give you either a hand out of a hole or the hand that pushes you in. I pray that you will choose your friendships wisely while making an effort to be a good friend to someone today.

Victor Marx
Founder and President, All Things Possible Ministries

SPIRITUAL GPS

Jesus said to him, "I am the way, the truth, and the life.
No one comes to the Father except through Me."

*f*or those of us who have GPS, you might appreciate one feature that I really like. After a trip, you push one button that says "Go Home," and the unit begins directing you the fastest way back home.

I believe that all of us have a built-in spiritual finder that brings us back to our relationship with God. The Word of God says, "But as many as received Him, to them He gave the right to become children of God, to those who believe in His name" (John 1:12). Once we receive Jesus, we become part of God's family. One of the blessings of being his children is knowing that we are continually being drawn back to our walk with Jesus.

The psalmist says in Psalm 119:105, "Your word is a lamp to my feet and a light to my path," like a spiritual GPS in our hearts. And again in Psalm 119:11, "Your word I have hidden in my heart, that I might not sin against You." Are you using God's Word in your heart, your spiritual GPS? Remember, no matter what road you are traveling, his Word will always guide you safely back to your heavenly home.

Jerry Foster
Senior Pastor, Calvary Chapel, South Lake Tahoe, CA

POVERTY, RICHES, DAILY BREAD

Two things I ask of you, Lord; do not refuse me before I die:
Keep falsehood and lies far from me; give me neither poverty
nor riches, but give me only my daily bread. Otherwise, I may have
too much and disown you and say, "Who is the Lord?" Or I may
become poor and steal, and so dishonor the name of my God.

PROVERBS 30:7–9, NIV

There is so much good theology about money packed into Proverbs 30:7–9 verses that it is hard to underestimate. There may not be another two verses in the Bible that cover money so deeply. Extreme riches or poverty can lead many away from God. It should be our goal to not be in extreme wealth or poverty. The author of the verses just asks that God give him his daily bread. Perhaps that was on Jesus's mind when he was teaching the disciples how to pray, when he said, "Give us this day our daily bread" (Matthew 6:11).

God has not designed us to live independent of him. Wealth can lead us to independence. It can lead us to the place of saying, "Look what I have built for myself. I don't need God." At the other end of the spectrum, there is trouble as well in the midst of poverty. If you are extremely poor, you may do something out of desperation. You may steal bread, deal drugs, or sell your body. You may do something you regret just for survival's sake.

"With everything I have, God, I want to honor you." Perhaps that is a prayer you can adopt day by day and ask, "God, give me neither poverty nor riches, but only my daily bread." It will keep you in a very healthy place in the financial-spiritual spectrum.

Mark Ashton
Senior Pastor, Christ Community Church, Omaha, NE

WORSHIP IN SPIRIT AND IN TRUTH

God is spirit, and his worshipers
must worship in spirit and in truth.

JOHN 4:24, NIV

What does it mean to worship God in spirit and in truth? The woman to whom Jesus is speaking immediately understands the implications of what to us seems a somewhat cryptic saying, by adding that when the Messiah comes he will explain everything. To worship in spirit and in truth is not to worship at this mountain or that, but to worship Christ himself, the Jesus of the Bible: "I who speak to you am He" (John 4:26, NKJV).

This truth—spiritually discerned, revealed in the Bible, that Jesus is the Christ, and that therefore true worshipers of God are not defined by location—is of enormous global religious significance. It is not only Medieval pilgrims who go on worship tours to Canterbury (or Jerusalem), but many people today who have their favorite shrines, or who argue as to whether Mecca or Medina, the Dome of the Rock, or some other site is the right place to worship. Jesus's saying does not mean that we are free to worship entirely individualistically, without incorporation with the local representation of the Body of Christ. That is a Western imposition upon the text. Jesus is simply making the world-changing claim that those who worship God rightly worship him. Today, orientate all of your life around the honoring, following, and proclaiming of Jesus as the Christ.

Josh Moody
Senior Pastor, College Church, Wheaton, IL

THE ANTI-MEDIA DIET

Whatever is true, whatever is noble, whatever is right,
whatever is lovely, whatever is admirable—if anything is
excellent or praiseworthy—think about such things.

PHILIPPIANS 4:8, NIV

*H*ave you ever suffered from food poisoning? If so, you'll never forget the experience. You probably remember the food that caused the "I'd rather be dead" feeling, and avoid it completely. In today's multimedia world, we can view a steady menu of violence and materialism, with alternative lifestyle choices for dessert. God never intended this kind of assault on our senses or this streaming garbage to fill our minds. A steady diet of multimedia trash can make our minds toxic for our children, our marriages, and our own spiritual health.

Yet changing one's media diet and lifestyle takes determination and discipline. Thankfully, Christians are not alone in this because God gave us a plan for a healthy mind and spirit in Philippians 4:8. When we daily ask God to help us focus all of our attention on what is true, noble, right, lovely, admirable, excellent, and praiseworthy, we won't have time for negative videos and websites. We can also find more excellent activities to occupy our time.

If you struggle with these issues, ask a trustworthy friend to pray for you and hold you accountable. The changes in your media diet will show in your relationship with God, with your family, and . . . in the mirror.

Pat Verbal
Manager of Curriculum Development, Christian Institute
on Disability, Joni and Friends, Agoura Hills, CA

UNSHAKABLE KINGDOM

*The words "once more" indicate the removing of
what can be shaken—that is, created things—so that what
cannot be shaken may remain. Therefore, since we are
receiving a kingdom that cannot be shaken, let us be thankful,
and so worship God acceptably with reverence and awe.*

HEBREWS 12:27–28, NIV

The kingdom of communism, socialism, or capitalism is shakable. The kingdom of the Republican Party or the Democratic Party is shakable. The stock market is shakable. Our health is shakable. But the kingdom of God is not shakable. What incredible news that we have received a kingdom that is unshakable!

The unshakable kingdom is the homeland of the soul for the followers of Jesus. When we discover his kingdom, we discover ourselves. For this reason, Jesus commanded us to pray, "Thy kingdom come, Thy will be done" (Matthew 6:10, KJV)—irrevocably linking the coming of the kingdom to his will. When we walk in the life and power of the kingdom of God, our lives become a reflection of Jesus. His unshakable Spirit living his life through us brings order and purpose to our lives. Today, "Seek first the kingdom of God" (v. 33) in your conversations, relationships, and activities. It won't be long before people notice an unshakable purpose and power to your life.

Steve Holt
*Founder, Word & Spirit Network, Founder and Lead Pastor,
Mountain Springs Church, Colorado Springs, CO*

WE WERE CREATED TO WORK

A worker is worthy of his food.

MATTHEW 10:10, NKJV

*J*esus Christ knew he had been sent to earth from heaven to save mankind from sin. Yet in his early years as a young man he worked in a carpentry shop in Nazareth. Talk about being overqualified for a job! And although the apostle Paul knew he had been sent from God to evangelize the world, he supported himself and others through tent making.

Very often people refuse to work unless it's in a job that meets their qualifications and goals. All around us are men and women who, when they are laid off, just sit around, send out resumés, and complain that they are out of work. It takes only a glance at the classified ads to know there is plenty of work out there if we are just willing to take on a job we may be very overqualified for or one that doesn't match our lifetime career goals. Any honorable, respectable job is better than no work at all. So . . . stop sitting, keep looking, and start working!

Anne Graham Lotz
Founder, AnGel Ministries, www.annegrahamlotz.com

PRAYER TO OUR FATHER

But when you pray, go into your room, close the door
and pray to your Father, who is unseen. Then your Father,
who sees what is done in secret, will reward you.

MATTHEW 6:6, NIV

*T*he discipline of setting aside some time to meet with the Lord each day may be one of the hardest for us to master. There are many reasons—or should we say excuses?—for why we succumb to the vices of this world.

However, this passage guarantees a reward when we go to our Father in prayer. I believe the enemy would do anything to keep you from praying. When you pray, all of heaven begins to move. The eager listening ears of our Father capture your words, and he begins to dispatch angels to answer your request.

Sometimes our prayers are simple to understand, while other times we are so moved by our circumstances that we cannot speak intelligibly. That must be what Charles H. Spurgeon meant when he said, "Groanings which cannot be uttered are often prayers which cannot be refused."

Brian A. Ross
Senior Pastor, Faith Chapel, Spring Valley, CA

WORSHIP THE CREATOR

👑 BIBLE READ: ECCLESIASTES 5:1–8

Guard your steps when you go to the house of God.
Go near to listen rather than to offer the sacrifice
of fools, who do not know that they do wrong.

ECCLESIASTES 5:1, NIV

One of the great teachings in the history of the church focuses on our purpose in this life. Why are we here? The answer to that question often has been, "To worship God and enjoy him forever" (Westminster Shorter Catechism). We read in Ecclesiastes something quite similar. We are invited to worship God, but not in a casual manner.

We dare not enter his presence as if he were merely another companion for life's journey (Ecclesiastes 4:12). Thus, we hear this warning: "Guard your steps when you go to the house of God" (v. 5:1). Our lives are to reflect the importance of God-glorifying worship.

Entrance into the presence of God should be characterized by faithfulness, awe, adoration, and fidelity, because this God is the sovereign Lord in heaven (v. 2). We would be unwise to be hasty or impulsive in our speech. In our worship, we would be wise to consider our words and not ramble with mindless or unending verbosity. He is in the heavens; we are not. Let us worship and adore the majestic God, Creator of the heavens and the earth.

David S. Dockery
President, Union University, Jackson, TN

JUST WORDS . . .

BIBLE READ: JAMES 3:1–12

*Likewise, the tongue is a small part of the body,
but it makes great boasts. Consider what a
great forest is set on fire by a small spark.*

JAMES 3:5, NIV84

avy warships are massive mechanical monstrosities costing billions of dollars to build. For example, the USS *Eisenhower* weighs about 91,000 tons, is 1,092 feet long, has a 280,000-horsepower nuclear-powered engine, and carries 6,000 crew members. But as immense as this ship is, it is piloted by one man controlling a rudder that is just 1/1000th the size of the ship.

In James 3:5, God's Word compares the words we use to the rudder of a ship and says, "Likewise the tongue is a small part of the body, but it makes great boasts." Don't underestimate the power of your words. Words have the capacity to change the direction of your life or someone else's.

How are you using the capacity for expression God has given you? Are you using it with wisdom? Proverbs 12:18 reads, "Reckless words pierce like a sword, but the tongue of the wise brings healing." Consider whether God might be calling you to adjust what kinds of words you use, what kind of tone you use, and why it matters. On one hand they're just words; but on the other hand, words have the power of life and death.

John V. Hansen
Lead Pastor, Centerpoint Church, Murrieta, CA

GOD IS YOUR SOURCE

I am the vine, ye are the branches: He that abideth in me,
and I in him, the same bringeth forth much fruit:
for without me ye can do nothing.

JOHN 15:5, KJV

It's easy to be dependent on God when you know you need help. Perhaps you aren't strong in dealing with conflict or financial issues, so you continually ask God for wisdom in those areas. It's much harder to ask for his help in areas where we are strong, have some ability and talent, and can handle things pretty well on our own. We often take care of life in these areas without ever thinking about the Lord.

The Lord will let you cruise along in areas you are proficient in until you finally hit a wall and are forced to recognize that God is your only source. The easiest way to avoid this type of situation is to continually recognize and admit that you are nothing without God, but with him you can do all things.

As you go through the day, take time to recognize that every gift and talent you have are from God. Just as a branch can't live without being connected to the vine, you truly live only when you stay connected to the Father.

Lord, I choose to acknowledge that all my talents, gifts, and abilities come directly from you. I recognize that without you I am nothing, but with you I can do all things. In Jesus's name, Amen.

Mac Hammond
Senior Pastor, Living Word Christian Center, Brooklyn Park, MN

THE POWER OF FAILURE

*If the LORD delights in a man's way, he makes
his steps firm; though he stumbles, he will not fall,
for the LORD upholds him with his hand.*

*f*ailure is a product of this fallen world. It's part of your story, I'm sure. I know it's part of mine. Oddly, Jesus seems to love to take our seeming failures and make a feast from them. He takes our brokenness and brings wholeness, if we let him.

And yet so many of us let failure dictate who we are, let it seep way down deep and taint our joy in today. It doesn't have to. It doesn't have that power.

Looking back, I can now attest that most of my recent growth was birthed from the time in my life where every day felt like a crushing blow. Have you experienced that? Are you experiencing that right now? Take courage. Failure can bring wisdom.

Failure is the crucible God uses to increase Jesus and decrease us. It's the venue God uses to increase our capacity for himself. "For You," the psalmist said, "will enlarge my heart" (Psalm 119:32, NASB). The funny thing is that I feel awfully small after failure. But my heart? It's growing.

Mary DeMuth
Speaker and Author, www.marydemuth.com

OUR HEAVENLY DADDY

*The Spirit you received does not make you slaves,
so that you live in fear again; rather, the Spirit you received
brought about your adoption to sonship. And by him
we cry, "Abba, Father." The Spirit himself testifies
with our spirit that we are God's children.*

ROMANS 8:15–16, NIV

Have you ever been looking for something, someone? We all have. We have walked through a store, hoping to find a spouse or a kid who has seemed to wander off, looked down a road waiting for a loved one, stood in line waiting for a clerk.

I heard a story about a disturbing situation in Spain that really shook me. When Francisco Franco became dictator, he removed children from the families of political rivals and placed them into families who were supporters of his cause. From around 1940 to 1980, doctors, the government, the church, and other authorities would tell families that their children had died at birth only to sell them to other families for profit. This sickening practice has recently come to light, and many families are now seeking their stolen children.

One father's diligence led him to seek out his son by gathering all the names of every baby boy born on his son's birthday. This father would not allow the passing of time to quench his passion to be this child's daddy. He said, "I want my boy to know that I am looking for him.... I will not give up.... He was not abandoned.... He is loved." Likewise our Heavenly Father has not abandoned or given up on us. He wants his children to know they have a daddy.

Scott Weatherford
Lead Pastor, First Alliance Church, Calgary, AB, Canada

SIN/REPENTANCE

For the wages of sin is death, but the gift of God
is eternal life in Christ Jesus our Lord.

*H*oliness is found in its purest sense in the person of God. And God's character sets the standard by which we are to live and become. The Bible says that we "all miss the mark" (see Romans 3:23), meaning that there is a target we are trying to hit but continue to fall short of hitting the bull's-eye.

Falling short is sin, and sin always separates us from God. It does more than separate; it is a condition of our hearts. Like the old saying goes, "Sin will take you further than you want to go. It will keep you longer than you want to stay, and it will cost you more than you want to pay."

Repentance isn't being sorry. True repentance allows us to live a free life in Christ without regret. That's why the apostle Paul said, "Yet now I am happy, not because you were made sorry, but because your sorrow led you to repentance. For you became sorrowful as God intended and so were not harmed in any way by us. Godly sorrow brings repentance that leads to salvation and leaves no regret, but worldly sorrow brings death" (2 Corinthians 7:9–10).

Are you ready for a new beginning with Jesus? Make a choice today to abandon the things that are not pleasing to him. God is waiting and wants to set your life free.

Brian A. Ross
Senior Pastor, Faith Chapel, Spring Valley, CA

51

CLOSED DOORS

Noah along with his sons Shem, Ham, and Japheth,
Noah's wife, and his three sons' wives entered the ark. . . .
Then the LORD shut him in.

GENESIS 7:13, 16, HCSB

God Almighty shut the door, sealing in Noah's family and the livestock. The rain came and the waters prevailed, and all flesh died that moved on the earth, save those who found grace in the eyes of God and found themselves behind a closed door.

Many times you pursue something and pray to be in God's will about a decision, only to face a shut door. A job falls through. The house you wanted was sold to someone else. An opportunity vanishes. Do you get angry, feel betrayed? Sometimes a shut door is evidence of God's grace and protection against taking the wrong path.

Oh, that God would shut more doors in my life! I pray that he would shut the door of evil thoughts, the door to unwanted sins and unwise decisions, the door to my impatience and anger . . . that God would shut the doors that lead me into the sea of sin, exposing me to destruction. May we all find God's grace behind shut doors!

David Wesley Whitlock
President
Oklahoma Baptist University, Shawnee, OK

COME, HEAR, DO

Whoever comes to Me, and hears My sayings and does them,
I will show you whom he is like: He is like a man building a house,
who dug deep and laid the foundation on the rock.
And when the flood arose, the stream beat vehemently
against that house, and could not shake it,
for it was founded on the rock.

LUKE 6:47–48, NKJV

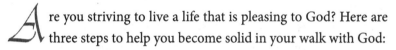re you striving to live a life that is pleasing to God? Here are three steps to help you become solid in your walk with God:

1. *Come to Jesus.* This does not simply mean becoming a Christian. Becoming solid requires a lifestyle of repeatedly coming to Jesus to hear instructions.
2. *Hear his sayings.* It's not enough to hear "about" God; we need to hear directly from God through the Bible—the Word of God. Proverbs 4:20–22 says, "My words . . . are life to those who find them."
3. *Do them.* The final step is to do what God's Word says. James 1:22 says, "But be doers of the Word, and not hearers only, deceiving yourselves." The process of becoming solid is not complete until you're doing what God says.

Is your life rock solid in Christ? Remember, your actions always speak louder than your words.

Jerry Dirmann
Senior Pastor, The Rock Church, Anaheim, CA

Active Faith

As Jesus passed on from there, He saw a man named
Matthew sitting at the tax office. And He said to him,
"Follow Me." So he arose and followed Him.

MATTHEW 9:9, NKJV

A farmer plows his field, sows the seed, fertilizes, and cultivates. God provides the rain and the sunshine to grow his crop. For a successful harvest, the farmer is utterly dependent on God to show up. Yet the farmer knows that unless he diligently pursues his responsibilities, he will have no harvest and reap no benefits. The farmer cannot do what God must do, and God will not do what the farmer should do.

We Christians greatly enjoy talking about the provision of God, how Christ defeated sin and gave us his Holy Spirit to walk victoriously over sin. But we do not as readily talk about our own responsibility to walk by faith, which requires great sacrifice. Many times we are simply reluctant to face up to our responsibility. We prefer to leave that to God. We pray for victory when we know we should be acting in obedience. When Jesus said those seemingly simple words, "Follow Me," it was a step of faith, but a lifetime of obedience.

When he speaks, are we eager to listen and respond? Faith is about action, and obedience demands sacrifice. Do what Jesus asks of you today and reap the harvest.

Matthew Cork
Senior Pastor, Yorba Linda Friends Church, Yorba Linda, CA

THE MOST IMPORTANT MOMENT

Why, you do not even know what will happen tomorrow.
What is your life? You are a mist that appears
for a little while and then vanishes.

JAMES 4:14, NIV

*L*et me ask you a thought-provoking question: What is the most important moment in the life of any human being? Is it the moment of birth? That certainly is an important moment. Is it the moment he or she is married, or the moment a person arrives on a new job? Those are big moments, but the most important moment, without a doubt, is the moment you and I die. That's the moment for which we all wait with bated breath as it draws closer and closer, like the ticking of an untimely clock, with every beat of our heart.

Such are fearful thoughts . . . if we have no faith. Never let that happen. Have faith in God. He is trustworthy. If you trust him, he will be there for you at the moment you pass from this problem- and pain-filled life into eternity. Until that happens, seek those who live without faith, and plead with them to get right with God. Let your heart go out to them, to a point where you go out to them, regularly.

Ray Comfort
Founder and CEO, Living Waters / The Way of the Master

WISE INVESTMENTS

But store up for yourselves treasures in heaven,
where moth and rust do not destroy, and where
thieves do not break in and steal.

MATTHEW 6:20, NIV84

There are plenty of ways to invest our resources. Some may prove more rewarding than others, particularly in certain financial environments, but investing requires a shrewd business-person to navigate the options and make wise decisions. However, let me remind you that investing in the kingdom of God is a sure bet.

There are two distinct blessings that come from investing in God's economy. The first is that God is honored. We bring glory to God when we are faithful and generous in taking care of others and building up his church.

The second is that our gifts impact others. When we surrendered our lives to Christ, we took up his mission to impact others with his love and his message of grace. When we give our resources, time, and talents to further the kingdom, everyone wins! Trusting God with all that we have is an investment we can stand on.

Dr. Tom Mullins
Founding Pastor, Christ Fellowship, Palm Beach Gardens, FL

INTEGRITY

*Whoever can be trusted with very little can also
be trusted with much, and whoever is dishonest
with very little will also be dishonest with much.*

LUKE 16:10, NIV

I don't envy young people today—often possessing a desire to be authentic and real, yet pounded with peer pressure to conform. What can a young man or woman do to survive with one's integrity intact?

In Daniel 3, we meet three young men who were teenagers when they were carried off captive to a pagan place called Babylon. They found themselves in a situation where their choice was to get with the program or die in the fiery furnace. Why not give in and fit in? After all, they were far from home! But fitting in meant denying the Lord, who had been faithful to them. They refused to give in and were thrown into the furnace. But the Lord stood with them in that place, rewarded their commitment, and delivered them.

Integrity is being the same person when nobody's watching as you are when everybody's watching, so walk with integrity before the Lord. In many respects, times may have changed, but the God who stood with these "young men of old" has not. And he'll stand with you—today!

Brian Bachochin
Senior Pastor, Calvary Chapel, Franklin, TN

OBEDIENCE

Now Jesse said to his son David, "Take this ephah of roasted grain
and these ten loaves of bread for your brothers and hurry to their
camp. Take along these ten cheeses to the commander of their unit.
See how your brothers are and bring back some assurance
from them. They are with Saul and all the men of Israel
in the Valley of Elah, fighting against the Philistines."

1 SAMUEL 17:17–19, NIV

We all want to find ourselves in a spot to accomplish something great in life. A game-winning hit, a great play, closing a big deal at the office. . . . We want to do something remarkable and unforgettable. We want history to remember our names, and we hope that we are wise enough to notice when the big opportunities happen. Where would David have been without Goliath? The question is, how did he end up there? The answer: obedience.

David was obedient to his dad regarding a small thing, and it put him in a place to accomplish something great. All David was doing was taking the food to his brothers, and he found himself in the face of a giant. Today, we find ourselves facing great opportunities the same way; we do the small things, and God still opens up the big doors! What are the small things that he is calling you to do, that if you do them may put you in the place to do something great for him?

Mike Linch
Senior Pastor, NorthStar Church, Kennesaw, GA

Is Jesus "Green"?

*The LORD God took the man and put him
in the Garden of Eden to work it and take care of it.*

GENESIS 2:15, NIV

Over the last thirty years, our world has been experiencing a rapidly growing ideology and burgeoning ethos to care for our land, eliminate pollution, promote ecology, preserve our environment, and conserve our natural resources, in consideration of the overall future of our planet.

This conscientious care of the planet God made for us is broadly referred to as being "green." It's a good thing for Christians to make lifestyle choices that lessen our impact on the environment. Christians are not only to care for the planet but everything God placed around us. We often call this "good stewardship." Since we belong to God, and not ourselves, we are called to be good stewards of our possessions, talents, and resources.

Are you a good steward? Are you green with God's stuff? Do you take good care of everything God allows your hands to hold, your mind to think—every place he allows your feet to trod?

I may be a good steward when I compare myself to others, but what matters is what God sees in me! A day will come when he says, "Give an account of your stewardship" (Luke 16:2, NKJV).

Gary Hoyt
Senior Pastor, Bellevue Christian Center, Bellevue, NE

FRIENDS OF
A DIFFERENT KIND

*A*ll of us have had those days when we wished we did not get out of bed. The next time you're having one of those days, remember that James has a unique and freeing take on bad days: "When all kinds of trials and temptations crowd into your lives, my brothers, don't resent them as intruders, but welcome them as friends! Realize that they come to test your faith and to produce in you the quality of endurance. But let the process go on until that endurance is fully developed, and you will find you have become men of mature character with the right sort of independence" (James 1:2–4, PHILLIPS).

Problems are my friends? They do produce in me the kinds of things a friend would want for me: stronger faith, perseverance, maturity, and the right kind of independence.

The next time a problem stares you in the face, try to smile and say, "Hello, friend!"

Jeff Jernigan
Senior Pastor, Corona Friends Church, Corona, CA

GOD'S FAITHFULNESS

Your unfailing love, O LORD, is as vast as the heavens;
your faithfulness reaches beyond the clouds.

PSALM 36:5, NLT

God's faithfulness is abundant and immeasurable.

Psalm 89:8 (NASB) says that "faithfulness surrounds" the Lord, and Isaiah the prophet says that "faithfulness [is] the belt about his waist" (Isaiah 11:5b, NASB). God's faithfulness is the basis of our confidence in him. God is just as faithful today as he has always been!

Having a faithful God is such a blessing to us. God is faithful in what he says:

- Titus 1:2 says God is the "God, who cannot lie" (NASB).
- Hebrews 6:18 says that "it is impossible for God to lie."

God is faithful in what he does. God would never lie to you. What he says is backed up by his faithfulness. Read the Bible to find out all God has promised you.

"The LORD's promises are pure, like silver refined in a furnace, purified seven times over" (Psalm 12:6, NLT).

Mark Martin
Senior Pastor, Calvary Community Church, Phoenix, AZ

TRANSFORMERS

On this rock I will build my church, and
the gates of Hades will not overcome it.

A pastor from Cuba recently wrote, "I live in a neighborhood where many people are involved with witchcraft and are sorcerers. One day I felt God moving my heart while I was visiting a home in this community. The man in the house was a sorcerer, so I explained the gospel to him and he accepted Christ. Together we threw away all the items from his witchcraft practice and today we have Sunday school in his home. Thirty people have come to Christ and meet there each week. I thank God because he is changing the neighborhood. He is transforming this community. The church still does not have a roof, we don't have chairs, but we have the presence of God, and that is most important."

No matter what opposition you face today, Christ can overcome and transform your life and community.

C. H. Dyer
President, Bright Hope, CHDyer.com

SOBERING STATISTICS:
72 AND 3:16

*J*ohn 3:16 states, "For God so loved the world, that he gave his only begotten Son, that whosoever believeth in him should not perish, but have everlasting life" (KJV).

Consider these sobering statistics. There are over 6.85 billion souls in the world. The World Health Organization reports there are 56,597,034 deaths per year. That's about 155,060 every day. Roughly 67 percent claim no affiliation with any form of Christianity. This means 4,328 die every hour—over 72 people every minute—rejecting any form of faith in Jesus. Over 72 souls every sixty seconds are swallowed up in an eternity forever separated from God, every minute of every hour of every day of every year . . . while we watch television, work, sleep, eat, email, blog, daydream, and Facebook. Look around you and realize the tremendous need for the world to hear John 3:16; to repent and seek forgiveness through Jesus; to trust in his death, burial, and resurrection. Seventy-two believing 3:16 will equal a much sweeter sound at the gates of heaven.

David Wesley Whitlock
President, Oklahoma Baptist University, Shawnee, OK

AT THE CENTER

*I*t is at the very center of what Christianity is all about. Without *it* there would be no church. Without *it* Jesus is just like every other man. Without *it* we would have no hope. What is "it"? It is the resurrection of Jesus Christ from the dead.

The apostles knew this. Every apostle except for John died a horrible martyr's death, going to his grave boldly proclaiming that they had been eyewitnesses to the fact that Jesus had risen from the dead. When Paul was arrested in Jerusalem and stood on trial before the Sanhedrin, he made it the cornerstone of his defense: "Men and brethren, I am a Pharisee, the son of a Pharisee; concerning the hope and resurrection of the dead I am being judged" (Acts 23:6).

Are you wondering what life is all about? Have you begun to ask yourself the tough questions of life, like, "Why am I here?" or "Is this all there is?" Are you beginning to search for answers and find yourself curious about this "Christian" stuff?

Stop and consider the resurrection of Jesus Christ. It shows us that he was more than just an ordinary man. He was more than even an extraordinary man. The resurrection shows us that this present life isn't all there is. There is another life after this life. Jesus is the one who offers us hope. He's made the way possible into God's arms and the hope of eternal life. Come and follow Jesus.

Rich Cathers
Senior Pastor, Calvary Chapel, Fullerton, CA

LORD, TAKE ALL OF ME

Just as the Son of Man did not come to be served,
but to serve, and to give his life
as a ransom for many.

MATTHEW 20:28, NIV

*T*he apostle John shares with us some very intimate details about the Last Supper of Jesus with his disciples. As supper ended, Jesus removed himself from the table, put on the garment of a servant, and took up a basin and towel.

Do you remember the words of Peter as Jesus approached him to wash his feet? After first refusing to allow Jesus to wash his feet, Peter said, "Lord, not my feet only, but also my hands and my head!"

I believe Peter wanted Jesus to have all of him. He wanted to surrender not only his feet but his hands and mind to Jesus as well. His feet signify the direction of his life. His head signifies the renewing of his willingness to have Jesus become Lord over his thought life. Offering his hands shows Peter's desire to have all that he does be in submission to Jesus and to his will.

What would you offer to Jesus if he were to stand before you today with a basin and a towel?

Steve DeNicola
Senior Pastor, Calvary Chapel, Foothill Ranch, CA

THE SCAPEGOAT

When he saw Jesus passing by, he said, Look, the Lamb of God!

JOHN 1:36, NIV

*O*n Yom Kippur, in the days of Messiah, the high priest had to perform a strange act. He had to lay his hands on the head of a goat, the scapegoat, as he pronounced over it the sins of Israel. A scarlet ribbon was then tied around the horns and a piece of it cut off and hung on the Temple. The scapegoat was then led out of the Temple, carrying Israel's sins into the wilderness where it was killed.

In the Talmud, the chief book of Rabbinical Judaism, it is recorded that every year when the scapegoat was killed, the scarlet thread that hung on the Temple would turn from scarlet to white, symbolizing that Israel's sins were forgiven. But an amazing passage written in the Talmud—Yoma 39—records that the "scarlet thread stopped turning white" and never turned white again. This change symbolized that God no longer accepted the sacrifice—that something of cosmic proportions had occurred. When did it happen? The Talmud records that it began about forty years before the destruction of the Temple. This is awesome, for the year that the rabbis record as being the year of the cosmic change regarding the atonement of God was AD 30. Amazingly that was the same time that the Messiah, the Scapegoat (the Lamb of God), was led to his death at Calvary to die for our sins once and for all.

So, my friends, walk in confidence and courage. For this salvation is more powerful and real than you could ever imagine!

Jonathan Cahn
Author, The Harbinger, *Senior Pastor and Messianic Rabbi*
the Jerusalem Center / Beth Israel, Wayne, NJ

SUFFERING ACCORDING TO THE WILL OF GOD

So then, those who suffer according to God's will
should commit themselves to their faithful
Creator and continue to do good.

1 PETER 4:19, NIV

There are two things that Peter says to those who are suffering according to the will of God. First of all, they are to commit their souls to him. The fact is that God does allow suffering, and we are to place our souls in God's charge during that time of need. The word "commit" means just that. Let God be in charge of you, and just like you would deposit something in the bank for safekeeping, so you can deposit your soul to him.

Second, we are to do good in the midst of our suffering. It's very easy to want to fight back, especially when someone is treating you unfairly or bringing trouble into your life when you don't deserve it. But remember that God wants us to keep doing what is right and what is good even when we are mistreated.

Last, notice what's said about God in this verse. He is a faithful Creator. That means he is dependable and trustworthy. You can count on him today in the midst of your suffering.

May God make his face shine upon you, especially if you are suffering and in need of his loving grace.

Bob Grenier
Senior Pastor, Calvary Chapel, Visalia, CA

CHOOSE TO OBEY

Now the word of the LORD came to Jonah the son of Amittai,
saying, "Arise, go to Nineveh, that great city, and cry out
against it; for their wickedness has come up before me."
But Jonah arose to flee to Tarshish from the presence of the LORD.
He went down to Joppa, and found a ship going to Tarshish;
so he paid the fare, and went down into it, to go with them
to Tarshish from the presence of the LORD.

JONAH 1:1–3, NKJV

*W*hat would possess Jonah to flee from the presence of the Lord and go in the opposite direction? Why would Jonah rebel against a direct order from the Lord? God had intended for Jonah to go into Nineveh, the capital city of Assyria, and declare that if Nineveh continued in its evil, it would be overthrown. The Assyrians had been brutal to the nation of Israel, and God wanted Jonah to call them to repentance.

Jonah's rebellion and disobedience cost him. The Word tells us he went out from the presence of the Lord. Losing fellowship with God is the greatest price we'll pay for disobedience. Whatever God calls us to do, no matter how difficult, may we choose to obey!

Eric Cartier
Senior Pastor, Rocky Mountain Calvary Chapel, Colorado Springs, CO

LET GO, LET GOD

Take My yoke upon you and learn from Me,
for I am gentle and lowly in heart, and you will
find rest for your souls. For My yoke is
easy and My burden is light.

*O*ne of the joys and blessings of being a Christian is being *underwhelmed*. When people hear this wonderful word when describing our lives it will point to the magnificent lives we have been promised in Christ Jesus. Try it. The next time someone asks you how you are doing, say politely, "I am so underwhelmed." There is a peace that comes from God that surpasses understanding, and it is ours in Jesus Christ.

To experience being underwhelmed, quit trying to be strong on your own and simply do what the Scriptures instruct us: "Casting all your care upon Him, for He cares for you" (1 Peter 5:7). The difference in being overwhelmed and underwhelmed is allowing Jesus to take all our burdens. Don't deny you have burdens, beloved of God; otherwise the Lord wouldn't be inviting us to cast them all on him. What are you waiting for? Let go and let God create in you a life that is *underwhelmed*!

Mike Osthimer
Senior Pastor, Calvary Chapel, Bakersfield, CA

RISING EARLY TO PRAY

👑 BIBLE READ: MARK 1:16–39

There are many good reasons for getting up early, but one stands head and shoulders above the others. Mark 1 records a single day in Jesus's ministry. He called Peter, Andrew, James, and John to discipleship. He then went into Capernaum and taught in the synagogue. Jesus healed a man with an unclean spirit. Then he went to Peter's house and healed Peter's mother-in-law. By evening, people were bringing sick and demon-possessed friends to be healed. Jesus must have been exhausted. I guess he decided to sleep in the next morning.

Guess again.

Mark 1:35 says, "Now in the morning, having risen a long while before daylight He went out and departed to a solitary place; and there He prayed" (NKJV). Jesus knew the secret to a day of power. It was to start his day with the power of prayer.

Don't just get up early to run, get the kids off to school, or get a jump on the work of the day. If you rise early, make an appointment to meet with God and you'll be amazed at how much better your day will be.

Woodrow Kroll
President, Back to the Bible, Lincoln, NE

IT IS FINISHED

When he had received the drink, Jesus said,
"It is finished." With that, he bowed his
head and gave up his spirit.

JOHN 19:30, NIV

Before giving himself unto death, our Lord proclaimed, "It is finished." This statement prompts the inquisitive to ask, "What is finished?" The guilt over my sin . . . it is finished! The feeling that I'll never measure up . . . it is finished! The shame of my selfishness . . . it is finished! The embarrassment over my shortcomings . . . it is finished! The death required for my offenses . . . it is finished! And so much more . . .

"It" is the fear of death, and "it" is finished!

"It" is the barrier that separated creation from Creator and "it" is finished!

"It" represents the punishment demanded for the combined failures of every person from all of time, and "it" is finished! For the Father has taken "it" away and has nailed "it" to the cross so that we may bear "it" no more!

The density of the word allows "it" to mean many different things to as many different people . . . yet this one thing remains universal: Brothers and sisters, "it" is behind us! And the Victorious Finisher now proclaims, "Behold, I make all things new!"

Brent Eldridge
Lead Pastor, First Baptist Church of Lakewood, Long Beach, CA

THE REASON FOR THE RESCUE

So that in the ages to come He might
show the surpassing riches of His grace in
kindness toward us in Christ Jesus.

EPHESIANS 2:7, NASB

*H*ave you ever asked yourself just why God decided to send his son so that we could be forgiven and live with him forever? The first answer that comes to our minds is usually that he did it all for us. He saved us so that we could know life as it was meant to be. But the truth is that God didn't save us for us; he saved us for himself. That's right. Paul declares the grand purpose behind God's redeeming work was that "He might show the surpassing riches of His grace in kindness toward us in Christ Jesus." Salvation is God's way of showing off just how great his grace and love are.

It surprises us to learn that God didn't save us simply so that we could feel good. In fact, he saved us primarily so that he could look good. And here's the best part: when he looks good in our lives, we will feel the very best in him. Imagine that! When he gets all the glory, we really do find life the way it was meant to be.

Dr. David W. Hegg
Senior Pastor, Grace Baptist Church, Santa Clarita, CA

JESUS:
THE LIVING WORD

When I was in Bible school I was so utterly fascinated with the Bible that I fell in love with it. Reading and studying was a breeze because I desired more and more knowledge. Then one day I was stopped dead in my tracks by what Jesus said:

You search the scriptures, for in them ye think
ye have eternal life, and these are they which testify of Me,
but you would not come to Me that ye might have life.

JOHN 5:39–40

I heard Jesus pleading with them not to yearn for more and more knowledge, but to remember the Bible is all about finding him. It shocked me to think I could become just like the Pharisees. They knew the Word of God cover to cover, and yet couldn't even see the Messiah standing in their midst!

This simple verse in John has transformed how I read my Bible. I don't read it like I'm cramming for finals, and piling up religious knowledge. Now I find myself seeking to know him, his opinions, his feelings, how he dealt with His people, looking for His direction.

Now I have more anticipation that God will speak to me through his Word, as I let the pages lead me to him, the Living Word. Like the hymn writer penned, "Beyond the sacred page . . . I seek Thee, Lord."

Lee Ezell
Author and Speaker, www.LeeEzell.com

A DEEP LOVE

Nevertheless I have this against you,
that you have left your first love.

REVELATION 2:4, NKJV

*T*he church in Ephesus was in many ways an exemplary church, having been planted by Paul, who spent the better part of three years there with them. This marvelous church could boast about their pastoral leadership from the likes of Paul, Timothy, the apostle John, Polycarp, and others who gave the saints remarkable teaching and examples. In John's day this church was large, busy, and fruitful, and yet Jesus took exception to the one thing only he could see: their motivation. In all that busyness and work, their hearts toward Jesus were no longer pure and driven by love for him. They had "left their first love." It is one thing to lose heart and be discouraged, yet quite another to leave behind the love for the Lord that once drove your service.

Many people start with a heart of service out of love for our Lord and yet over time they leave or forget their very reason for ministry. At this point we are left with nothing but a religious work that is habitual, perfunctory, and loveless in origin.

I hope the words of Jesus here to the Ephesian church will be a lesson to each of us that God is far more interested in the heart motivation than the busyness of our service to him.

Examine your heart! Anything you do out of a love for Jesus will stand his test. Anything done for any other reason or purpose will not be rewarded.

Jack Abeelen
Senior Pastor, Morning Star Christian Chapel, Whittier, CA

PLACE OF REST

👑 BIBLE READ: HEBREWS 4

*So there is a special rest still waiting
for the people of God.*

HEBREWS 4:9, NLT

ebrews 4 reveals that rest is a precious commodity, stemming first from a promise (v. 1). God's promises can give us rest and soothe our minds when we are troubled. After we receive the promise, however, we must combine it with faith (v. 2). Faith is the fuel in our engine that brings the promise to life. A promise without faith has no power, in the same way that an engine without fuel has no active energy.

We know that our faith is activating a promise when the result is *rest*. "For only we who believe can enter his place of rest" (v. 3). The moment our faith mixes with a promise, a perfect rest enters our hearts. All anxiety, frustration, fear, and worry depart, as God's rest is ours.

God is not anxious about problems! When we believe his Word, we enter into his rest. Therefore, when we are troubled we must bring a promise to God's throne, mix it with faith, and sit quietly in the rest of God until he performs it.

"Let us do our best to enter that place of rest" (v. 11)!

Larry Stockstill
Teaching Pastor, Bethany World Prayer Center, Baton Rouge, LA

SERVING THE SAVIOR COMPLETELY

BIBLE READ: EPHESIANS 4:5–16

We will speak the truth in love, growing in every way
more and more like Christ, who is the head of his body, the church.
He makes the whole body fit together perfectly. As each part
does its own special work, it helps the other parts grow,
so that the whole body is healthy and growing and full of love.

EPHESIANS 4:15–16, NLT

When I was a kid growing up in New Jersey, we used to always get gas at the full-service Sunoco station in town. As soon as we drove in across the little hose, it made a bell ring. Then a couple of guys would come out, dressed in official blue gas station uniforms. One would come to the window and ask us what kind of gas we wanted while another began washing our car windows. The other attendant would then fill up our tank and check the oil and the tire pressure while we sat in our car. Before the attendant was done he'd offer to top off the windshield washer fluid. That gas station was a full-service kind of experience!

In the same way, God wants his church to be a full-service experience, and every one of us has a part to play. When we finally realize that we were created to serve the Savior by serving his church, it can bring a huge blessing into our hearts and lives. When we serve the Savior, we are strengthened, fulfilled, and made more complete in Christ. Even more, the Savior's church is strengthened, stabilized, and brought to further maturity, further toward being the complete church the Body of Christ is meant to be. So what kind of experience will you have the next time? Will it be self-serving or full-service?

John V. Hansen
Lead Pastor, Centerpoint Church, Murrieta, CA

CRITICS

BIBLE READ: 1 SAMUEL 17:26–30

Blessed is the man who does not walk
in the counsel of the wicked or stand in the way
of sinners or sit in the seat of mockers.

PSALM 1:1, NIV84

There are times in life when God calls someone to a position to do something for him by stepping out in faith from your normal pattern of existence. When those times come, you can expect that there will be some pessimistic people lurking nearby. Oftentimes, the people who are closest to us become our greatest critics. They remind us of who we really are and of our weaknesses and flaws. The reality is that most of them have stood close by and just chosen not to do anything, and therefore they do not want anyone else to step up either.

How do you handle a critic when you are ready to step out? Do exactly what David did with his critical brother: "He turned away" (1 Samuel 17:30). David did not focus on his brothers or their opinions; he found people who had the information he needed and made the decision to get involved. The irony is that if David had done nothing and listened to his critics, Goliath would have been the champion of the valley!

What's God calling you to do today that is causing your critics to rise up? May God give you the strength to stand tall, stay focused, and turn away from your critics.

Mike Linch
Senior Pastor, NorthStar Church, Kennesaw, GA

GOD'S BIGGER PLAN

*O*ne of the saddest verses in the Bible is Genesis 42:36, in which the patriarch Jacob concludes, "Everything is against me!" (NIV).

Have you ever felt that way? Have you felt like your family, friends, the economy, the weather, and maybe even God were all against you? This is how Jacob felt—with good reason—and he was convinced his future held only sorrow.

Yet here is the surprise: While Jacob was whining, God was about to give him the greatest blessing of his life. He would soon receive not just food and prosperity but also be reunited with his son Joseph, whom he thought had died years before. What a turn of events!

This is why Genesis 42:36 is, strangely, also one of the most encouraging verses in the Bible for me. Just when I think all is lost and everything is against me, I am reminded that Jacob felt the same because he could not see God's bigger plan. Because of this, when I am discouraged, I choose to believe that God's plan is bigger than my limited vision perceives.

Rick Stedman
Senior Pastor, Adventure Christian Church, Roseville, CA

DAILY EXERCISE FOR THE SOUL

One of my greatest treasures is a small New Testament that my grandmother left for me the summer before she passed away. She was not wealthy as the world judges wealth, but she was one of the wisest people I have known. And my grandmother managed to communicate that wisdom in language that even a child could understand. In the days before email, she wrote to each of her grandchildren once a week, showing interest in all that we were doing and encouraging us to be open to the adventures that God would have for us as we got older.

Knowing that I had always been a worrier, she specifically marked Philippians 4:6–7 as "my verses": "Do not worry about anything, but in everything by prayer and supplication with thanksgiving let your requests be made known to God. And the peace of God, which surpasses all understanding, will guard your hearts and minds in Christ Jesus" (NRSV). The problem with worrying is that we are trying to find strength for all the thousands of things that *might* happen. My grandmother's point was always that God promises strength for the things that actually *do* happen, so we can be at peace.

Practicing the peace of God is one of the most helpful daily exercises for the soul. I hope that you find a way to exercise your soul today.

Shirley A. Mullen
President and Professor of History, Houghton College, Houghton, NY

PRACTICAL WISDOM

👑 BIBLE READ: 1 KINGS 3:1–28

How much better to get wisdom than gold!
And to get understanding is to be
chosen rather than silver.

PROVERBS 16:16, NKJV

*T*hese sentiments of Solomon, regarding the preference for wisdom over wealth, stem from a strange dream he had that changed his life. Solomon attended a solemn procession to the altar at Gibeon. Here the king celebrated an elaborate religious festival. While at Gibeon, Solomon received a dream from the Lord in which God demanded, "Ask! What shall I give you?" (1 Kings 3:5).

Solomon asked for practical wisdom, the ability to make decisions based on truth. God was pleased with Solomon's request, granted it, and added riches, honor, and length of days as well.

The incident with the two prostitutes each claiming a still-living child was theirs soon tested Solomon's practical wisdom. It appears that Solomon's wisdom went well beyond mere practical shrewdness in everyday affairs. He displayed the kind of spiritual shrewdness that Paul speaks of in 2 Corinthians 2:11. This is the kind of wisdom we often lack but can receive from God, if we but ask (James 1:5). Is there godly wisdom you seek to know today? Then ask!

Woodrow Kroll
President, Back to the Bible, Lincoln, NE

LOOK UP

Set your minds on things above,
not earthly things.

COLOSSIANS 3:2, NIV

*H*ave you ever had a time when your heart ached so much that even the thought of food made you sick to your stomach?

I had one of those days a few years ago. My teenage daughter and I had become separated on the ski slopes of a mountain resort. I came upon a ski accident as they were taking the victim away in a black body bag. With thousands of people on the slopes, I did not want to imagine the person in that bag could be my daughter, but moments later my cell phone rang with some bad news. "Mr. Willis," the voice said with a grand sense of urgency. "You need to report to the first aid shelter immediately."

My heart dropped. And in the short, yet excruciatingly long moments between the time I received the call and the moment when I saw my little girl, well, as you can imagine, food was the last thing on my mind. I didn't think about a car payment, home repairs, or even that next raise. Thank God, it was only a broken leg, but that experience served as a stark reminder of what is important in life— and what isn't.

Dear God, help me be focused on that which is eternal. By your grace, may the things of this world fade away so that your will might be preeminent in my life.

Steve Willis
Lead Pastor, First Baptist Church, Kenova, WV

WHY SERVE?

*Present your bodies a living sacrifice, holy, acceptable
to God, which is your reasonable service.*

*I*n Romans 12 we come to an important turning point in this epistle. The theme for the first eleven chapters of Romans is "knowing" what God has done to save his people from their sins. But starting in chapter 12, the theme shifts to "doing" as the command comes to serve sacrificially.

Notice the order. It starts with what God "has done" for us and then comes the command for us "to do" for God. That always has to be the order when we serve the Lord. What we do for him has to be a response to what he's already done for us. If not, our service to him becomes a loveless routine of trying to earn his favor and forgiveness.

True favor and forgiveness always begin with his grace, not with anything we attempt to do in order to earn or deserve it. The very structure of the book of Romans cries out its great theme, "Grace saves!" Now let's sacrificially live in light of that.

Bob Coy
Senior Pastor, Calvary Chapel, Fort Lauderdale, FL

SPIRITUALLY RIPPED

Therefore, take up the full armor of God, so that you
will be able to resist in the evil day, and having
done everything, to stand firm.

EPHESIANS 6:13, NASB

In Ephesians 6, Paul calls us to be trained, prepared, and ready to fight. Verse 13 says that an "evil day" will come; the battle is imminent. In Luke 4, Jesus withstands Satan's onslaught with God's Word. The section ends with verse 13, "When the devil had finished every temptation, he left Him until an opportune time." It is not a question of "if," but rather a question of "when." The devil will come at you at an opportune time. Therefore we need to be fully armed and ready.

We need to exercise our hearts and minds to be in the best possible spiritual condition. Ephesians 6:13 says we are to have "done everything" to stand which literally means to "work out."

The primary reason for people being physically out of shape is that they are unwilling to exercise. This is the primary reason for people being in weak spiritual shape as well. Some Christians hope that somehow, with no effort on their part, they will wake up one day with a strong faith. According to Scripture, this is not possible. For faith to increase, we need to be completely obedient to the Lord (Luke 17).

To stand firm in the evil day, we must be spiritually ripped. To withstand, we must be in top spiritual condition. To stand firm, we must go through the correct preparation. Are you ready to exercise your faith?

Chuck Booher
Senior Pastor, Crossroads Christian Church, Corona, CA

MAJESTY OF GOD

👑 BIBLE READ: PSALM 93

Great is the LORD and most worthy of praise;
his greatness no one can fathom.

PSALM 145:3, NIV84

The first time I visited St. Paul's Cathedral in London, the church was surrounded by barricades, British bobbies, and armed guards.

"What is going on?" I asked.

"Today is a special day," an official replied. "This is the Bank of London's 500th anniversary, and there is a commemorative service today in St. Paul's."

"Aw, man!" I exclaimed. "I wanted to see the cathedral."

He replied, "Stand right here and you will see something even better. You will get a rare glimpse of Her Majesty, herself."

Queen Elizabeth passed right by me with a royal escort. As I have told that story, many people have remarked, "I have been to London several times and never actually seen the Queen. You were so lucky!" I know now how fortunate I was.

With all due respect, an earthly monarch doesn't compare to the King of Kings! Our God is seated today on an eternal throne. He is the unparalleled, unprecedented, incomparable, immovable, unchanging, ever-present, all-knowing, almighty, majestic, glorious, righteous, holy, eternal God of the ages.

How fortunate we are to know and serve our God.

Dennis R. Wiles, PhD
Senior Pastor, First Baptist Church, Arlington, TX

GOING HOME

Through all generations you [God] have been our home.

PSALM 90:1 (A PRAYER OF MOSES), NLT

Moses was a wanderer. He grew up away from home, lived away from his people, and then was called by God to lead the Jewish people into the Promised Land—to lead them "home." It is ironic that the man who knew no home was the leader toward home. But Moses knew something that we don't know.

This past week I went back to the only consistent place that I or my family has known as home: the house my parents filled with love. The sweetness of home flooded my heart and filled my eyes with tears. I felt the warm embrace of my mother and the steadying hand of my father. I recalled the nights I lay in bed and prayed for my wife Tara and our future together . . . the Christmas gatherings . . . Calah running backward hitting the wall and the stitches that followed . . . the nights spent sleeping with Caleb on a blow-up bed in the living room.

As I pondered, I could not help but recall Moses's words: "Lord, you are home." We all have a longing to find the place where we belong. But it is not a place; it is a person . . . a people . . . a purpose. It is God who is making us a family. We are looking for home, and it has been God all along.

One day I will be home. God will whisper to me once again and call me to himself, and I will discover the truth that Moses, the wanderer, knew all along. I think the first words I'll hear will be "Welcome home."

Scott Weatherford
Lead Pastor, First Alliance Church, Calgary, AB, Canada

BE ANGRY

Be angry, and do not sin.

EPHESIANS 4:26, NASB

During Nehemiah's time the people of Israel were overburdened with taxes and mortgages on homes, vineyards, and grain fields. Their stress at home and at the office became too much to bear. They cried out to Nehemiah for relief. He became very angry when he heard their outcry and distress. After serious thought, Nehemiah rebuked the nobles and rulers and called for a town hall meeting (Nehemiah 5:7).

He did not rebuke them until he had given the matter serious thought. Was this a valid complaint? Are the people to be trusted? What is the track record of the rulers? After serious thought he corrected them and demanded a response. They repented and corrected their methods, plus they restored money to the people.

Anger has a place in our lives. However, we must try to be slower to anger, leaving room for serious thought before we say something we might regret.

Garry Ansdell
Senior Pastor, Hosanna Christian Fellowship, Bellflower, CA

THE GREAT EQUALIZER

*Just as people are destined to die once, and after that
to face judgment, so Christ was sacrificed once to take away the
sins of many; and he will appear a second time, not to bear sin,
but to bring salvation to those who are waiting for him.*

HEBREWS 9:27–28, NIV

A friend of mine is facing serious cancer. There is something about sickness and tragedy that reminds us about the frailty of life. It is healthy for our soul to face its own mortality periodically. Death is the great equalizer. We brought nothing into this world, and we can take nothing out except the story of how we have lived our life. To realize this in the land of living is to gain an edge on the great majority of humanity, who live oblivious to the reality of eternity.

For the believer in Christ, every funeral and hospital visit are reminders of a couple of important things. First, life is short, so engage in the mission of Jesus without delay. Second, there will be a day of judgment, so walk as one who will give account. Third, the troubles and hardships in this world are nothing compared to the glory to come. Fourth, we are a people full of hope because we know our destiny, so be a living hope carrier wherever you go. Remember, "Death has been swallowed up in victory" (1 Corinthians 15:54b).

Mark Jobe
Senior Pastor, New Life Community Church, Chicago, IL

SAVED BY THE LORD

Who is like you, a people saved by the LORD?

o you know who you are this day, and are you rejoicing in the God of your salvation? Are you dwelling in the place of darkness and sin where you have come from, or are you dwelling in the light, in Christ—loving, adoring, and cherishing the Lover of your soul, the bright morning Star, the risen King of Glory?

O believer, stop today. Take note of the mercies and love of God that have bought and brought you to this place. You are no longer a child of Satan, laden with sin and having the payment of death due. Sing for joy, child of God: you are the people saved by the Lord. He redeemed you, paid the penalty of death you owe, and is seated at the right hand of the Father forever, making intercession on your behalf. "Redeemed, how I love to proclaim it. Redeemed by the blood of the Lamb. Redeemed by His infinite mercy. His child forever I am." (From "Redeemed, How I Love to Proclaim It," the hymn by Fanny J. Crosby.)

Tom DeSantis
Senior Pastor, Calvary Chapel, Santa Clarita, CA

GO FORWARD

*And the L*ORD *said to Moses, "Why do you cry to Me?*
Tell the children of Israel to go forward."

As Moses led the Israelites out of Egypt, he must have felt the weight of the world on his shoulders. Trapped by the Red Sea and pursued by the Egyptian army, with over a million terrified Israelites complaining and placing blame on him, Moses cried out to the Lord for direction.

But God said, "Why do you cry to me? Go forward."

Moses simply needed a reminder. It was God who "went before them . . . in a pillar of cloud . . . and . . . a pillar of fire" (Exodus 13:21). Moses's only task was, literally, to follow God. Each day, he pursued the pillar of cloud by day and the pillar of fire by night. His destination each day was not a city, landmark, or border; it was the pillar itself.

You see, God doesn't just point us toward our destination. He *is* our destination. When we live a life in pursuit of God, his will becomes our only aim and his provision our only need. Today, take your eyes off the oceans of problems before you, make Jesus your destination, and, like Moses, "Go forward."

Mike Macintosh
Senior Pastor, Horizon Christian Fellowship, San Diego, CA

THE SOLDIER'S PSALM

Thou shalt not be afraid.

PSALM 91:5, KJV

A miracle of God's protection comes out of World War I that gave Psalm 91 the title "The Soldier's Psalm." The books *Life Understood* by F. L. Rawson and *The Mighty Hand of God* by K. P. Carter record this story.

The Ninety-First Infantry Brigade of the U.S. Army was preparing to enter combat in Europe. Its commander, a devout Christian, called an assembly where he gave each soldier a little card on which was printed Psalm 91. They agreed to recite this psalm daily. The Ninety-First Brigade was engaged in three of the bloodiest battles of the Great War. While other units similarly engaged had up to 90 percent casualties, the Ninety-First Brigade did not suffer a single casualty. Truly God gave his angels charge over these soldiers to keep them in all their ways.

Holy Father, protect our soldiers who protect our country. Place a hedge of love around our soldiers in harm's way and pray for people to turn to the Lord Jesus Christ. Amen.

Dr. Roger Freeman
Senior Pastor (Retired), First Baptist Church, Clarksville, TN

Be Humble

*H*umility is one of the most important and most attractive qualities a person can have. Humility can be defined as having a right view of God, yourself, and others.

Have a right view of God. Like most of us, you may have much too small of an understanding of who God is. He is the most high God (Daniel 4:24, 34), the Almighty One (Genesis 17:1), the Creator of everything (Genesis 14:19, 22; Colossians 1:16). He is your loving Father, but he is also the all-powerful Ruler of the universe.

Have a right view of yourself. Compared to God you are nothing. Yet you are also of incredible value because you are made in God's image. Despite your high value, God clearly wants you to walk in humility. Scripture promises many benefits when you walk in humility: grace (Proverbs 3:34), guidance (Psalm 25:9), wisdom (Proverbs 11:2), honor (Proverbs 15:33), and many more.

Have a right view of others. Success in life depends on success in relationships. Nothing contributes more to successful relationships than being humble, respectful, and loving toward others. God desires you to consider others better than yourself (Philippians 2:3–4), to honor others above yourself (Romans 12:10), and to treat others as you want to be treated (Matthew 7:12).

My prayer is that you will increasingly find joy, friendship, and success as you walk humbly before God and others.

Judy Douglass
Author, Campus Crusade for Christ

UNDER HIS FEET

Now about the fourth watch of the night He came to them,
walking on the sea, and would have passed them by.

MARK 6:48, NKJV

What an incredible scene this is: A raging storm, terrified disciples, and a heroic, all-powerful Savior, Jesus, walking on the water. What amazes me is that the very storm that had them so terrified was *under his feet*. I also find that last part of the verse interesting: "and would have passed them by."

The implication is that if they had not cried out, he would have walked right by! I wonder how often the Lord stands ready to work in a mighty way in our lives. He is just waiting for us to come to the end of ourselves and confess our need of him. Remember that today: The storm that you are in is under his feet. Cry out to him today. Tell him you need him. He is there, waiting to work in your life in a mighty way!

Rob Salvato
Senior Pastor, Calvary Chapel Vista, Vista, CA

Does Anybody Really Know What Time It Is?

An old song asks, "Does anybody really know what time it is? Does anybody really care . . . about time?" In Ephesians 5:15–16 we hear God's challenge about time management: "Be very careful, then, how you live—not as unwise but as wise, making the most of every opportunity, because the days are evil" (NIV84).

How do you redeem time? One Christian man currently undergoing radiation treatments for prostate cancer prays that God will use his illness as a witness for Christ. The radiation treatments force him to get up five or six times during the night. Such inconvenience and sleep deprivation would make most of us irritable and angry. This gentleman uses that time to pray for different individuals in his life. As these people are sleeping, a brother in Christ is interceding for them.

So, the next time you are stuck on hold, trapped in snarled traffic, or jammed into a packed waiting room, choose to redeem that time. Time is never wasted when God's people are praying. "Does anybody really know what time it is?" Yes. It's time to pray!

Scott Miller
Senior Pastor, Graceland Baptist Church, New Albany, IN

CISTERNS, NOT AQUEDUCTS

I will bless you; I will make your name great,
and you will be a blessing.

GENESIS 12:2, NIV

God promises much to Abram in the beginning of Genesis
12: "I will show you. . . . I will make you a great nation. . . .
I will bless you. . . . I will make your name great. . . ." These are God's
pledges in the promise.

But from out of this promise there must be a response: "And you
will be a blessing."

This charge to Abram in Genesis is the first biblical appearance of
the Great Commission, something we attribute to Jesus's words in
Matthew 28 ("Go and make disciples of all nations").

But the Great Commission to bring the good news to all nations is
not a New Testament concept. It begins in Genesis 12.

It is the nature of God's call to beckon us—as disciples of Christ
today—to leave something behind to embrace the claims of God on
our lives.

Abram was blessed to be a recipient of that grace, but he was also
called to be a dispenser of that grace . . . "through your offspring all
nations of the earth will be blessed" (Genesis 22:18).

Christians should view themselves not just as beneficiaries or col-
lectors of grace but as agents of grace. We are not designed to be
cisterns; we are designed to be aqueducts.

Dr. Barry H. Corey
President, Biola University, La Mirada, CA

Going Down the Right Path

Blessed is the man who walks not in the counsel
of the ungodly, nor stands in the path of sinners,
nor sits in the seat of the scornful; but his delight is in the
law of the Lord, and in his law he meditates day and night.

PSALM 1:1–2, NKJV

Sometimes we hold on too tight to material things that could be hindering us from totally following the will of God. Whenever we want more or less than the will of God, we're in trouble.

Remember, there is a path that God wants us to go down. We may not always understand that path, but that path will always take us the way of Jesus Christ. God's will for our lives might be a cross to bear, a period of suffering, or a time of uncertainty. But there is a path that God wants us to take in our lives. Sometimes it's not what we want, but it's what he wants. Are you accepting the plan that God has for your life?

The problem is that we think we can find something better than what God's doing for us. But what will happen if a man gains the whole world and loses his own soul (see Mark 8:36)? God, help us to be content with your plan and obedient to your call. Lord, let us understand the principles of life. God, we need to be faithful and trustworthy, and more than anything else in our lives, we need to be thankful.

Steve Mays
Senior Pastor, Calvary Chapel, South Bay, CA

95

LIVING ON PROMISES

And the peace of God, which transcends all understanding,
will guard your hearts and your minds in Christ Jesus.

PHILIPPIANS 4:7, NIV

If you're like most people nowadays, your head is probably spinning, and maybe your heart is even sinking as you try to understand the times we're living in. It's easy to be shaken when you discover that the ground which you thought was so firm under your feet turns out to be more like shifting sand. We're looking for something to hold on to and maybe even someone to explain the seeming unfairness of our circumstances.

In Psalm 73 Asaph was shaken as he wrestled with similar questions. As he tried to understand the world he saw, it became too painful for him . . . until he went into the sanctuary of God. Interestingly, God didn't give Asaph an explanation. God instead reminded Asaph of the promises God had made to him.

The Lord knew that Asaph wouldn't find peace simply in an explanation, but he would find it when he rested in God. Isaiah put his trust in God when he wrote, "You will keep him in perfect peace, whose mind is stayed on you, because he trusts in you" (Isaiah 26:3 ESV). Trust in God's promises today and you will find his peace.

Brian Bachochin
Senior Pastor, Calvary Chapel, Franklin, TN

THE LORD IS MY SHEPHERD

👑 BIBLE READ: PSALM 23

*I am the good shepherd. The good shepherd
lays down his life for the sheep.*

JOHN 10:11, NIV

As a youth I raised sheep on our small farm. One night a tornado came through and literally lifted the barn from my flock, leaving them exposed and in grave danger. My father and I quickly cleared our attached garage, spreading fresh, dry straw knee-deep. We set up heat lamps and set out fresh grain and water, preparing a safe, dry shelter for the lambs. I called and called to no avail. The lambs stared blankly, refusing to move, bleating in fear. One by one I gathered them as my father guarded the door to keep them from escaping back into the stormy night.

Only years later did I realize the spiritual truth of that long night. Jesus is the Good Shepherd, who prepares for us a place of peace, safety, and redemption from the storms of life. Yet like lambs we would still be lost had not the Shepherd rescued us one by one, and had not the Father kept us from our tendency to return to danger. What a blessing that the Lord is my Shepherd!

David Wesley Whitlock
President, Oklahoma Baptist University, Shawnee, OK

FOR OUR GOOD

For I know the thoughts that I think toward you, says the LORD,
thoughts of peace and not of evil, to give you a future and a hope.
Then you will call upon Me and go and pray to Me,
and I will listen to you. And you will seek Me and find Me,
when you search for Me with all your heart.

JEREMIAH 29:11–13, NKJV

The children of Judah had been taken into captivity by the Babylonians, and many found themselves in Babylon wondering what would come next. The false prophets told them all would soon be rectified and to refuse the government and stand in rebellion. Yet God had other plans. He had told them they would be spending some seventy years (Jeremiah 29:10) here so they might learn that false gods serve no purpose and are no substitute for faith in and obedience to their God. Jeremiah's verses above were meant to encourage these captive people and to let them know that God loved them and that he had a plan.

God will indeed take whatever course is necessary in our lives to bring us to the place where he is glorified and we are bowed before him in love. His children in Babylon needed to learn that God was thinking of them, that his thoughts were good and designed to give them a future and a hope. His ways are for our good, even when we do not understand. May our attitude be that of submission to his working, as God leads us to a place of willful and joyful obedience.

Jack Abeelen
Senior Pastor, Morning Star Christian Chapel, Whittier, CA

TRAIN UP A CHILD

*Train up a child in the way he should go, and
when he is old he will not depart from it.*

PROVERBS 22:6, NKJV

*M*ore than anything in the world, I want two things for my kids: to love Jesus and make wise choices. If those things happen, everything else will fall into place.

Even though there are exceptions to the proverb above, it really is true that the investment you make in your children pays off for the long haul in their lives. The things you influence them to do when they are young are the things they will continue to do when they are older.

What kind of a model are you for your kids at home? Are you humble and kindhearted? Do you speak well and are thoughtful of other people? If so, your kids will pick these things up as they grow. Are you angry, disrespectful of your spouse, or joyless? If so, your kids are likely to choose that path for their life. Do you make your own spiritual walk with God a priority and do your kids know it is a priority for your life? Do you make it a priority for your kids to be involved in kids' ministries at your church? These things will mold them for the rest of their lives. If you invest in your children in these ways, the likelihood of their walking with God for the rest of their lives dramatically increases.

Mark Ashton
Senior Pastor, Christ Community Church, Omaha, NE

PREPARED TO WIN THE VICTORY

Raise the battle flag against Babylon! Reinforce the guard
and station the watchmen. Prepare an ambush,
for the LORD will fulfill all his plans against Babylon.

JEREMIAH 51:12, NLT

Sometimes there are those who will set up ambushes against you, but the Lord turns the tables, and now he is setting up the ambushes against them to bring them down. It's time to be ready with the plans of the Lord, to plant your flag and proclaim the victory—that instead of them having taken you captive, now God is bringing them into captivity.

Are you ready? Are you guarded? Are you watching? Are you reinforced with the armor of God? God has some battle plans. There are things you will have to do in this war if you are to escape with your life.

God sometimes gives forewarning of impending doom. The apostle Paul's nephew told him and the Roman commander that more than forty men would be lying in wait to kill Paul. This information was pertinent to the spiritual warfare against the gospel. Paul's life was secured, and the enemy was foiled. "When the enemy comes in like a flood, the Lord raises up a standard against them" (Isaiah 59:19). You, too, will face trials, temptations, or persecution, and God has a strategy for you to win. What preparations is he calling you to make today?

John Schaffer
Senior Pastor, First Love Calvary Chapel, Whittier, CA

LEARNING TO WAIT

Wait on the LORD; be of good courage, and
he shall strengthen your heart; wait, I say, on the LORD!

PSALM 27:14, NKJV

It's much easier to ask for help when you think you need it. After all, if you're driving a car and you assume you're headed in the right direction, why would you pull over to ask someone for help? Often, it's only when things go wrong that we seek help. We ask God to lead us out of emergencies, rather than into his will.

But if the only time we ask for the Lord's help is in emergencies, we will never learn to wait on him—and we will never grow stronger in him. How could we? In an emergency, we need an answer right away. We need action immediately! And yes, God can take action immediately. He is able to guide you through whatever emergency you face today. But what about tomorrow? God does not simply want to deliver you, but to strengthen you.

Today, may I encourage you to wait on the Lord Jesus? He is "able to do exceedingly abundantly above all that we ask or think" (Ephesians 3:20), but we must be willing to wait.

Mike Macintosh
Senior Pastor, Horizon Christian Fellowship, San Diego, CA

SAFE PATHS

But when he, the Spirit of truth, comes,
he will guide you into all truth.

JOHN 16:13, NIV

Long gone are the days of ripped-up and outdated paper maps. Many cars have GPS packages, and it is a fairly common feature on most smartphones nowadays. You can get most anywhere if you have GPS to lead you.

Likewise, God has given us an internal GPS—the Holy Spirit—designed to guide us through life and keep us from dangerous situations. If we set our course with the wrong coordinates, we could wind up spiritually lost or hurt. The Holy Spirit is there to provide us with the wisdom we need to avoid such disasters.

To receive the full benefit of the Holy Spirit, we must confess any attitudes or actions that put self in the driver seat and send him to the backseat. Then we must prayerfully invite him to take control of our lives. When we allow the Holy Spirit this place in our lives, he is able to lead us down safe paths.

Dr. Tom Mullins
Founding Pastor, Christ Fellowship, Palm Beach Gardens, FL

LOT'S WIFE

Remember Lot's wife!

LUKE 17:32, NIV

*R*emember Lot's wife?

Lot's wife looked back. She took her eyes off the path of the Lord. She looked back to the world instead of forward to God's plan for her life.

Prior to God's destroying Sodom and Gomorrah, Abraham pleaded with him on the people's behalf. Abraham bargained with God until it was clear there was no one righteous.

In God's mercy, he allowed Abraham's nephew Lot and his family to escape, but God gave strict instruction to them not to look back. Lot's wife, consumed perhaps with the sin in the city she was leaving behind, looked back and was instantly turned into a pillar of salt.

Jesus told us to remember Lot's wife. When we look back, when we fail to see Jesus, we are taken from the blessings and protection that come from following God exclusively and left to our own defense. Our independence causes us to miss the mercy of God.

Remember Lot's wife today!

Ron Edmondson
Senior Pastor, Immanuel Baptist Church, Lexington, KY, RonEdmondson.com

GUILT—YES;
CONDEMNATION—NO

*There is therefore now no condemnation to those who
are in Christ Jesus, who do not walk according
to the flesh, but according to the Spirit.*

ROMANS 8:1, NKJV

Please try to understand my need to be completely frank about the following statement: Sometimes people just need to shut up and quit lying to themselves and others by making excuses for their poor choices and resulting behavior!

For example, suppose it's a Saturday, and your conscious is giving you the negative vibe for stupid choices you made last night. Great! Guilt is a good thing to bring you to the place of confession and repentance before a Holy God. I do not mean condemnation after repentance, but pure, good conviction and confession, especially if you call yourself a follower of Christ. My prayer is that you will be miserable, completely miserable, until you repent and make things right before God and others.

Victor Marx
Founder and President, All Things Possible Ministries

TRUE POTENTIAL

If you were going to put together a leadership team, what sort of qualities would you look for in a potential candidate? Jesus assembled the most influential ministry team in history with arguably the most ordinary men of his day. Primarily composed of fishermen, Jesus even included a tax collector and some other outcasts from society who, in many instances, didn't even get along with one another. Amazingly, Jesus knew this about the crew he was assembling, and yet he chose them anyway. That seems like a counterproductive approach, but somehow Jesus made it work—and that was the key. It was *Jesus* who made it work.

Healing the sick and raising the dead weren't in their skill set before they came to Jesus. But in the hands of the Master Potter, they went on to turn the world upside-down.

Second Chronicles 16:9 says, "The eyes of the LORD run to and fro throughout the whole earth, to show Himself strong on behalf of those whose heart is loyal to Him" (NKJV). So when it comes to serving the Lord, I wonder if it isn't so much about ability as it is availability. Imagine what the Master Potter might fashion if you let him set his skillful hands to work on you!

Brian Bachochin
Senior Pastor, Calvary Chapel, Franklin, TN

OUR IDEA OF GOD

👑 BIBLE READ: PSALM 139

You have searched me, LORD,
and you know me.

PSALM 139:1, NIV

What is your idea of God? A. W. Tozer, in *The Knowledge of the Holy*, concludes that this is the most important thing about you. He proposes that perhaps the most important question you will answer is, "What comes into your mind when you think about God?"

I remember reading about a homiletics professor at a seminary on the eastern seaboard whose standard practice was to go listen to his students preach after they had graduated. He said that he needed to know if they were "big Godders" or "little Godders." He was concerned that the God they proclaimed might not "measure up" to the actual God of the Bible.

I also teach preaching in a seminary. I share that professor's concern—and not just with the students in my preaching classes. Unfortunately, many Christians fail to realize that God is grander than we could ever imagine. He is more glorious than we have supposed. He is more majestic than we have dreamed!

May your vocabulary of praise be enhanced as you grow in Christ. May your worship life be deepened and your vision of God expanded.

Dennis R. Wiles, PhD
Senior Pastor, First Baptist Church, Arlington, TX

OUR CHOICE

👑 BIBLE READ: LUKE 8:26–39

They sailed to the region of the Gerasenes,
which is across the lake from Galilee. When Jesus stepped
ashore, he was met by a demon-possessed man from the town.
For a long time this man had not worn clothes or lived
in a house, but had lived in the tombs.

LUKE 8:26–27, NIV

What a powerful story in Luke 8 of a demon-possessed man who lived in the tombs, gouging himself with stones. Jesus cast out the demons into a herd of pigs, which then ran off into the lake and drowned. What a pitiful story when the people of the city came out and asked Jesus to leave. It was swine over souls, profit over people. What a contrast: "Jesus deliver me" or "Jesus depart from me." Our choice.

Joe Coleman
Senior Pastor, Calvary Chapel, Palm Desert, CA

SOW AND REAP

Do not be deceived; God is not mocked,
for whatever a man sows, that will he also reap.
For the one who sows to his own flesh will from the flesh
reap corruption, but the one who sows to the Spirit
will from the Spirit reap eternal life.

GALATIANS 6:7–8, NASB

very day you and I get to choose the path we walk. We can choose to make our best decisions based upon our own perceptions and understanding, or we can choose to let the Spirit be in charge, guiding our decisions based upon his discernment and eternal wisdom. Remember, God is not mocked. Whatever option we choose, we will achieve that result. The reality is that we cannot have one kind of life by living the other way. Whichever way we decide leads to the result we experience.

When we choose to be in charge and live life in the flesh, then we reap the earthly result of that decision: corruption, decay, sin. We experience a life that is full of turmoil and lacks peace. But when we choose to let the Spirit empower and direct and enlighten us, then we reap eternal life—a life that is satisfying and fulfilling and significant . . . a life of peace that is glorifying to God.

The options are pretty simple: your kind of life or God's kind of life. So today, which sort of life are you choosing?

Mike Bickley
Senior Pastor, Olathe Bible Church, Olathe, KS

FACING GIANTS

*C*ounting on. Resting in. Relying on. Hoping for. Leaning on. Trusting in . . . Different phrases that describe the word we call "faith." As Christians, we claim to be people of faith. What does that really mean? What does that look like?

For the young shepherd named David, we get a glimpse of his faith as he faced the giant Goliath in battle. David wasn't just a braggart who talked a good talk around the campfire. Consider carefully David's words as he actually charged the behemoth in battle: "Then David said to the Philistine, 'You come to me with a sword, with a spear, and with a javelin. But I come to you in the name of the LORD of hosts, the God of the armies of Israel, whom you have defied'" (1 Samuel 17:45, NKJV).

David's faith was demonstrated by what he took to the battle. David wasn't really counting on those five little stones and his sling. David was counting on God. He wasn't alone as he faced the nine-foot soldier. He had God at his side.

Goliath had his own kind of faith. Goliath was counting on his own ability, his years of experience, and, most important, the awesome weaponry that he and his armor-bearer were carrying.

There will be battles ahead. I'm not writing this prophetically, but practically. We all face giants through our lives. The issue is this: What are you counting on? Are you armed with Goliath's kind of weapons or David's? Have faith in God. He will never abandon you no matter how big the battles are in your life.

Rich Cathers
Senior Pastor, Calvary Chapel, Fullerton, CA

GOD WITH US

👑 BIBLE READ: LUKE 2:1–7

*The virgin will conceive and give birth to a
son, and they will call him Immanuel
(which means "God with us").*

MATTHEW 1:23, NIV

We stood in a hushed line in a musty church building, ready to see the very place where Mary birthed Jesus. My skepticism was at an all-time high, and my gregarious behavior had made the attending Orthodox priest grumpier than usual.

Nevertheless we stood in line, for we were looking for the miracle —the place where God appeared from the womb of a virgin and changed the course of human history. Somewhere in my heart I longed to see, to feel, to embrace the historical reality of Jesus.

We wound down a serpentine staircase to view a silver star marking the place of the divine birth. The air was thick with incense mixed with the hushed prayers of the devout. We were not alone in our quest. Others were looking for a miracle as well.

We long to see God, not just the place of his birth, but the intersection of his life with ours.

Today we will look for a miracle as found in Luke's account of the birth of Christ. We will not stand in line in a musty old building, but we will see the place where God came to be born—be born in you. Are you looking for a miracle? Well, he is here: Christ the Lord.

Scott Weatherford
Lead Pastor, First Alliance Church, Calgary, AB, Canada

BREAKING FREE

Moses my servant is dead. Now then, you and
all these people, get ready to cross the Jordan River into the
land I am about to give to them—to the Israelites.

JOSHUA 1:2, NIV

What sets the boundaries of your life? Often when we get trapped spiritually it is because of a past scar—possibly some disappointment, some hurt, a wound, the loss of a dear friend or loved one. We find ourselves saying, *I would like to believe for so-and-so, but when I was sixteen or six or thirty-six, this happened to me and I can't. It altered my possibilities.* It is amazing how yesterday flavors our tomorrow. It is a fact: Whatever it is in your past that has shaped your life doesn't have any claim on your future.

Anything that may have been intimidating, restricting, negative, disappointing . . . it is dead! The cross declares it! The grace of the cross buries our past so that we can possess our tomorrows.

Second Corinthians 5:17 says, "Therefore, if anyone is in Christ, he is a new creation; the old has gone, the new has come!" (NIV84). Make that tough decision to press on into the full possibilities Jesus has for you right now. Ask the Father to break off the past and all that hinders you from pressing into the future that God has ordained for you.

Dan Carroll
Senior Pastor, Water of Life Community Church, Fontana, CA

ALWAYS FORGIVE

But if you do not forgive, neither will your Father
in heaven forgive your trespasses.

MARK 11:26, NKJV

he Bible teaches us that God has forgiven us a *huge* debt of sin, and that no one on Earth could ever offend us as much as we have offended God. Because God has forgiven us, he expects us to forgive others for what they've done to us.

Because God commands us to forgive, unforgiveness is sin, and sin keeps us out of fellowship with God. To follow God and hear his instructions for our lives, we must be in fellowship with him.

Unforgiveness does not hurt the other person as much as it hurts us. Carrying unforgiveness is like having cancer. Unless we remove it, it continues to grow until we are consumed by it. Many good people ended their lives as bitter and isolated people because they chose not to forgive.

If you have anything against anyone, ask God to give you the strength to forgive them right now.

Jerry Dirmann
Senior Pastor, The Rock Church, Anaheim, CA

SUFFERING

The Lord is not slow in keeping his promise,
as some understand slowness. Instead he is patient
with you, not wanting anyone to perish, but
everyone to come to repentance.

2 PETER 3:9, NIV

In the face of human suffering, pain, and injustice, the psalmists and prophets repeatedly cry out with a heartfelt question for the Sovereign One: "How long, O Lord?" They struggle, as do we, with the apparent passivity of God, who could—and arguably should—intervene to rectify the egregious wrongs in the world. "Will you hide yourself forever?" they ask (e.g., Psalm 89:46, NKJV). The rest of Scripture tells us that God's unequivocal answer is most certainly "No!" He won't wait forever. There will be a definite end to sin and injustice. All wrongs will one day be made right.

What we often fail to see in God's delayed justice is his incredible grace. Peter reminds us in 2 Peter 3:9 that though God is just, he does not take pleasure in judgment of the wicked, but longs to see more people come to repentance. His continued patience will mean salvation for more and more people as it did for us (v. 15). God will indeed make things right, but, in the meantime, it is our prayer and our ardent endeavor that more people would turn from their sin to God and find the grace and forgiveness that we so richly enjoy.

Mike Fabarez
Senior Pastor, Compass Bible Church, Aliso Viejo, CA

THE RESURRECTION—
THE LAMB WINS!

Jesus said to her, "I am the resurrection and the life.
He who believes in me will live, even though he dies."

Billy Graham wrote, "In Germany, it was my privilege to visit then Chancellor Adenauer. He startled me by asking, 'Young man, do you believe in the resurrection of Jesus Christ?' I replied, 'Yes, sir, with all my heart.' He said, 'So do I. It is absolutely the only hope that the human race has.'"

The resurrection declares the victory of Jesus Christ. The Lamb wins!

After forty-plus years of the rule of atheistic communism over Eastern Europe, the communist bloc fell in 1989.

In Prague, Czechoslovakia, on November 27, 1989, the great city church opened its doors for the first time in over forty years! These Christians, the spiritual descendants of the early evangelical Moravian Christians who helped found the modern missions movement, began to worship the risen Christ publicly again without government interference.

The church bells rang! The doors and windows of the church flew open. Christians rallied to the town square to sing hymns of faith. A banner was unfurled from the upper window of the newly opened church. It read, THE LAMB WINS!

Dr. Roger Freeman
Senior Pastor (Retired), First Baptist Church, Clarksville, TN

WORD OF GOD

The earth was formless and void, and darkness was
over the surface of the deep, and the Spirit of God
was moving over the surface of the waters.

GENESIS 1:2, NASB

We see the Holy Spirit moving, hovering—but not yet working. What's he waiting for? Why doesn't the Holy Spirit create light in this darkness? Here's why: The Holy Spirit is waiting for the Word of God to be spoken. The Holy Spirit doesn't work where there is no Word. There is no Word until verse 3. Where there is no Word of God, there is no work of God.

As the Word comes to you, the Spirit works in you. Where there is no Word of God there is no work of God. So many experience emptiness in their lives and wonder why the Holy Spirit doesn't come and do something. He works where there is the Word. Is the Word of God flowing in your life? He is waiting for you to take up the Word even now! God has a word to speak to your finances/faith/emotions/marriage/health. . . . He is waiting for you to take up the Word.

Bible reading and Bible study are so strategic. Listening for the voice of God is crucial, because the Word of God releases the work of God in you by his Spirit!

Tim Brown
Senior Pastor, Calvary Chapel, Fremont, CA

PATIENCE IN WAITING

*Be patient, then, brothers and sisters, until the
Lord's coming. See how the farmer waits for the land to
yield its valuable crop, patiently waiting for the autumn
and spring rains. You, too, be patient and stand
firm, because the Lord's coming is near.*

JAMES 5:7–8, NIV

The Message version of James 5:7 reads, "Meanwhile, friends, wait patiently for the Master's Arrival."

Much of life is about waiting patiently on the Lord's timing. We might as well accept it and learn how to do it! We do it by trusting him and surrendering to him. When there's no longer a battle between our will and his, calmness settles in. Peace comes with the absence of striving. In our waiting, we must "stay steady and strong" (v. 8).

Just like the farmer tending his crops, God will give us things to do while we're waiting (even if it's "just" the crucial job of praying or the act of worshiping him). He may show us little ways to bless others, such as a friendly hello to a stranger, a phone call, a note, and so on. Simply do what he says without rushing him. Rest in his time schedule.

Jorja Stewart
Cofounder, www.musicthatblessesothers.com,
Author, Relation Tips blog (jorjastewart.com)

HE IS THE FATHER TO THE FATHERLESS

A father to the fatherless, a defender of
widows, is God in his holy dwelling.

PSALM 68:5, NIV

There are many kinds of earthly fathers in the world; some are loving, supportive, merciful, and faithful. The reality of today is that more and more have abandoned the forms and ideals of marriage and parenthood. This may result in societal breakdown, which often produces abusive, angry, and disconnected fathers.

My father suffered from alcoholism for many years. Growing up in that environment caused me to develop trust issues and feelings of abandonment. During my adult life I was seeking the Scriptures for healing, so when I read those words with great joy, "He is the Father to the fatherless," I began to realize that God loved me as his own. I could trust him with my past, present, and future. He was my very foundation, and I wanted to know his presence.

In Matthew 6:9, Jesus directs us to pray, "Our Father who art in heaven" (ASV). These words bring to us the hope that God is our Father. He sees our wounds and our weaknesses with eyes of compassion and mercy.

No matter where you came from or what you have done, you have a Heavenly Father that waits for you to call out for him.

Paige Junaeus
Founder, Paige Junaeus Ministries, International Speaker,
Columnist, and Creative www.turn2paige.com

THE PENDULUM SWING

When the woman saw that the fruit of the tree was good for
food and pleasing to the eye, and also desirable for gaining wisdom,
she took some and ate it. She also gave some to her
husband, who was with her, and he ate it.

GENESIS 3:6, NIV

One of my earliest ministries was in the affluent suburbs of North Dallas. During our time there, my wife and I were shocked to find that nearly a third of the girls in our area struggled with either anorexia or bulimia. We would be on retreats, and these skinny girls would either not eat or run to the restroom to purge themselves right after dinner.

As the young ladies opened up to us, we found the root of their self-image problems was a result of societal pressure to look thin.

Eventually we ended up doing youth ministry in Huntington, West Virginia. The girls here had self-image problems as well, but their issues had a different manifestation. In 2009 the CDC released a report stating that our city was the most obese city in America. We had moved from one extreme to the other.

Isn't that Satan's way? Just as with Eve in the Garden of Eden, he takes something that is good (in this case, food) and perverts it to extremes. It's no accident that Satan's first temptation for both Jesus and Adam revolved around the misuse of food (see Matthew 4:3).

God, help us to be on our guard today and use your gifts the way you designed them—for good.

Steve Willis
Lead Pastor, First Baptist Church, Kenova, WV

WILL YOU FIND REST?

*Thus says the LORD: "Stand in the ways and see, and
ask for the old paths, where the good way is, and walk in it;
then you will find rest for your souls. But they said,
'We will not walk in it.' Also, I set watchmen over you,
saying, 'Listen to the sound of the trumpet!'
But they said, 'We will not listen.'"*

JEREMIAH 6:16, NKJV

God wants us to return to our first love of him and his saving grace. He wants us to look to the paths of the saints of the Old and New Testaments and walk in their footsteps of faith. He wants us to listen to those who love us and watch over us as their own sheep protecting us from the presence of our enemy.

Will you walk? Will you listen? Will you find rest?

Garry Ansdell
Senior Pastor, Hosanna Christian Fellowship, Bellflower, CA

THREE STEPS OF A DISCIPLE

Then Jesus said to his disciples,
"If anyone wants to come with Me, he must deny
himself, take up his cross, and follow Me."

MATTHEW 16:24, HCSB

*J*esus gave us three steps to be a disciple.

First, we must deny ourselves. Jesus is not telling you to deprive yourself of vacations. He is telling you to step aside from the desires of the world and place your desires on his will, not yours. He is saying to prioritize your life around him.

Second, Jesus said to take up our cross. I'm not sure about you, but I don't have a cross, at least not literally. Jesus is talking about carrying forth the mission of Christ. We are to be the salt of the Earth. We are to spread the good news. The message and wonder of the cross are to be evident in us.

Third, Jesus told us to follow him. That may seem the easiest, but it is perhaps the most difficult.

I remember when I was younger, playing follow-the-leader. The guy in front made all the moves. The object was to follow the leader exactly.

Jesus is our leader. Each and every day we need to mimic the Savior. If we want to be disciples, we need to apply each of these three steps in our daily walk!

Ron Edmondson
Senior Pastor, Immanuel Baptist Church, Lexington, KY, RonEdmondson.com

SUFFERING IS NOT WASTED

Our light and momentary troubles
are achieving for us an eternal glory that
far outweighs them all.

2 CORINTHIANS 4:17, NIV

As the Potter molding—or remolding—you, using . . . pressure or problems? Stress or suffering? Hurt or heartache? Illness or injustice? Has he now placed you in the fire so that circumstances are heating up with intensity in your life? Then would you just trust the Potter to know exactly what he is doing?

For the child of God, suffering is not wasted. It's not an end in itself. Scripture reminds us, "For our light and momentary troubles are achieving for us an eternal glory that far outweighs them all." The spiritual principle is that in some way God uses suffering to transform ordinary, dust-clay people into vessels that are strong in faith . . . vessels that are fit for his use . . . vessels that display his glory to the watching world.

So don't waste your sorrow. Trust God!

Anne Graham Lotz
Founder, AnGel Ministries, www.annegrahamlotz.com

ASK GOD FIRST

Ask and it will be given to you;
seek and you will find; knock and the door
will be opened to you. For everyone who asks receives;
the one who seeks finds; and to the one who knocks,
the door will be opened. Which of you, if your son asks for bread,
will give him a stone? Or if he asks for a fish, will give him a snake?
If you, then, though you are evil, know how to give good gifts
to your children, how much more will your Father in
heaven give good gifts to those who ask him!

MATTHEW 7:7–11, NIV

Scripture says that God knows our needs before we even ask him. And we know that God is able to meet every one of those needs. Ever wonder why a loving and wonderful Father God just doesn't provide the answer without our asking? Let me offer this one thought: Maybe it's because he loves hearing our voices.

"To be a Christian without prayer is no more possible than to be alive without breathing" (Dr. Martin Luther King Jr.).

Prayer should be as much a part of our lives as our need to eat or sleep. When you place God first in your life, he knows how to make the rest of your life truly worth living. Let's start making it a habit to spend time in prayer with the One who loves us the most.

Brian A. Ross
Senior Pastor, Faith Chapel, Spring Valley, CA

WHO AM I?

👑 BIBLE READ: PSALM 8:1–9

> *LORD, our LORD, how majestic is your name in all the earth!*
> *You have set your glory in the heavens.*
>
> PSALM 8:1, NIV

When is the last time you looked into the sky on a clear night? Of course, the view is better out in the country where the darkness is not diffused by the lights of the city. On those rare occasions of nighttime star gazing, the beauty is breathtaking. The longer you look, the more your eyes are able to focus on the clusters of stars that form the constellations in our galaxy. In those moments, we often begin to feel really small and rather insignificant. If we ponder the vastness of the universe for any length of time, we find ourselves asking the ancient question of David, "What is man that you are mindful of him, and the son of man that you care for him?" (Psalm 8:4, NIV84).

The answer to that question is recorded for us as David celebrates the reality of God's love in the following comments:

- We are *created* by God (v. 5).
- We are *crowned* by God (v. 6).
- We are *cared* for by God (vv. 7–8).

Take this moment to think about how precious you are in God's eyes. Thank him for his everlasting love toward you.

Danny Sinquefield
Senior Pastor, Faith Baptist Church, Bartlett, TN

GOD'S REST

For he giveth his beloved sleep.

PSALM 127:2, ESV

*O*ur life should not be a life of anxiety and worry but a life of happy faith. Our Heavenly Father can and will meet the needs of his children. He knows our needs before we ask him.

There is no need to spend exhausting hours into the night planning what to do and say. Go to bed early learning how to trust and depend on our God, leaving our anxiety and worries on him. If we do this, we will never sleep with anxiety and fear that torments our hearts. He will give us healthy and quiet sleep. Our tongues will sing praises to his name.

It is a great honor to be God's beloved. Everyone who has this privilege should know that our bodies do not wish for more than that. Let us depart from our selfish desires. What is greater in heaven than the love of God?

Rest, oh my soul, in spite of the many waves of life that toss us left and right. God will not only show us how to rest but he will give us rest itself. We will sleep safely on his chest in life or death because he has sprinkled us with the blood of forgiveness.

We will rest in the bosom of God, in the chest of our Savior in happy sleep!

Dr. Elias Malki
Founder and President, Middle East Gospel Outreach

A Look in the Mirror

You shall love the LORD with all your heart,
with all your soul, with all your strength, and
with all your mind, and your
neighbor as yourself.

LUKE 10:27, NKJV

*L*oving yourself is sandwiched between loving God and loving others and is inextricably linked to both. In other words, how you feel about yourself impacts your ideas about God and other people. Is God cantankerous or critical, pushy or invasive? Perhaps a look in the mirror is all you need to adjust your attitude for the day. When we see ourselves as God does, his love can flow through us to those around us without the spin our frame of mind can put on it. God always sees us as members of his family: imperfect yet totally acceptable, totally loved.

Jeff Jernigan
Senior Pastor, Corona Friends Church, Corona, CA

THE CORNERSTONE

See, I lay a stone in Zion, a chosen and precious
cornerstone, and the one who trusts in
him will never be put to shame.

1 PETER 2:6, NIV

*A*ncient buildings all began with one large rock called the cornerstone. It was laid as a guide to line up the rest of the structure. Without the foundation stone, the entire building would be off-kilter—unsound and unsafe. This is a popular biblical metaphor describing Jesus, the Messiah, as the Cornerstone of our lives.

As God incarnate, Jesus promises that if anyone puts his Word into practice, their lives will be as solid as a well-built house—that when the storms of life rage, those trusting in him would be completely safe in life or in death. These lives are solid because they are living by God's wisdom, protected by God's power, and energized by God's love. What can destroy what God has established? Line up your life with me and my word, Jesus says, and in the end, you'll never be put to shame. Are you building on the Cornerstone?

Dr. Ross Reinman
Senior Pastor, The Rock, Santa Rosa, CA

THE DANGEROUS TONGUE

And the tongue is a fire, a world of iniquity.
The tongue is so set among our members that it defiles the
whole body, and sets on fire the course of nature;
and it is set on fire by hell.

*H*ave you ever wished you could take back the words you said to someone, only afterward feeling remorse and needing that person and Christ's forgiveness? Christians tend to be conscientious about what proceeds from their lips: "death and life are in the power of the tongue" (Proverbs 18:21). We have seen God use us in ministering to others, and we have seen the damaging effects of a loose, uncontrolled tongue. Idle words can be dangerous, and it can be more than difficult to reconcile after unguarded words have been spoken.

Maybe you've hurt someone with your words. It is important that you go back to them and apologize in sincerity. Remember, "Be quick to listen and slow to speak" (James 1:19, NIV), while being led by the Spirit. Make an effort to find the right words to say that are seasoned with God's grace. God has called you to build up and speak life-giving words. You might have the one word that brings healing to a broken relationship. Are you ready to be that vessel of God's grace? I hope so, because someone is waiting. Someone is watching. Someone might need a kind word spoken from you today.

John Schaffer
Senior Pastor, First Love Calvary Chapel, Whittier, CA

GIVE US THIS DAY

Give us each day our
daily bread.

LUKE 11:3, NIV

A dear friend of mine received terrible news from a recent physical examination. His blood and bones showed signs of an aggressive cancer undetected at another complete examination just six months prior. While he felt fine, the prognosis proved grim. After making a fruitless trip to a national cancer institute, he returned home to face a powerful regime of cancer treatments.

As the illness progressed along with the grind of painful treatments, he found the Lord's Prayer ever on his mind. He felt led to concentrate on the phrase "Give us this day our daily bread," with the focus on the word "day." His prayer was to survive one more day and to experience one more day of God's grace, of God's creation, and of the love around him. While he remained confident in his faith and in the love of God, he sought in prayer strength for one more day, and then the next day. So may God give us all each day and each next day in his good will.

Dr. Lee G. Royce
President, Mississippi College, Clinton, MS

I'M ALL IN

Now a certain man [was lying near the pool of Bethesda]
who had an infirmity for thirty-eight years. When Jesus saw him
lying there, and knew that he had been in that condition
a long time, he said to him, "Do you want to be made well?"
The sick man answered him, "Sir, I have no man to put me into the
pool when the water is stirred up; but while I am coming,
another steps down before me." Jesus said to him,
"Rise, take up your mat, and walk."

JOHN 5:5–8, NKJV

We live in a country where close to 87 percent of people say they are Christian. I don't know what that means for them; I can only speak for myself. I was a Christian most of my life, but didn't really know what it meant to be a follower of Jesus. There is a difference! I needed to be healed from playing the role of Christian and fulfilling my religious duties. I had to admit I wasn't following Jesus anywhere. He was just along for the ride.

What Jesus was doing to the man at Bethesda was calling him into a love relationship with the living God. The man was healed physically, but what goes unnoticed is that he was healed spiritually as well. "Sin no more" (John 5:14). Today, Jesus is calling you into a relationship, not into being more religious. The question is: Will you follow? Will you lay down your life and follow no matter the cost, no matter the place, no matter the change? If yes, you are on your way to becoming a fully devoted follower, and Jesus invites you to walk with him.

Matthew Cork
Senior Pastor, Yorba Linda Friends Church, Yorba Linda, CA

FEARFULLY AND
WONDERFULLY MADE

The word of the LORD came to me, saying,
"Before I formed you in the womb I knew you,
before you were born I set you apart."

JEREMIAH 1:4–5, NIV

God told Jeremiah that he "formed" Jeremiah in the womb. While we may think that God created Adam and Eve and backed off, Scripture tells us that he is intimately involved with every one of us even before we exist.

God not only forms us in the womb, he knows each of us as individuals before we are created. He told Jeremiah that before he formed him, he knew him and set him apart as a prophet. Even before our conception, in the eyes of Almighty God each of us is a personality with worth and purpose.

Psalm 139 adds, "You formed my inward parts; you covered me in my mother's womb," and that we are "fearfully and wonderfully made" (vv. 13, 14, NKJV). How does God form our inward parts? How does he create eyes that can see and relate what is seen to a brain? How do our brains independently think endless thoughts? Or how does he make life-giving blood that flows through a mass of amazing vessels that make the complex freeways of Los Angeles look simple? How does he give us an invisible soul with its own unique personality? We are truly "fearfully and wonderfully made."

Ray Comfort
Founder and CEO, Living Waters / The Way of the Master

A SPECIAL BLESSING

When you give a banquet, invite the poor, the crippled,
the lame, the blind and you will be blessed.

LUKE 14:13, NIV

ou can find thousands of web sites on how to plan a dinner party or church picnic, but you would be hard pressed to find one with ideas on how to include families affected by disabilities. Yet, it is estimated that these families make up about 20 percent of every community, and few attend church. They are often stressed out with demanding schedules and isolated from activities that most families enjoy. In a parents' survey, families coping with disabilities said the one thing they needed the most from a church was to simply be accepted.

The people of God have often been call on to be caregivers. Jesus modeled caring for others throughout his ministry on earth. He stopped to touch the blind, the crippled and the lame, healing many of them. In the Parable of the Great Banquet, Jesus honored the disabled by instructing the host to invite them into his house so it would be full. In the same way, our church doors should be open wide to these families because they need to know Jesus Christ and use their spiritual gifts in his service.

People with disabilities want your friendship—not your pity. Genuine compassion comes when we recognize our own weaknesses and enter into authentic, mutual relationship. If you want to deepen your faith, make it your prayerful goal to get to know one person with a special need. As promised, it will be a special blessing.

Pat Verbal
Manager of Curriculum Development, Christian Institute on Disability
Joni and Friends, Agoura Hills, CA

HOPE AND FORGIVENESS

Be kind and compassionate to one another,
forgiving each other, just as in Christ God forgave you.

In the stillness of the morning the religious leaders brought before Jesus a barely covered woman caught in adultery. One of the accusers said, "Teacher, this woman was caught in the act of adultery. The Law of Moses commands that we stone such a woman. What do you say about this?" (John 8:5, NIV) Jesus did not answer the question but instead bent down and started to write on the ground with his finger. As the crowd kept pushing the issue, Jesus stood up and said to the mob, "If anyone in this group is without sin, let that person be the first one to throw a stone at her." (John 8:6, NIV) Jesus glared at the crowd and stooped down to write on the ground again. You could hear the echo noise in the temple courtyard as the crowd dropped their rocks of judgment and left.

Have you ever felt like you were being unfairly judged or misinterpreted by others because of a social gaffe or a past mistake? You hear the gossip, you sense the social distancing, and feel the pain of rejection. Like the woman caught in adultery, we can find hope, forgiveness, and understanding from Jesus. Remember, your new beginning is just one prayer away.

Steve M. Woods
Chairman, Board of Directors, www.WoodsMasteryLearningFoundation.org

STRATEGICALLY PLACED

In the year that King Uzziah died, I saw
the Lord seated on a throne, high and exalted, and
the train of his robe filled the temple.

*J*udah had lived for fifty-two years under the rule and reign of one of its best and brightest: King Uzziah.

Uzziah became king at the ripe age of sixteen! Imagine the pressure. Imagine the responsibility on such young shoulders. However, by God's grace, King Uzziah led the people of Judah into five decades of prosperity. The Bible tells us that Uzziah was victorious in war, built up cities, and fortified the land. He sought the Lord, and the Lord was with him!

Uzziah was a people's king. The nation loved him—and for good cause. He was benevolent and brave, having great leadership among his people. He cared for them, and they loved him back. And then, Uzziah, the beloved king, *died*.

After fifty-two years of leadership, fifty-two years of success and fame, fifty-two years of serving the people of Judah, King Uzziah died! Imagine the loss and grief the people must have felt. But in those days, God called one of the greatest prophets of all time into his service. Isaiah 6:1 tells us it was "in the year that King Uzziah died" that God called Isaiah to serve his people. That timing brings an important truth to the surface: God uses his people at strategic times. You are where you are for a reason. There are no mistakes in God's master plan.

Brent Eldridge
Lead Pastor, First Baptist Church of Lakewood, Long Beach, CA

LEARNING TO WAIT ON THE LORD

Tell the priests who carry the Ark of the Covenant:
"When you reach the edge of the Jordan's waters, go and stand
in the river." . . . And it shall come to pass, as soon as the
soles of the feet of the priests who bear the ark of the LORD . . .
shall rest in the waters of the Jordan, that the waters
of the Jordan shall be cut off, the waters that come down
from upstream, and they shall stand as a heap.

JOSHUA 3:8 (NIV), 13 (KJV)

It is interesting to note that in the passage above the Lord asked them to put their feet in the raging spring river and then to stand and wait for a miracle. They had to literally step out in faith. How long did they stand still in the Jordan? It was dammed up seventeen to nineteen miles north. They obeyed but didn't realize their miracle immediately.

So often as we walk by faith, Jesus asks us to obey and then wait to see him move. Waiting is certainly not in our nature, but it is his call for us. Over and over Scripture declares it, "But those who wait for the LORD, they will inherit the land" (Psalm 37:9, NASB). "Make me know your ways, O Lord; Teach me your paths. Lead me in your truth and teach me, for you are the God of my salvation; for you I wait all the day" (Psalm 25:4–5). Are you ready to step out by faith and wait on the Lord? Waiting is our means to a deeper, trusting relationship with Jesus.

Dan Carroll
Senior Pastor, Water of Life Community Church, Fontana, CA

LIVING IN TENTS

👑 BIBLE READ: HEBREWS 11:8–22

When Abraham left his home of comfort and wealth in Ur, he did so in faith, and in so doing, Hebrews 11:2 says he obtained a good testimony. Abraham lived a certain nomadic pilgrim existence (v. 9), dwelling in tents as did Isaac and Jacob, his son and grandson, heirs of the same promise.

Abraham waited for his glorious dwelling in the city that has foundations whose builder and maker is God (v. 10). Why did he give up so much to live a life of faith, like a nomad, dwelling in tents, moving from place to place, not looking back at what he once owned before he encountered God?

Because he trusted in the promise of God—that God would do as he said.

Faith for Abraham and his descendants meant they would live their lives and dwell not in permanent homes but in permanent hope, daily striving (some days better than others) to live in the consciousness of an eternal destiny.

Lord, let us walk in obedient faith as people daily seduced to do otherwise.

Lord, let us never forget there is a city whose Architect and Builder is you, so that it's okay to live in tents and to see life as a pilgrimage.

Dr. Barry H. Corey
President, Biola University, La Mirada, CA

DECIDE!

But if you refuse to serve the LORD, then choose today
whom you will serve. Would you prefer the gods your ancestors
served beyond the Euphrates? Or will it be the gods of the
Amorites in whose land you now live? But as for me
and my family, we will serve the LORD.

JOSHUA 24:15, NLT

God's people, the Israelites, had come through many difficult times and were at the edge of a spiritual cliff. Over a period of many years, God had miraculously set them free from slavery in Egypt, brought them through the Red Sea on dry ground, provided food and water for them while wandering in the desert, helped them survive attacks from enemies, and brought them into an amazing new Promised Land. Now they stood at the precipice of decision.

The congregation had started to intermarry with people from surrounding regions who had pagan mystical belief systems and values that were contrary to God's law. Intermarrying is a metaphor for our decisions to morally wed ourselves to things other than God. Joshua was very straightforward. Choose today and settle it! Decide *now!*"

There comes a time for all of us when we must stop kicking the can down the road and decide where we're going to stand! God is challenging you to make a decision. It might be a moral decision or a fundamental choice once and for all to surrender your life completely to him. There comes a time when God asks, "Is that your final answer?"

Gary Hoyt
Senior Pastor, Bellevue Christian Center, Bellevue, NE

GLAD NEWS FOR EVERYONE

I have other sheep that do not belong to this fold.
I must bring them also, and they will listen to my voice.
So there will be one flock, one shepherd.

*M*any experienced missionaries to the Muslim world are sharing that dreams and visions are leading Muslims to Jesus in unprecedented numbers. One out of four people living in the world today is a Muslim. More Muslims have come to Christ in the past fifty to sixty years than in the past 1,400 years.

Most Muslims are spiritually thirsty, searching for the truth and a sincere desire to have a right relationship with their Creator. Most of them never had a good chance to understand the biblical teaching. Yet God promised Abraham that He will bless Ishmael (Genesis 17:20). God told us in 1 Chronicles 1:28–29 that Ishmael's first two sons are Nebaioth and Kedar. We know from Isaiah 21:13–17 that the Arab people came from Kedar. God told us in Isaiah 60:7 that the descendants of Kedar and Nebaioth will know God.

God loves the Muslim and you so much that he is willing to do whatever it takes to reach us. Jesus often told parables about hidden treasures, lost coins, lost sheep that someone would be willing to give up everything to find. That's the kind of love God has for you. Jesus was willing to leave heaven and give up everything, even his own life, to bring you back home.

Samy Tanagho
Founder and President of Glad News for Muslims Ministry
www.gladnewsministry.com

First of All

Therefore I exhort first of all that supplications,
prayers, intercessions, and giving of thanks be made for all men,
for kings and all who are in authority, that we may lead a
quiet and peaceable life in all godliness and reverence.

1 TIMOTHY 2:1–2, NKJV

In this passage, Paul describes a grace-shaped life. It is first of all devoted to prayer for all people. There's no one beyond the scope of God's grace, including seemingly godless authorities. Consider the Roman emperor when Paul penned this: Nero.

According to conventional wisdom, Nero was someone you prayed against, not for. He was an enemy of the church who made sport of torturing Christians before putting them to death in the most diabolical ways. Nero had Paul arrested and executed. Yet here Paul calls Christians to pray for him.

Paul wasn't spinning out an idealistic but impractical call here. He knew firsthand how important prayer for hostile leaders was. He'd been one! He began as a Christian-hating agent of the Sanhedrin who'd officiated at the execution of the first martyr, Stephen. He heard Stephen's dying prayer, "Father, forgive them." God answered that prayer and turned Paul into an apostle, who would himself one day be martyred for his faith.

God delights in turning Sauls into Pauls. No one is beyond the reach of God's grace. So pray!

Lance E. Ralston
Senior Pastor, Calvary Chapel, Oxnard, CA

STAY IN THE RACE

Let us not grow weary while doing good,
for in due season we shall reap if
we do not lose heart.

GALATIANS 6:9, NKJV

In the Christian life, when you finish, you win!

The race is not to the fastest or strongest. The race is won by the faithful, the one who finishes.

We remember the tremendous movie *Ben Hur* and the famous chariot race scene. On the day for the chariot scene, actor Charlton Heston said to director William Wilder, "I think I can drive the chariot all right, but I'm not sure I can actually win the race." Smiling slightly, Wilder said, "Heston, you just stay in the race, and I'll make sure you win."

Our loving Father says the same to you. "Stay in the race. Run the race I have assigned you. Be faithful, and I will give you the crown of life. I will make sure that you win!"

When you finish, you win.

Dr. Roger Freeman
Senior Pastor (Retired), First Baptist Church, Clarksville, TN

GOD'S KIND OF LOVE

👑 BIBLE READ: GENESIS 50:15–21

When Joseph's brothers saw that their father was dead,
they said, "What if Joseph holds a grudge against us and
pays us back for all the wrongs we did to him?" . . .
"This is what you are to say to Joseph: 'I ask you to forgive
your brothers the sins and the wrongs they
committed in treating you so badly.'"

GENESIS 50:15, 17, NIV

We have all been at one time or another where Joseph's brothers are here in Genesis. We have wronged somebody and they have forgiven us, but the relationship is still strained in a sense due to our inability to believe we are truly forgiven. Sometimes we will say that we have forgiven someone, only to bring up the offense again at a later date. Joseph's brothers are assuming that is the case here. They have this suspicion that their brother will finally be able to get even, now that their father has died.

But Joseph is a portrait of grace and how we should all respond when others treat us unfairly. It has been said that when we forgive, we stop trying to play God. I like that analogy. God is the Judge—the only righteous Judge.

Is there someone you need to forgive? Like Joseph, is there someone you need to show unmerited kindness and forgiveness?

Mike Osthimer
Senior Pastor, Calvary Chapel, Bakersfield, CA

The Street Preacher

But you will receive power when the Holy Spirit comes on you;
and you will be my witnesses in Jerusalem, and in all
Judea and Samaria, and to the ends of the earth.

ACTS 1:8, NIV

While attending seminary I had a friend who loved to street witness. One night he talked me into going down to the French Quarter of New Orleans and witness to some random folks. I have never felt so out of place. My friend was really good at this— me, not so much.

As he was passionately sharing the love of Jesus with two guys, I was standing there looking really uncomfortable when I heard someone saying, "Hey you, you with the preacher." I turned and searched for the voice and didn't see anyone. The voice came again, "Hey you, big guy." I thought I was having a Samuel experience only to notice a guy standing right by me; he was about three feet tall. I stooped down, and he said, "Man, you don't belong down here. What are you doing?" I explained why I was there, and we struck up a conversation.

He was super-interesting—super-broken—needing Jesus. We had a great chat, and he shared his story and his struggles. I promised to pray for him, and I did. I gave him my Bible and I went home.

When we decide to follow Jesus as intentional disciples, we no longer live for ourselves but we are on a mission from God. God invites you into the assignment of making him known—making him famous. The assignment is the call to all of us who claim the name of Jesus. I hope you will choose to make Jesus known to someone by your words or your deeds.

Scott Weatherford
Lead Pastor, First Alliance Church, Calgary, AB, Canada

THE IMPORTANCE
OF PRAYER AND FASTING

Is not this the kind of fasting I have chosen:
to loose the chains of injustice and untie the cords of
the yoke, to set the oppressed free and break every yoke?
Is it not to share your food with the hungry and to provide the
poor wanderer with shelter—when you see the naked, to
clothe him, and not to turn away from your own flesh and blood?
Then your light will break forth like the dawn, and your
healing will quickly appear; then your righteousness
will go before you, and the glory of the
LORD will be your rear guard.

ISAIAH 58:6–8, NIV

Prayer and fasting are important because we prepare for them by humbling ourselves, confessing our sins, and opening up to God's will for our lives. Second, the book of Acts tells us that praying and fasting strengthen and guide us in our calling. Third, they offer the most powerful way to deal with satanic forces. Prayer and fasting are what Jesus did when he was tempted by the devil. The flesh is diametrically opposed to the Spirit, and when we fast and pray, we deny the flesh. No wonder this blesses God. I hope that you make prayer and fasting a regular part of your spiritual walk with God.

Steve Price
Senior Pastor, Calvary Chapel, Bear Creek, CA

FREE FROM CONTROL

Obviously, I'm not trying to win the
approval of people, but of God. If pleasing
people were my goal, I would not
be Christ's servant.

*T*he Bible teaches us that the bondage of people pleasing can keep us from fully serving Christ. Paul always sought to please God. He always wanted God's smile, even if that meant he wouldn't have the smile of the world.

Let's determine, because we have God's acceptance, to live our lives looking only for the Lord's smile and approval. We can live with man's disapproval as long as we know that we have the Lord's approval and smile.

The way to become free of controlling people is to live as a servant of God.

Mark Martin
Senior Pastor, Calvary Community Church, Phoenix, AZ

GOD AND CREATION

👑 BIBLE READ: PSALM 19

*In the beginning God created the
heavens and the earth.*

GENESIS 1:1, NIV

$\mathcal{T}$he above passage says it all. How's that for succinct? After Genesis 1:1, Moses elaborates in just six to eight paragraphs (depending on the translation you choose) what Paul Harvey might have called "the rest of the story."

Just when you thought he couldn't be any more concise, Moses almost deadpans, "Thus the heavens and the earth were completed in all their vast array" (Genesis 2:1).

Such incredible truth in so few words! The Bible opens with a statement of faith—not an argument for intelligent design. We immediately encounter the presence of an involved, creating, designing, intentional God. We discover a God who is to be met, not studied. He is a God who has left his mark on the universe. Indeed, the span of the galaxies and the scope of history bear his signature.

When the first two pages of Genesis are complete, we have a universe in place, complete with an inhabited earth. Human beings are living in community with each other, creation, and the Creator. It is an idyllic paradise where tranquility is a given and shame, a stranger. Let us appreciate God's creation this and every day.

Dennis R. Wiles, PhD
Senior Pastor, First Baptist Church, Arlington, TX

THE POWER OF FELLOWSHIP

They devoted themselves to the
apostles' teaching and to fellowship, to the
breaking of bread, and to prayer.

ACTS 2:42, NIV

God doesn't want us to simply exist in our journey of faith. He wants us to thrive. A thriving Christian life was not designed to be lived out alone. If we want to have the power and insight of the early church, we need to have the perspective and priorities of the early church.

Acts 2 tells us that the early Christians "devoted themselves to the apostles' teaching and to fellowship, to the breaking of bread and to prayer . . . Everyone was filled with awe. . . ." Today we seem to understand the priorities of being devoted to the apostles' teaching (the Bible) and to prayer (our conversations with God). But our generation has gotten very casual about fellowship. We have forgotten that God designed his church in the context of community. In fact, the early Christians couldn't even conceive of a Christian outside of a Christian community. They knew there is enormous power in community. That's why the early believers didn't just *have* fellowship; they *devoted* themselves to it! Since there is no substitute for it, don't forsake it. Pursue it, get involved, and thrive as God calls you deeper in his community of faith.

Brian Cashman
Senior Pastor, Valley Metro Church, Sherman Oaks, CA

Becoming Informed

We love each other because he loved us first.

1 JOHN 4:19, NLT

While God wants us to love one another, he does not ask us to put our brains on the shelf and become doormats for other people. He does ask us to put their considerations before our own, but not in the way you might think. "Do nothing from selfishness or empty conceit, but with humility of mind regard one another as more important than yourselves; do not merely look out for your own personal interests, but also for the interests of others" (Philippians 2:3–4, NASB). Our interests are important to God. However, when it comes to solid relationships, Paul encourages us to put our interests aside long enough to allow the interests of others to influence our own.

Hear someone out today, listening carefully, before you put your agenda on the table. If you take time to listen, something they say may make a difference to you that could have been missed if you were merely looking out for your own interests.

Jeff Jernigan
Senior Pastor, Corona Friends Church, Corona, CA

NOT RULED BY RULES

Who is my neighbor?

LUKE 10:29, NKJV

"Who's my neighbor?" That's the question a man asked Jesus, wanting to know how to be right with God. Initially, Jesus told him it takes a loving relationship with God that naturally overflows to touch those around you. But this wasn't enough for the man. He wanted Jesus to define who his neighbor was, as if doing the right thing was a matter of following a rigid set of rules.

So Jesus shared a story about a man who was robbed and left on the roadside. Two people passed him by, while another man mercifully stopped to take care of him. Then Jesus asked the man who the true neighbor was. The man correctly answered that it was the one who showed mercy. So the Lord tells him, "Go and do the same" (Luke 10:37, NASB).

The Lord's point was this: Being right with God isn't about following some rulebook. It's about allowing the mercy and love that he's shown us to flow through our lives to as many people as possible. I hope you will take the time to make a difference in someone's life today.

Bob Coy
Senior Pastor, Calvary Chapel, Fort Lauderdale, FL

YESHUA

Therefore God exalted him to the highest place and gave him the
name that is above every name, that at the name of Jesus every knee
should bow, in heaven and on earth and under the earth.

PHILIPPIANS 2:9–10, NIV

What was Jesus's real name? It's *Yeshua*, a beautiful-sounding name. But even more beautiful is its meaning. The name of Jesus means "God is salvation." But the name is also beautiful because you're in it. Think about it: Why does God have anything to do with salvation? Because of one word—*you*—and another word—*me*. In fact, for all of us, the name Yeshua means God is salvation.

Whose salvation? Our salvation. Better than that, *your* salvation. You're in his name! Your salvation is in his name.

Whatever your name is, Yeshua and his love for you are in his name. God has, with all his heart, become your salvation—the answer to all of our needs. And there is no doubt that if you were the only one in the world who needed salvation, he still would have given his life. What a wonderful gift that your Yeshua gave his life to save you personally. And personally is the only way you can know him. He is not Jesus until you can call him "my Jesus." It's not salvation until you can say, "my Salvation, my Savior, my Joy, my Friend, my Life."

Is Yeshua your Savior? If not, make him so today at this moment. Remember, his holy name already has you in it! Yeshua—a beautiful name.

Jonathan Cahn
Author, The Harbinger, *Senior Pastor and Messianic Rabbi*
the Jerusalem Center/Beth Israel, Wayne, NJ

NEVER GIVE UP

And above all these [put on] love and enfold yourselves
with the bond of perfectness [which binds everything
together completely in ideal harmony].

COLOSSIANS 3:14, AMPLIFIED

*S*ome years ago my hairdresser mentioned to me that his younger gay brother was in the hospital dying of AIDS as we spoke about Christ and his teachings. He asked me to pray for his brother. I said yes, asking if I could possibly go to the hospital to pray for him in person as well.

As I continued to pursue a visit, the call came that his younger brother passed away. My heart felt very heavy for his loss. His family believed in God but didn't have a grasp on the knowledge of the salvation of Christ and the power of his resurrection. The entire family felt hopeless.

Never give up on yourself. Only the Lord knows what's in a person's heart. Upon his death, as they prepared to move him, the nurses discovered that the young man had torn Scriptures out of a Bible, clutching them in his hands and tucking salvation Scriptures between his mattresses. God was there in that hospital room working on his heart!

Never give up on anyone else. Family, friends, and a nurse from the hospital gathered at the burial site to say their last good-byes. The nurse shared with the brother that she cared for his younger brother until the end. She also shared with a smile that his younger brother gave his life to the Lord. She put on love, and Christ was made perfect in this situation.

Paige Junaeus
Founder, Paige Junaeus Ministries, International Speaker, Columnist, and Creative
www.turn2paige.com

The Fragrance of Christ

There is a story about a press correspondent in Europe who went to eat in a small restaurant. While he was there, a group of men entered for their lunch break. Immediately the room was permeated with the smell of perfume. When the men left, the correspondent asked the restaurant owner who those men were. The owner replied, "They are the workmen from the perfume factory, and they bring the scent of perfume in with them every time they come to eat."

In 2 Corinthians 2:15 Paul writes, "For we are to God the fragrance of Christ among those who are being saved and among those who are perishing" (NKJV). In other words, we are to permeate the world by bringing the fragrance of light and life to men. Every time we leave a room, we should be leaving the scent of Christ. Every time we leave a family gathering, we should be leaving the scent of Christ. Every time we leave a conversation, we should be leaving the scent of Christ.

May we be continually alert to the Holy Spirit working in and through us so that we will exude the godly, influential fragrance of Christ! Let that fragrance linger and permeate the lives of those we've touched.

"To follow truth as blind men long for light, To do my best from dawn of day till night, To keep my heart fit for His holy sight, This is my task" ("To Love Someone More Dearly," Maude Louise Ray).

Ron Hindt
Senior Pastor, Calvary Chapel, Houston, TX

THE EXTRA MILE

You have heard it said, "Eye for eye, and tooth for tooth."
But I tell you, do not resist an evil person. If someone strikes you
on the right cheek, turn to him the other also. And if someone
wants to sue you and take your tunic, let him have your
cloak as well. If someone forces you to go
one mile, go with him two miles.

MATTHEW 5:38, NIV84

The Jews didn't like this new law of love very much. It meant they would have to sacrifice their afternoon plans or give up their best clothing or suffer a few black eyes for the sake of their enemy. Some of them probably said, "No thanks, Jesus. I'm not walking the extra mile today!"

But what if Jesus hadn't lived by his own law? What if, at some point along the way, he had decided that wearing the garb of humanity wasn't worth it? What if, instead of stumbling up the hill to Golgotha, he had dropped the cross off his shoulders and gone back to his Father in heaven? Thank God we never have to know the answer to that!

Jesus didn't just tell us to walk the extra mile. He showed us how to walk it. So let's follow his footsteps today. It might require a little sacrifice. It might not seem convenient. But it will be worth it in the end.

Dr. Stephen Davey
Senior Pastor, Colonial Baptist Church, Cary, NC

THE LORD'S BATTLE

👑 BIBLE READ: 2 CHRONICLES 20:1–27

Not by might nor by power, but by my Spirit,
says the Lord Almighty.

ZECHARIAH 4:6, NIV

The quarter-century reign of Jehoshaphat is one of the rare bright spots in Judah's checkered history. When Jehoshaphat ascended the throne in 873 BC, he continued the religious reforms of his father, Asa. But when someone attempts to serve God, Satan usually becomes active. As 2 Chronicles 20:1 indicates, the peace of Judah was suddenly interrupted by a confederacy of the Moabites and Ammonites.

What would King Jehoshaphat do? Would he fight or would he knuckle under? Jehoshaphat "set himself to seek the LORD, and proclaimed a fast throughout all Judah" (NKJV). When the king finished praying, a little-known man named Jahaziel began to prophesy by the Spirit of the Lord. His message was simple: "Thus says the LORD to you: 'Do not be afraid nor dismayed because of this great multitude, for the battle is not yours, but God's'" (v. 15).

That's a lesson we all need to learn. It doesn't matter how formidable our enemy is or how tough our trials are, as long as we recognize we are not fighting alone. The battle is not yours, but God's. Knowing that makes all the difference.

Woodrow Kroll
President, Back to the Bible, Lincoln, NE

LIVING IN GOD'S TIME

Get your supplies ready. Three days from
now you will cross the Jordan here to go in and
take possession of the land the LORD your
God is giving you for your own.

JOSHUA 1:11, NIV84

*T*he Israelites, after forty years of wandering and waiting, heard God declare in no uncertain terms, "The time is now. Go forward." God has given you a destiny, a possibility of life you have never had, and you must get ready in three days.

Timing has always been central to all God has done and will do. Jesus warned in Matthew 24 and 25 that no man knows the hour or the day he will return, but it was obvious that the day and hour had been established in the Father's heart. It is no different in our lives. God has our purposes established. But we must often wait—not usually forty years, but it seems like it when we are impatient.

Remember the Word of the Lord to those who would honor and serve him: "Wait for the LORD; Be strong and let your heart take courage; Yes, wait for the LORD" (Psalm 27:14, NASB).

Father, I confess that waiting is hard to do. Holy Spirit, build your patience in me. Jesus, teach me not to force my time on your plans, but to wait until you say the fruit is ripe.

Dan Carroll
Senior Pastor, Water of Life Community Church, Fontana, CA

THEY THAT SOW IN
TEARS SHALL REAP IN JOY!

Those who sow with tears will reap with
songs of joy. Those who go out weeping, carrying
seed to sow, will return with songs of joy,
carrying sheaves with them.

PSALM 126:5–6, NIV

*T*he time of weeping is the best time to sow, because the ground needs to be flooded with our tears so that the crop will grow quickly. The small amount of salt from our tears will protect the seed from infestation by insects living in the soil. The truth we speak in faith gives power that helps the seed to germinate and grow.

It is the time of tears and not the time of laughter that provides the best conditions for sowing, because the deep sorrow and concerns for other souls is closer to Jesus's teaching. We have heard about the soldiers who go to war with little concern for their commitment and end up deserting the battle. The same will happen to those who do not sow in tears and sincere concern for lost souls.

Come, my heart, and sow with tears and remember God's promise to see the fruit of joyful harvest. Seed will not grow without water, and we will not see the joy of the harvest. Remember that when tears fall from our eyes, the golden harvest will welcome and bear all the tribulations with an open heart. The harvest is near; do not wait, it is growing late. Behold the fields are ripe. It's harvest time!

Dr. Elias Malki
Founder and President, Middle East Gospel Outreach

GOD CARES, THROUGH US

👑 BIBLE READ: JOHN 6:1–14

*The generous will themselves be blessed, for
they share their food with the poor.*

PROVERBS 22:9, NIV

Jesus didn't just see a "multitude" that day on that hillside; He saw *people*: hungry men, women, and children who'd been traveling all day along dusty roads. Their need for food was real. They were weak and faint. They needed sustenance. He was moved by their need and moved to meet it.

God knows your needs. He sees when your pantry is bare because you're out of work. He knows when the bills are due and there's no money in the checking account. He knows, and he cares.

While it's true our greatest need is spiritual, that doesn't lessen the reality of the physical. God wants to prove he's sufficient to meet our spiritual need by taking care of our physical needs.

Jesus fed the hungry that day through a miracle he worked through the hands of his followers. They were the ones who passed out the food. Jesus sees not only our needs but those of others as well. Just as he used the disciples to feed the hungry, he wants to use us to meet the needs around us.

Lance E. Ralston
Senior Pastor, Calvary Chapel, Oxnard, CA

SHINE BRIGHT

In the same way, let your light shine before men,
that they may see your good deeds and
praise your Father in heaven.

*J*esus was clear that he has no interest in covert Christians. He expects our commitment to him to "shine" forth in everything we do. He has no tolerance for tasteless garnish and lamps with opaque shades (Matthew 5:14–15). He says that Christians who blend in are "good for nothing" (v. 13, NKJV). It is no surprise that Jesus was not impressed with Nicodemus, who wanted to chat with the Christ under the cover of darkness (John 3:2). Jesus knows that our standing up and standing out would make a difference for eternity, as those rightly affected will one day "praise your Father in heaven" (Matthew 5:16, NIV84).

So, if those around you do not know why you think, live, or talk the way you do, be sure to fill them in that you have been changed. Let them know proudly and boldly that this lifelong journey of transformation is because you have become a follower of Christ.

Mike Fabarez
Senior Pastor, Compass Bible Church, Aliso Viejo, CA

ON THE POTTER'S WHEEL

The vessel that he made of clay was marred . . .
so he made it again another vessel, as
seemed good to the potter to make it.

JEREMIAH 18:4, KJV

A preacher who preaches from a wheelchair signs all his letters "On the Potter's Wheel." That is his way of saying that his Christian life is still in process and he is trusting God to mold him daily. Our life is clay in the divine Potter's wise and loving hands.

Louis Braille (1809–52) invented the method of raised dots on paper to symbolize letters of the alphabet, which permits blind persons to read. Braille was blinded as a child when he was playing with his father's awl. He fell on the awl and it struck his eye, blinding him. Years later Braille used the same awl that blinded him to create the Braille alphabet. Suffering was turned into blessing for others. Like the cross of Jesus, an instrument of death gave life to needy souls.

"Have Thine own way, Lord! Thou art the potter, I am the clay!"

Dr. Roger Freeman
Senior Pastor (Retired), First Baptist Church, Clarksville, TN

HOLY HUNGER

*But when you fast, put oil on your head and wash your face, so
that it will not be obvious to others that you are fasting, but
only to your Father, who is unseen; and your Father,
who sees what is done in secret, will reward you.*

*J*esus told his disciples, "*When* you fast," not "*If* you fast." The
implication is that Jesus expected fasting to be a normal part
of his followers' lives. Fasting is the voluntary abstinence from food
for a set period of time in order to seek God concerning an important or specific matter. The secret of fasting is that it creates physical
hunger that is designed by God to fuel a holy hunger.

Let your appetite for nourishment and craving for food be a picture
of how your soul should be stirred to desire God. Augustine (AD 354–
430) described the effects of his fasting this way: "Fasting cleanses the
soul, raises the mind, subjects one's flesh to the spirit, renders the heart
contrite and humble, scatters the clouds of concupiscence, quenches
the fire of lust, and kindles the true light of chastity."

Is there an issue in your life that God is leading you to fast and
pray about? Fasting and prayer prepare the spiritual environment
for breakthroughs like nothing else can do. May God stir our holy
hunger.

Mark Jobe
Senior Pastor, New Life Community Church, Chicago, IL

GOD GIVES US WHAT
IS BEST FOR US

No good thing will he withhold from
those who walk uprightly.

PSALM 84:11, NASB

The psalmist here is reveling in the glory of corporate worship as he speaks of the grandeur of the Temple and the joy of praising God with all the people. And at the end of worship he comes to realize that God, being God, always does what is best and right. God always has our best in mind.

Yet it often doesn't seem that way. Things come into our lives bringing pain, confusion, and often despair. Where is God? Why has pain invaded our lives?

In this psalm the author has come to understand, through the act of corporate worship, that God's agenda doesn't always match up with his. And when this happens in our lives, we have to make a choice. Will we trust that God's plan to make us more like Jesus is our very best option? Or will we get mad at God because his blessings didn't come in the packages we felt we deserved? In those hard times, remember this: God is good all the time, and he gives us only what he knows is ultimately for our best, and for his glory.

Dr. David W. Hegg
Senior Pastor, Grace Baptist Church, Santa Clarita, CA

STRANGERS IN THIS WORLD

Peter, an apostle of Jesus Christ,
to God's chosen strangers
in the world.

1 PETER 1:1, CEB

*L*iving as a foreigner in another country can be filled with adventure, but it's certainly not without its difficulties. The necessary adjustment period is called "culture shock" for a reason. The Bible frequently uses the term "foreigner" to describe the Christian who, by virtue of being born again, immediately becomes an expatriate in his own country. The new life we're raised to is completely out of step with the world around us, from which we came. Suddenly we have opposing customs, language, and core values; right is wrong, and now wrong is right. Talk about culture shock—but Jesus reminds us that we don't fit in the world any more than he did. So, of course, we stand out, don't fit in, and rub people the wrong way; we've got heaven in our hearts. But one day, when God's kingdom comes, we'll be right at home.

Dr. Ross Reinman
Senior Pastor, The Rock, Santa Rosa, CA

What to Do and Not to Do with God's Word

*Do not merely listen to the word, and so
deceive yourselves. Do what it says. Anyone who listens
to the word but does not do what it says is like someone who
looks at his face in a mirror and, after looking at himself,
goes away and immediately forgets what he looks like.
But whoever looks intently into the perfect law
that gives freedom, and continues in it—
not forgetting what they have heard, but doing it—
they will be blessed in what they do.*

JAMES 1:22–25, NIV

Having received God's Word into our lives, it's very important to also respond to it by being what the Bible calls "doers of the Word." We must recognize the tendency to hear and not do. If we are hearing and not doing, then we are deceiving or betraying ourselves. Here's what happens if we just hear and don't do.

Hearing without doing is like looking in the mirror (God's Word does mirror our lives to ourselves) and seeing who we are and what we need to change. But without responding to God's Word, we will forget what we ought to do. We will remain unchanged.

But if we look into God's Word, and if we continue in it or respond to it—and not forget what it says—we will be blessed. God will work in our lives, changing us, transforming us, and then using our lives for his glory.

Bob Grenier
Senior Pastor, Calvary Chapel, Visalia, CA

THE END OF YOUR ROPE

He remembered our utter weakness.
His faithful love endures forever.

PSALM 136:23, NLT

*T*he One who remembers us in our times of trouble also remembered Elijah and Peter at their lowest points. Elijah was suffering from burnout after fighting the victorious battle on Mount Carmel (1 Kings 19:4), but an angel of the Lord came and strengthened him. God gave him new vision and direction for his life. Peter, also in dire straits, had an angelic visitation and was rescued from prison the night before he was to be executed.

You can learn from these examples that God remembers you in your human frailty when you are worn out in mind, body, and spirit from the fatigue of spiritual warfare. When you are at the end of your rope, tie a knot and hang on. Help is on the way!

God receives the greatest glory when his servants come to the end of their resources and can only look up. Ask him to strengthen you in your weakness, for his love truly endures forever.

Larry Stockstill
Teaching Pastor, Bethany World Prayer Center, Baton Rouge, LA

IMITATE JESUS AND PAUL

If you are a Christian, make sure you do what Jesus did when you present the gospel to a lost and dying world. If they are humble and have a knowledge of sin, give them grace (John 3:1–5). If they are proud and self-righteous, give them the Law to humble them and bring the knowledge of sin (Mark 10:17–22). Do what Paul did in Romans 2. He said to his hearers,

> *You, therefore, who teach another, do you not teach yourself? You who preach that a man should not steal, do you steal? You who say, "Do not commit adultery," do you commit adultery? You who abhor idols, do you rob temples? You who make your boast in the law, do you dishonor God through breaking the law?* (Romans 2:21–23, NKJV)

Imitate Paul. Do what Jesus did. Open up the divine Law as he did in the Sermon on the Mount, and show sinners the seriousness of sin and its fearful consequences. To fail to do so is the ultimate betrayal, the terrible repercussions of which will only be seen in eternity.

Ray Comfort
Founder and CEO, Living Waters / The Way of the Master

SENIOR MOMENTS

*Nevertheless I will remember My covenant with you
in the days of your youth, and I will establish
an everlasting covenant with you.*

It's happening. My birthday is fast approaching, and already I have been plagued with "moments" that remind me I am becoming someone affectionately known as a "senior"!

I have always felt that the aging process is one of God's ways of allowing us to understand our need for him. As I mature, I am constantly being confronted with my many limitations.

This graying cloud on the horizon of our lives does have a silver lining. That silver lining is that although we grow weak, God is strong still. Although we tend to forget things more often, God has not forgotten anything that has have ever happened or been said. God has not forgotten any of the prayers that we have prayed.

In light of this, I have a new way to pray for my family members: that God would remember his covenant with them that they made in the days of their youth.

Steve DeNicola
Senior Pastor, Calvary Chapel, Foothill Ranch, CA

BLESSED STRUGGLES

⚜ BIBLE READ: 2 CORINTHIANS 12:6–9

But he said to me, "My grace is sufficient for you,
for my power is made perfect in weakness."

2 CORINTHIANS 12:9, NIV

We all will experience difficult times, trials, feelings of despair, and hardships in life. As Christians, we can call those difficult times "blessed struggles," because we know that trials make us strong.

We all have weak areas in our lives. But we should not allow our weaknesses to keep us from living life to the fullest and serving God faithfully. The thorn in Paul's flesh might have been relational, physical, mental, spiritual, or psychological in nature. We have a thorn, and whatever that thorn represented, as Christians we know that God's grace is sufficient to us. The grace that is unmerited (not deserved), unbridled (all-powerful), unlimited (sufficient).

Can we boast in our weaknesses? The answer is yes, because the power of Christ dwells in us through his grace. Circumstances don't determine whether we experience peace or joy or contentment, or prevent us from knowing God and following him. The circumstances in our lives are not to make us miserable or tear us away from God, but to help us grow closer to him.

Let us continue to trust and submit to God's will. We must remember that the safest place in the whole wide world is in the will of God.

Dr. Rosemary Ricks-Saulsby
Wife to the Late Rev. Dr. B. S. Saulsby and Chairperson, Department of Nursing, Chicago
State University, Messiah Temple MB Church, Chicago, IL

LESSONS OF LOVE IN THE LETTER TO PHILEMON

I prefer to appeal to you on the basis of love.

PHILEMON 1:9, NIV

Paul's letter to Philemon breathes the spirit of Christian love. In the deepest sense, this is a family letter about a family matter, from brother to brother concerning a third brother.

I believe this letter contains three models whom we can follow in our own Christian lives. First, be like Philemon, who was asked to forgive Onesimus and to take him back because Onesimus has since become a Christian. Second, be like Onesimus, who shows true repentance and willingness to undo the wrong he has done. These two men—one rich and one poor—were both willing to do something they would never have considered doing before accepting Christ as their Lord. Paul asks both Onesimus and Philemon to demonstrate the Christian virtue of loving forgiveness, which demands humility from both.

And third, be like Paul, who was called to facilitate peace in the *koinonia* of our Christian life. Paul knows that *koinonia* demands reconciliation, peace between the people of God who have harmed each other. Like Paul, we must recognize that Christian love should be the first rule of human action.

Dr. Barry H. Corey
President, Biola University, La Mirada, CA

GOD SPEAKS

An old Puritan preacher once asked two very profound questions: "Does God speak? And if so, what does God say?" Profound indeed!

As Isaiah begins his prophecy, we're told that his ministry spanned the reigns of four kings of Judah. Isaiah himself had a lot to say for God during these many years as well. He was a prophet of God with a tremendous calling to bring the hearts of God's people back to the Lord.

All that said, it becomes immediately obvious whose voice is preeminent: "Hear, Oh heavens, and give ear, O earth! For the LORD has spoken" (Isaiah 1:2, NKJV).

I am amazed at how often and how clearly the Lord spoke to his people in Scripture—leading them, teaching them, instructing some in such minute detail as to leave us with the impression that these followers of old were hearing from the Almighty as we would hear someone across the coffee table. How can it be that we seem to hear him so little?

Does God speak? The answer is a resounding yes. The answer to the old Puritan preacher's second question is a treasure to be discovered by those who can heed the words of another prophet, who said, "The LORD is in his holy temple; let all the earth be silent before him" (Habakkuk 2:20, NASB).

Brian Bachochin
Senior Pastor, Calvary Chapel, Franklin, TN

VESSEL OF HONOR

But in a great house there are not only vessels of
gold and silver, but also of wood and clay,
some for honor and some for dishonor.

2 TIMOTHY 2:20, NKJV

How can you become a vessel of honor rather than dishonor? Well, you need to disassociate yourself from bad influences, being very careful whom you allow to influence your life. The people you hang around with are going to influence you either for the good or the bad. So, if your friends are not walking in the Spirit of God—if they don't love his Word, if they are not sharing their faith with others and basically have no earmarks of a maturing Christian—then you need to be careful because they can undermine your walk with the Lord.

Be diligent to maintain godly fellowship with believers who are like-minded, with those who love the Lord and call upon him out of a pure heart.

My encouragement to you today is to make a decision on whether you are going to be a vessel of gold and silver or a vessel of wood and clay. A vessel of honor or a vessel of dishonor. Speaking for myself, I want to be that vessel of honor—the china and not the paper plate. It's up to you. The decision is yours.

David Rosales
Senior Pastor, Calvary Chapel, Chino Valley, CA

BE BETTER AT LIFE

In Mark 1:32–34, after Jesus had healed Peter's mother-in-law and driven out an evil spirit from a man in the synagogue, he was asked for more. "That evening after sunset the people brought to Jesus all the sick and demon-possessed. The whole town gathered at the door, and Jesus healed many." These extra events probably took him the better part of the night. No one could accuse Jesus of kicking back on the job.

But look at the other side of the story. The very next morning Jesus got up early and went away to pray, to be alone and away from the demands of ministry.

Perhaps Jesus took his cue from his heavenly Father. Thousands of years before Jesus took a break in Mark 1, God himself rested. After creating the world and all that inhabits it, "God blessed the seventh day and made it holy, because on it he rested from all the work of creating that he had done" (Genesis 2:3, NIV).

Stop what you're doing right now and come apart before you come apart. Grab hold of the reality that when you invest in rest, you invest in making yourself a better person, a better spouse, a better parent, a better worker, and a better friend.

Want to be better at life? Rest.

Elisa Morgan
Author, Speaker, Publisher, www.fullfill.org
President Emerita, MOPS International

Not Common to Him

Even the sparrow has found a home,
and the swallow a nest for herself, where she
may have her young—a place near your altar,
Lord Almighty, my King and my God.

PSALM 84:3, NIV

What worth does a sparrow have in the eyes of the world? Not much. It is too small to eat for food. It doesn't have an impressive plume of feathers. It doesn't make a very distinctive sound. It isn't known for its aerobatic maneuvers. It is a very *common* creature. But the sparrow has found a home at the house of the Lord.

You may not be much in the eyes of others. You may be considered very *common*. But you are special to the Lord. You are loved by the Lord. You always have a home at the house of the Lord.

Jeff Miles
Senior Pastor, Touchstone Christian Fellowship, Sacramento, CA

LOVE ONE ANOTHER

Owe no one anything, except to love each other,
for the one who loves another
has fulfilled the law.

ROMANS 13:8, NKJV

ove is like water; it is a prerequisite for a healthy life. Love is one of the simplest human needs. God so loved the world that He gave His only son that through Him the world might be saved. The ability to love does not rest in one's riches but in one's ability to share the goodness of God. To feel love is to enjoy the other person's enjoyment of you. This love is felt only when the message of love is heard. When we really love a person, we give that person the power of attorney to make decisions for us.

If you love God, please give him the power to make decisions concerning your life. Love is a luxury that everyone must be willing to purchase. How much are you willing to pay?

Dr. Le'on M. Willis I
Reverend, Wesley United Methodist Church, Chicago, IL

GOD AT WORK

When the men came to Jesus, they said,
"John the Baptist sent us to you to ask, 'Are you the one
who is to come, or should we expect someone else?'"

LUKE 7:20, NIV

In this passage, John the Baptist has been imprisoned by King Herod. All his adult life, John the Baptist has lived in the wilderness. Now, in this smelly and dark prison cell, doubts about Jesus loom. Most Christ-followers have experienced something similar, times when our faith seems small—our God-given vision reduced to almost nothing—and doubt pervades. Jesus responds to John's honest misgivings with these words: "Tell John what you hear and see: the blind receive sight, the lame walk . . . the deaf hear . . . and the good news is preached to the poor" (Matthew 11:4–5, NIV84).

When I struggle similarly, I also look to the active work of God for encouragement. In absolute dependence, I ask God to reveal himself in Scripture, the fellowship of his church, and his ongoing work in my life. On each occasion, God has used my honest doubt to build my faith and trust in him.

Jon R. Wallace, DBA
President, Azusa Pacific University, Azusa, CA

SELF-DECEPTION

Do not think of yourself more highly than you ought,
but rather think of yourself with sober judgment,
in accordance with the faith God has
distributed to each of you.

ROMANS 12:3, NIV

Sometimes it's rather sad to see the local high school football sensation who feels like he's on the way to the NFL, but when he gets to college he sits on the sidelines. As kids we laughed at "The Emperor's New Clothes" and at the silliness of a self-deceived man who refused to see that he was naked.

Isaiah the prophet is talking about this problem of self-deception when he addresses the issue of the people's idolatry. Isaiah talks about the incredible irony of the person who takes a piece of wood and uses half to burn in the oven to bake his bread, while he carves the other half into an image that he will bow down to and worship. Isaiah writes, "The poor, deluded fool feeds on ashes. He trusts something that can't help him at all. Yet he cannot bring himself to ask, 'Is this idol that I'm holding in my hand a lie?'" (Isaiah 44:20, NLT).

With self-deception, I refuse to look at the reality of my situation. Maturity comes when I face the truth and deal with it. The truth I need is not my truth, but God's truth.

Rich Cathers
Senior Pastor, Calvary Chapel, Fullerton, CA

CONTROLLING YOUR THOUGHTS

For God did not give us a spirit of fear,
but of power and of love and
of a sound mind.

2 TIMOTHY 1:7, NKJV

o you realize how your thoughts, emotions, and feelings seem to dictate your decisions and control your behavior? Does your thinking make you stumble on your walk with God at times? If so, do you want to learn how to control your thoughts? First, identify what you are thinking. When Peter was depressed, Jesus asked, "What do you think, Simon?" (Matthew 17:25). Now test your thoughts with the Word of God. Scripture teaches that you are to "test all things" (1 Thessalonians 5:21).

Next, you must choose to refuse what is contrary to God's Word. God commands us not to think certain things in our hearts. He declared, "Do not think in your hearts . . ." (Deuteronomy 9:4). Jesus said, "Do not think . . ." (Matthew 10:34). Therefore, you need to make a choice about what you will think.

Last, bring your thoughts captive to God in prayer. Ask the Lord to help you focus on what is true, good, and virtuous (2 Corinthians 10:3–5; Philippians 4:6–9). As you take these simple steps, you will find the peace of God will be with you. Draw near to him and take captive your thoughts!

Steve Carr
Senior Pastor, Calvary Chapel, Arroyo Grande, CA

RACHAMIM

The grace of our Lord was poured out on me abundantly,
along with the faith and love that are in Christ Jesus.
Here is a trustworthy saying that deserves full acceptance:
Christ Jesus came into the world to save sinners—of whom I am
the worst. But for that very reason I was shown mercy so
that in me, the worst of sinners, Christ Jesus might display
his immense patience as an example for those who
would believe in him and receive eternal life.

1 TIMOTHY 1:14–16, NIV

God does not simply have mercy for you. In the original Hebrew the word for "mercy" isn't singular but plural—*rachamim*. God doesn't have mercy on you. What he does have is *rachamim*, more than mercy . . . mercies, loads and loads of mercy, mercy upon mercy. And not just for one time, but for every time you need it. Not just enough for the bad sins, but enough for the very, very bad sins. Not just for the sin we fell into, but for the sins we did over and over again—even years of being cold to God. Our sins may be great, but rest assured his *rachamim* is greater. We ask for mercy, but God doesn't give us what we ask for. He gives us *rachamim*—mercies, overflowing, able to fill up and cleanse every sin and failure, and with mercy to spare with leftovers, with extra mercy, surplus mercy!

So don't let the past keep you down. Open your heart real wide, for he has mercies upon mercies upon mercies, and then some, more than enough for you to live a life of abundant joy and victory.

Jonathan Cahn
Author, The Harbinger, *Senior Pastor and Messianic Rabbi,*
the Jerusalem Center / Beth Israel, Wayne, NJ

IT'S TIME WE GO

God blessed them and told them,
"Be fruitful and multiply. Fill the earth."

GENESIS 1:28, NLT

God's plan was bigger than staying put in Eden. He told Adam and Eve to multiply and [go] fill the Earth. That is the Meta-level Commission: to go and make disciples of all people. But Adam and Eve stayed and they fell. God had to make them leave. They multiplied all right—as a fallen race.

That's when God took his Commission to the next level. He flooded the Earth and started over again with Noah. "Multiply and fill the Earth," he said. Noah's family multiplied, but eventually rebellion prevailed; men snubbed their noses at the Commission. "Let's build a great city. . . . This will keep us from being scattered all over the world" (Genesis 11:4, NLT). In other words, they said, "No. We won't go. We'll build a holy huddle right here!" But, God thwarted their plans as he scrambled their one language into 7,000.

Soon afterward, God established covenant with Abraham; his "seed" would bless all nations. That Seed was Jesus, and his last instruction to the disciples was the Great Commission. They were to multiply, fill the Earth with God's Word, and bring people into his kingdom "from every nation, tribe, people, and language" (Revelation 7:9).

It's time we go.

Roy Peterson
President and CEO, The Seed Company

LIGHTEN A LOAD

Brothers, if someone is caught in a sin,
you who are spiritual should restore him gently.
But watch yourself, or you also may be tempted.
Carry each other's burdens, and in this way
you will fulfill the law of Christ.

GALATIANS 6:1–2, NIV84

I am amazed at what people around the world can carry on their heads! I have seen women in India and Africa balance the most unbelievable loads of food, wood, or supplies on their heads as they walk down the street. I am more amazed at the heavy relational, physical, and financial burdens people carry around. Sometimes they seem more than what any person should be able to bear. When you see them weighed down, it makes you want to ask, "Can I lighten your load and carry that for you?" Paul says we should do more than ask; we should go and lift that burden off them. After all, that is one of the things a person who is spiritual does.

Going to a Bible study or attending another small group is not just to get strong enough to make it to the next study. One reason we grow spiritually is to be able to support others as they live through the challenges of life. Are you growing? And are you using your growth to lighten the load of others?

Terry Sanderson
Senior Pastor, Calvary Church, St. Peters, MO

PUT ON LOVE

And above all these put on love, which binds
everything together in perfect harmony.

When relationships fall apart, it hurts deeply whether it is in a family or in a church.

The fracturing can always be traced back to the absence of love. Jesus said that the world would be able to identify his followers by their love for one another. Paul wrote that love is the fulfillment of the law.

The love we are to have for others is found in God's love for us. When this love is absent from our relationships, they begin to fall apart. The love that God has shown to man is unconditional and inexhaustible. This love that we have received from God, we are to show toward one another. As John wrote, "If God so loved us, we also ought to love one another" (1 John 4:11).

May we be reminded daily to "put on love."

Aaron Newman
Senior Pastor, Calvary Chapel, Paso Robles, CA

TRUE REPENTANCE

Yet now I am happy, not because you were made sorry,
but because your sorrow led you to repentance. For you became
sorrowful as God intended and so were not harmed in any
way by us. Godly sorrow brings repentance that leads to
salvation and leaves no regret, but worldly sorrow brings death.
See what this godly sorrow has produced in you:
what earnestness, what eagerness to clear yourselves,
what indignation, what alarm, what longing, what concern,
what readiness to see justice done. At every point
you have proved yourselves to be
innocent in this matter.

2 CORINTHIANS 7:9–11, NIV

"I'm sorry I got caught!" True repentance is the exact opposite. It leads to a desire to turn from sin and have a relationship with God. It's at the heart of salvation and proves one's salvation. Repentance continues in the life of a believer, restoring joy and blessing. It changes our attitude from complacency about sin to eagerly pursuing the right path. It leads to anger over my sin, the hurt it caused loved ones, and the shame it brought upon my Lord, whom I love. Repentance moves me from being sorry I was caught to not wanting to do anything to harm the objects of my love.

Brent Wagner
Senior Pastor, Voyage Calvary Chapel, Fountain Valley, CA

INSIDE-OUT FAITH

👑 BIBLE READ: PHILIPPIANS 2:1–11

In your relationships with one another,
have the same mind-set as
Christ Jesus.

PHILIPPIANS 2:5, NIV

One of the all-time great TV commercials is from the sports drink company that displays rugged athletes on various playing fields being jolted and jostled about. The colored sports drink is seen oozing from their pores like perspiration—splashes of green and purple juice drip off their brow as they compete. Then the classic question at the end simply asks, "Is it in you?" The idea, of course, is that their product is the fuel that produces energy for success on the playing field.

In a similar fashion, followers of Jesus compete on the field of ministry and mission service every day. When we are bumped and shoved in life, something good is supposed to come out of it. We are asking the question in this devotional guide: "Is it in you?" Do you have the life of the Lord Jesus deeply dwelling in your inmost being? You are going to be tested and pushed by life physically, emotionally, and spiritually. When game time comes, what will come splashing out from the inside?

Danny Sinquefield
Senior Pastor, Faith Baptist Church, Bartlett, TN

GOD'S MASTERPIECE

For we are his workmanship,
created in Christ Jesus for good works,
which God prepared beforehand that
we would walk in them.

In Florence's Academia museum stands perhaps the greatest example of statuary the world has ever known. Hewn out of a cast-off piece of marble, Michelangelo's *David* has enthralled onlookers for years with its unmatched beauty, simplicity, and strength. Yet as spectacular as the statue is, all the glory goes to the artist whose vision and skill brought a masterpiece out of stone thought to be unworkable.

The apostle Paul told the Ephesian believers something we all need to know and remember daily. All who have denied themselves, taken up the cross, and followed Christ have been re-created as intentional displays of God's transforming grace. Once unworkable castaways, we are now his intentional work of art, designed to declare his glory as the great Artist of the soul. The authenticity of our faith will be seen in the good works that he has designed for us to display. You might even say that these are the chisel marks of the Master, declaring that we are authentic works of his hand. May our lives display his craftsmanship so that the world may acknowledge his greatness.

Dr. David W. Hegg
Senior Pastor, Grace Baptist Church, Santa Clarita, CA

CLOUD OF WITNESSES

Therefore we also, since we are surrounded by
so great a cloud of witnesses, let us lay aside every weight,
and the sin which so easily ensnares us, and let us run
with endurance the race that is set before us, looking unto Jesus,
the author and finisher of our faith, who for the joy that was set
before him endured the cross, despising the shame, and has
sat down at the right hand of the throne of God.

HEBREWS 12:1–2, NKJV

After spending ten chapters showing us and the Hebrew saints that Jesus was the fulfillment of all the Old Testament sacrifices and types and pictures, Paul in Hebrews 11 chronicles some examples of those who in times past had lived their lives in faith, pleasing God! He then calls on us to consider their testimonies and examples as they, the cloud of witnesses, now challenge us to walk by faith in our generation and lay aside any weight or sin that easily besets us and run our race with endurance, following Jesus our Lord. Like Abel, Enoch, Noah, Abraham, and others, we also must keep our eyes on the Lord and live for him in these uncertain times.

How are you living today? With a heavenly hope, with an eye on the eternal, with a faith that sees God and pleases him daily? Come on, saints. Run to win, keep your eyes on Jesus, and be the generation that exemplifies what living by faith in him really means! What a glorious addition to Hebrews 11 you can be as God continues to work mightily through those sold out to him.

Jack Abeelen
Senior Pastor, Morning Star Christian Chapel, Whittier, CA

THE GOD/MAN

When it was evening, the boat was in the middle of the sea,
and He [Jesus] was alone on the land. Seeing them straining at the
oars, for the wind was against them, at about the fourth watch
of the night He came to them, walking on the sea;
and He intended to pass by them.

MARK 6:47–48, NASB

*M*ost Christians when they read this passage are fascinated by this miraculous event. I find this story interesting because Jesus is "walking" on water. If God is all powerful, why walk? Walking on water took energy, which meant Jesus would have gotten tired eventually. But if God is all-knowing, why did he wait to leave until later on that night, and then almost walk right by the disciples? Have you ever felt like the disciples, wondering why God seems to wait when you need him?

In this one passage we get a small glimpse into the God/man all rolled up into one person: Jesus. Jesus was fully God and fully man. The apostle Paul said this about Jesus: "Who, although He existed in the form of God, did not regard equality with God a thing to be grasped, but emptied himself, taking the form of a bond-servant, and being made in the likeness of men" (Philippians 2:6–7). You see, even though Jesus was fully God, he chose purposefully to limit his prerogatives as God. Jesus laid aside his eternal heavenly, Kingly heritage in order to take on a humble human nature, even to the point of death on a cross.

If you are struggling right now, don't look at the circumstances or unanswered questions in your life. Remember, God's timing is perfect. He knows what he is doing, and he is still in control.

Steve M. Woods
Chairman, Board of Directors, www.WoodsMasteryLearningFoundation.org

TAKE CAPTIVE EVERY THOUGHT

I will refuse to look at anything vile and vulgar. . . .
I will reject perverse ideas and stay away from every evil.

PSALM 101:3–4, NLT

*W*hat we look at shapes our lives. David said he would not set before his eyes any vile thing. In this world we live in, our minds are bombarded daily with vile and vulgar images. From television, magazines, movies, and even the daily lives of others comes constant portrayal of the perverse, proud, deceptive, profane, and slanderous.

What can we do about it? We can do as David did and be totally intolerant of filth. Whenever something from the enemy came before David's eyes, he immediately cast it from his mind. We cannot afford to meditate passively on unclean and worthless things that our minds conceive. Rather, we must follow Paul's instructions to "take captive every thought" (2 Corinthians 10:5, NIV) and David's admonishment to "stay away from every evil" (Psalm 101:4, NLT).

Analyze your environment. Conduct spiritual housecleaning, if necessary, and do not let evil enter your presence (v. 7). Your mind will clear, temptation will lift, and you will dwell in safety.

Larry Stockstill
Teaching Pastor, Bethany World Prayer Center, Baton Rouge, LA

DEO VOLENTE

👑 BIBLE READ: JAMES 4:13–17

If it is the Lord's will, we will live and do this or that.

JAMES 4:15B, NIV

A beautiful sign hung upon the archway of a friend's vacation home by the lake. It read, "Deo Volente," Latin for "God willing." After an economic downturn, my friend lost the vacation home. His response? "Oh well, *Deo volente.*" The fact is, even as we make our own plans we must hold them loosely. In James 4:15, we are told that our settled heart should conclude, "If it is the Lord's will, we will live and do this or that." It is wise to make plans for "this and that," but we must know that God is sovereign over all, and it is ultimately his will that prevails, not ours. In fact, as we are making our plans and decisions, *Deo volente* needs to become a question. What is it that God wills for this circumstance? How can I make plans and choices that most align with the will of God? When this is our posture, we are more likely to move toward the perfect will of God. Then, whether we experience gain or loss, we can confidently say, *"Deo volente!"*

John V. Hansen
Lead Pastor, Centerpoint Church, Murrieta, CA

THE MAJESTY OF GOD

On the glorious splendor of Your majesty
and on Your wonderful works,
I will meditate.

PSALM 145:5, NASB

A new heart and a new life start here: recognizing the power and majesty of God. It might seem counterintuitive to think that way. Wouldn't it make more sense to boost our self-esteem and think about how cool we are?

The two ideas aren't mutually exclusive. Think big thoughts about God and find amazement that he loves and cares for you. Big God = big love for you.

God is our Creator. He created everything you see, taste, touch, smell, and hear. He spun the universe into existence. He gave you breath. Knowing that reconfigures our days, doesn't it? When life feels too hard or stress mounts, we can rest in knowing that God is bigger than us, that he is powerful and capable of running the universe without us.

Rest there. Nestle into the beauty and otherness of God. Lift your eyes from the worries of today to the steadfastness and unchangeableness of him. And remember that Jesus, who saved you, represents everything lovely about God.

Mary DeMuth
Speaker and Author, www.marydemuth.com

BATTLEGROUND, HOLY GROUND

The Lord is my light and my salvation—whom shall I fear?
The Lord is the stronghold of my life—of whom shall I be afraid?
When evil men advance against me to devour my flesh,
when my enemies and my foes attack me, they will stumble and fall.
Though an army besieges me, my heart will not fear; though war
break out against me, even then will I be confident.

PSALM 27:1–3, NIV84

*D*avid was a man after God's own heart. He understood how important it was to have the presence of God with him. He won many battles as king over Israel, and in each one of them he gave God the honor. He also experienced many challenges and personal failure in his own life. At one point the Scriptures describe how he cried out to God in prayer: "Take not thy Holy Spirit from me" (Psalm 51:11, KJV). The psalm goes on to describe that life can go from bad to worse, each battle stronger than the last. However, in our battles there is still hope in Christ. The psalmist continues, "Even then will I be confident" and "not give up" (27:3, NIV84). Why? Because he is my Light and my Savior! It's a daily decision in our hearts that causes us to be steadfast, walking in the grace that only he can and will provide day by day. His presence through Christ is with you, you can be sure of that!

He will prepare you for the battlegrounds of life, teaching you his ways step by step. David's life was one of passion and courage. Take courage in his salvation.

Paige Junaeus
Founder, Paige Junaeus Ministries

Cast Your Net

"Cast the net on the right side of the boat,"
He told them, "and you'll find some."
So they did, and they were unable to haul it in
because of the large number of fish.

JOHN 21:6, HCSB

Cast your net on the right side!

The disciples had struggled all night and caught nothing.

Suddenly a voice cries out to them, "Cast the nets on the right side." When they do, they are unable to haul in the catch.

The disciples were given a visual reminder. They should never forget that on the right side of the boat is where the fish are—and in life, on the right side is wherever Jesus is.

The right side is where Jesus is! The right side is where the Creator and Sustainer of all is located. The right side is where you and I find the hope of the world. The right side is the place of grace.

Are you casting the net of your life on the right side of the boat?

Throw your net on the right side today! Choose Jesus.

Ron Edmondson
Senior Pastor, Immanuel Baptist Church, Lexington, KY
RonEdmondson.com

ABUNDANTLY MORE

[God will] do exceedingly abundantly
above all that we ask or think.

EPHESIANS 3:20, NKJV

Most of us have a pretty active imagination when it comes to our interests—fantasy football, the car of our dreams, what we'd do with an extreme home makeover. What about when it comes to picturing what God has in store for our future—or beyond this life?

The combined creative force of Steven Spielberg, Steve Jobs, and Walt Disney isn't enough to begin to tell the story. The Bible says it is simply . . . "unimaginable."

It's not just "life everlasting" that's beyond our understanding. God's plans for today and tomorrow—as well as his magnificence and greatness as an almighty God—these things, too, are "too wonderful" and "too high" for us to attain (Psalm 139:6).

But once you have him in this life, he begins to reveal his wonders to us in treasures great and small. There are over 7,000 promises in the Bible; this is one of them. You can count on it. All you have to do is believe it and continue on the journey with him to start discovering what only a Magnificent Creator, Wonderful Counselor, and Gracious Redeemer like our God has imagined for you in this life and the one to come.

Shawn Mitchell
Senior Pastor, New Venture Christian Fellowship, Oceanside, CA

WISDOM AND RICHES

I love those who love me, and those who seek me find me.
With me are riches and honor, enduring wealth and prosperity.

PROVERBS 8:17–18, NIV84

roverbs teaches that all who would live godly must seek God's wisdom. To seek divine wisdom is to seek to know God more intimately. Wisdom is equated with God in the book of Proverbs, and God says, "I love those who love me, and those who seek me diligently will find me" (Proverbs 8:17). When we demonstrate to God that we love him by seeking him early and often, he demonstrates to us that he loves us by filling our day with his wisdom.

Seeking God and his wisdom doesn't mean we have to be paupers. Proverbs 8 continues, "Riches and honor are with me, enduring riches and righteousness" (v. 18). The world's wealth is temporal and often a deterrent to godliness. Divine wisdom is eternal and an everlasting aid to godliness. Should God allow us both wisdom and wealth, our attitude toward our possessions should be, "As for every man to whom God has given riches and wealth . . . this is the gift of God" (Ecclesiastes 5:19, NKJV).

Don't despise wealth, but don't allow wealth to become a substitute for godly wisdom.

Woodrow Kroll
President, Back to the Bible, Lincoln, NE

HOMESICK AND HEARTSICK

But the time will come when the bridegroom will be
taken from them; in those days they will fast.

LUKE 5:35, NIV

On the summer of 1989 my heart was lovesick. I was in Spain, counting down the days until I could return home and propose to the woman who is now my wife of twenty-two years. It would not be an exaggeration to say that there were days when I had little appetite due to my yearning to be with her. My bride-to-be had been taken away from me, and my desire to be with her was greater than all the delicacies of the Iberian Peninsula.

Have you ever felt that way about heaven? Do you long to be with Jesus to the point that you have no desire to have a meal? I believe that is what Jesus was talking about when he told his followers that a day would come when he would no longer be with them. By choosing to fast, they demonstrated a longing of the heart, a longing for heaven, that was greater than anything this world had to offer.

I encourage you to make fasting a part of your prayer life. Each and every time you feel the pangs of hunger, may it be a reminder of a greater spiritual need that dwells in all of us—a hunger to be in the presence of God.

Dear God, may my desire for you always be greater than my desire for my next meal. When I fast, may each twinge of hunger point me to the day when I will feast around the heavenly table with you.

Steve Willis
Lead Pastor, First Baptist Church, Kenova, WV

TEMPTATIONS

Let no one say when he is tempted, "I am tempted by God";
for God cannot be tempted by evil, nor does He Himself
tempt anyone. But each one is tempted when he is drawn away
by his own desires and enticed. Then, when desire has conceived, it
gives birth to sin; and sin, when it is full-grown, brings forth death.

God helps us rise above our confusion about temptations. Temptations are different from trials, and God is not the one who tempts us. Temptation occurs when we are drawn away by our own sinful nature; and if we give in to it, then we sin. When we sin, there are consequences. So God allows trials, for the testing of our faith, but he would never tempt us to sin.

Jesus taught us to pray, "Lead us not into temptation, but deliver us from evil" (Matthew 6:13, NASB). God will help us with our temptations. He will deliver us not only from them but from the devil himself.

The interesting similarity between trials and temptations is that we can grow through either one of them. Both will always be with us, and both are normal—and can be productive if we let them.

The Lord never condemns us for our failures in times of trials or temptations. He only seeks to build us up, help us, comfort us, and forgive us, and help us to grow. May you be blessed by Jesus Christ in your trials and temptations.

Bob Grenier
Senior Pastor, Calvary Chapel, Visalia, CA

COMPLAINERS GET FIRED
. . . LITERALLY

Now the people became like those who complain of adversity in
the hearing of the LORD; and when the LORD heard it,
His anger was kindled, and the fire of the LORD burned among
them and consumed some of the outskirts of the camp.

NUMBERS 11:1, NASB

When I think of the things that anger God, I think of things like murder, sexual impurity, and abuse. In this passage of Scripture, we see that complaining ranks just as high in the category of things that anger God. Many of us complain even when things are going well. We complain about the weather, people driving too slow, our spouses or children, our employees, and so on. The apostle Paul says that we are to "do all things without grumbling or complaining" (Philippians 2:14) so that we may stand out as children of Christ.

You may say that the children of Israel had reason to complain. After all, they had been wandering around in the desert for quite some time while eating the same meal day after day. They felt they had a reason to complain, but God did not see it that way. He tells us in James 1:2 that we are to "count it all joy when we face trials of various kinds." We are guaranteed trials and adversity in life, and when they come, we are never to complain.

Ask God to help you with your attitude today when you are tempted to complain. Instead of complaining, turn your circumstances into thanksgiving, knowing that God is refining you.

Chuck Booher
Senior Pastor, Crossroads Christian Church, Corona, CA

ARE YOU PREPARED?

*Run from anything
that stimulates youthful lusts.*

2 TIMOTHY 2:22A, NLT

When we allow the Lord to clean up our lives, then we'll be ready for the Master to use us for every good work. We'll be utensils or instruments "for honor, sanctified, useful to the Master, prepared for every good work" (2 Timothy 2:21, NASB).

You know what? That's what I want to be! I want to be a vessel God can use for his purpose. I want to be ready for the Master to use at any moment.

Paul gives the practical command in verse 22: "Run from anything that stimulates youthful lusts" (NLT). This is talking about a continuous action as a habit of life.

Are there things in your life that stir up lust? Maybe the TV programs you watch or the places you go online? Do you read books or magazines that cause you to stumble? Sometimes the people we're hanging out with cause us to stumble into lust. The Bible says to continually run from anything that stimulates youthful lust.

Mark Martin
Senior Pastor, Calvary Community Church, Phoenix, AZ

DRIVING BY THE RULES

Who among you is wise and understanding?
Let him show by his good behavior and his
deeds in the gentleness of wisdom.

JAMES 3:13, NASB

remember the excitement I felt upon beginning the driving portion of drivers' ed. With my instructor seated next to me, I started the engine, put the car in first gear, pressed the gas pedal, eased off the clutch, and began to drive.

Suddenly the car screeched to a halt. I looked over and discovered that my instructor had a set of brakes on his side of the car. He looked at me and said, "Young man, we're not here to race anybody. You're gonna learn to drive according to the rules."

Frankly, learning to walk as a Christian is much like learning to drive. We have to do it by God's rules. As we grow in our faith, our understanding of the Bible is constantly tested through our application of it. So James is telling us that in order to grow up in Christ we have to take what we learn from God's Word out onto the open road.

Are you ready to take your faith for a spin?

Dr. Stephen Davey
Senior Pastor, Colonial Baptist Church, Cary, NC

WORK HARD

All hard work brings a profit,
but mere talk leads only to poverty.

*C*onsistent success in life requires consistent hard work. Although hard work is not the only secret of success, the lack of hard work almost always guarantees failure.

Be willing to work. It is easy to be lazy, to get by with as little work as possible, or to let others do more than their share. But the book of Proverbs not only shares the reward of hard work, it repeatedly warns about the harmful results of laziness (Proverbs 6:6–11).

Do your work well. Do your best; do quality work. As good work produces good results, shoddy work produces a shoddy product. Paul tells us to do everything, including our work, to the glory of God (1 Corinthians 10:31) and in the name of Jesus (Colossians 3:17). Doing things for his glory and in his name means to do it as he would, in order to be a blessing to others.

Keep at it! A truly successful person doesn't quit, even when things get tough, work is tedious, or there is failure. When you want to give up, push through instead. Persevere and keep going to the end. Be diligent, staying at it until the work is done.

Judy Douglass
Author, Campus Crusade for Christ

Seek God and Find Him

But from there you will seek the LORD your God,
and you will find Him if you seek Him
with all your heart and with all your soul.

DEUTERONOMY 4:29, NKJV

ook at what Moses said: If you seek the Lord, you will find him. He is not hidden from us. He is always there for us.

What happens when people feel like God has forsaken them? Where is God? I will tell you; he is right there beside them. He is waiting for them to turn to him. When we cannot see or feel God, it is not because he has left us; we have left him. We have turned our backs on him.

Our God is a gentleman. He will never force himself on us. He is a holy God, so when we turn to worldliness, God waits for us to turn back and seek him. What a great promise from God: when we seek him, we will find him. He does not hide from us. He welcomes us with open arms.

Remember, if you get sidetracked, all you need to do is repent and come back to God. He will receive you. He loves you and is waiting for you to seek him, so that he can restore fellowship.

Raul Ries
Senior Pastor, Calvary Chapel Golden Springs, Diamond Bar, CA

FRUIT THAT REMAINS

👑 BIBLE READ: COLOSSIANS 1:9–15

> *For this reason, since the day we heard*
> *about you, we have not stopped praying for you.*
> *We continually ask God to fill you with the*
> *knowledge of his will through all the wisdom*
> *and understanding that the Spirit gives.*

COLOSSIANS 1:9, NIV

As I considered the role of prayer in our lives, I was inspired by the thought of prayer being something that is eternal in nature. There is no limit to our prayers because our prayers are precious to God.

Jesus told us that we were chosen and appointed by him to bear fruit and that our fruit should remain (John 15:16). Have you ever considered the remaining fruit of your prayers? Prayers outlast your lifetime. Many prayers have been answered long after the person praying had died and gone to be with Jesus. Prayers spoken in this life plant seeds that may not spring up until long after the sower has died.

Prayer is eternal in nature because our prayers ascend into heaven and are before the throne of God (Revelation 5:8; 8:4). Too often we think that, because we don't see the fulfillment of our prayers, they were spoken in vain. Yet the truth is that, like the seed in the ground, they take time and the right conditions to germinate and grow. May your prayers continue to sow seeds of peace and grace.

Steve DeNicola
Senior Pastor, Calvary Chapel, Foothill Ranch, CA

WELCOME TO CHAOS

You have never traveled
this way before.

JOSHUA 3:4, NLT

*M*iracle after miracle, God proved his faithfulness to Israel by delivering them from the bondage of Egypt. He set them on a path of faith leading to the Promised Land. It was a way they'd never traveled before. God was setting the stage for our Savior.

Sure, there were challenges ahead: walled cities, pagan practices, organized armies, and giants! God had invited them into certain chaos, but he knew something they didn't. If they acted on his word, he knew they would be different people by the time he finished fighting their battles.

Forty years later, the nation of Israel was still in the wilderness. All those who had refused to believe God's promise were dead. For the new generation, it was time to stop circling and climb out of that well-worn rut in the desert.

When it's time for us to get out of a rut—step into a different job, a new facet of ministry, or a new relationship—every step toward God's promise will bring aspects of growth. Our faith will be stretched to the limit and our minds put to the test as we walk toward our promised land.

Walking with our Lord Jesus, we can say as Caleb did, "Let us go up at once . . . we are able!" (Numbers 13:30, NKJV).

Roy Peterson
President and CEO, The Seed Company

SELFISHNESS

Love . . . does not seek its own.

1 CORINTHIANS 13:4–5, NKJV

have good news and bad news. The good news is that you are the best thing that could possibly happen to your relationships with others. The bad news is that you could also be the worst thing that could possibly happen in those relationships. How can both of these be true? Well, it comes down to whether you will die to yourself for the sake of others, or whether you will be selfish, insisting on taking care of yourself first. Hands down, selfishness is the number-one problem in relationships, the biggest reason for divorce. Selfishness is a black hole whose desire is never fulfilled. Selfishness is never happy, never satisfied, and never whole.

Love, on the other hand, does not seek its own. It seeks to benefit others. And when we actually embrace love in a relationship or marriage, not only will our needs be met, but trust and true intimacy are built over time. This will make our marriages and our families rock-solid pillars of love in our communities. God designed us so that the blessings come when we die to ourselves, and this is especially true in a marriage.

Building a strong, devoted family is the ultimate witness for Christ, and it starts when we reject selfishness and choose love.

Bob Botsford
Senior Pastor, Horizon Christian Fellowship North, Rancho Santa Fe, CA

TOTAL OBEDIENCE

♕ BIBLE READ: GENESIS 22:1–14

What does Scripture say?
"Abraham believed God, and it was
credited to him as righteousness."

ROMANS 4:3, NIV

It was an unusually exciting day for young Isaac. He and his dad were going on a trip—one of his favorites—to offer a sacrifice to God. He had witnessed this process many times before as father Abraham carefully explained each step to his son. Something was different this time. Young Isaac began to notice that his father, now well up in years, had forgotten a few things. In fact, he had forgotten the most important item on the list—a lamb for the actual sacrifice.

As they approached the base of the mountain of sacrifice, Abraham instructed the servants to stay while he and Isaac went to worship. He added these words spoken by faith, "We will worship and then we will come back to you" (Genesis 22:5b, NIV). Scholars agree that Abraham fully intended to take the boy's life following God's command, and he was totally trusting God to bring him back to life again. That is total obedience.

Danny Sinquefield
Senior Pastor, Faith Baptist Church, Bartlett, TN

CAN YOU BIND?

Can you bind the cluster of the Pleiades,
or loose the belt of Orion?

JOB 38:31, NKJV

hy would God ask Job, in the midst of his trial, such a rhetorical question? Elihu had prepared the way by telling Job to "listen" and to "stand still and consider the wondrous works of God" (Job 37:14), and in his conclusion in verse 24 Elihu gave an exhortation to be "wise in heart."

But now God himself was confronting Job with some tough questions. You would think this would be a great time for God to speak words of comfort to such a needy man. Instead, he says to Job, "Prepare yourself like a man to give an answer" (Job 38:3). Job is now brought lower than his emotional and physical pain and sees himself as vile (v. 40:4).

Isaiah, Peter, and Moses all were made painfully aware of God's majesty and might before they could be used in a mighty way. "Therefore men fear him; He shows no partiality to any who are wise of heart" (Job 37:24). If you want to be used by God, remember that the road to serve might lead to a cross.

Garry Ansdell
Senior Pastor, Hosanna Christian Fellowship, Bellflower, CA

BIRD ZOO

You open your hand and satisfy the
desires of every living thing.

PSALM 145:16, NIV

In the home where we raised our boys, we had a bird zoo in our backyard. We had two birdhouses, several feeders, and perfect places to build a nest.

We went through a lot of bird seed in those days. We purchased it in twenty-five-pound bags, and it seemed every month I was buying another.

I noticed something once while we were out of town for a few days. We had forgotten to fill the bird feeders, and they were completely empty on our return. Yet our birds were still pleasantly chirping their favorite song. Our absence didn't send them into a starvation frenzy.

Do you know why? Because our Heavenly Father feeds them. Our God, the Creator and Sustainer of all the atoms and molecules in the universe, opens his mighty and powerful hands and feeds these tiny, feathered creatures. The same God, using the same hands that hold the stars in place, provides meals for the smallest of the whistlers.

If God will care for birds like this, imagine what he will do for you and me!

Ron Edmondson
Senior Pastor, Immanuel Baptist Church, Lexington, KY
RonEdmondson.com

THE UMPIRE

If only there were a mediator who could
bring us together, but there is none.

JOB 9:33

*T*he cry of man throughout the ages has been for someone who could act as an umpire in the game of life. Job envisioned a mediator who could be on equal terms with both God and man and could reconcile us to the Father.

In Christ's resurrection, Paul presents a picture of the man Job was looking for. "So you see, just as death came into the world through a man [Adam], now the resurrection from the dead has begun through another man [Christ]" (1 Corinthians 15:21, NLT). Only a "God/man" could come to earth, die for our sins, and be resurrected as the Son of God.

Jesus, the second Adam, is the Umpire, the one who can stand between God and man to reconcile us. His resurrection has assured us that, in the end, he will humble "all his enemies beneath his feet" (v. 25, NLT).

Let us look to Jesus as our Hope, both now and forever!

Larry Stockstill
Teaching Pastor, Bethany World Prayer Center, Baton Rouge, LA

ARE YOU DEPRESSED?

Why, my soul, are you downcast?
Why so disturbed within me? Put your hope
in God, for I will yet praise him, my
Savior and my God.

PSALM 42:11

At times, all of us have experienced depression in our lives. Even the greatest men and women in the Bible struggled with depression, discouragement, and sometimes even despair. How can you conquer your depression? The Bible teaches, "Anxiety in the heart of man causes depression, but a good word makes it glad" (Proverbs 12:25, NKJV). To conquer depression you must first listen to God's good word. You can receive a good word from a person who knows the Scriptures, or from personally reading the Word of God. Solomon declared, "Where there is no counsel, the people fall" (v. 11:14). Jesus also said, "My sheep hear My voice" (John 10:27). Therefore, hear his word and receive his counsel.

However, after receiving his good Word, you must then obey it. Jesus said, "If you know these things, blessed are you if you do them" (v. 13:17). The word "blessed" means happy. True happiness in life will always be found as you hear God's truth and obey it. Why not open his Word today and obey what God says, no matter how you feel?

Steve Carr
Senior Pastor, Calvary Chapel, Arroyo Grande, CA

TRIALS

Consider it pure joy, my brothers and sisters,
whenever you face trials of many kinds, because you know
that the testing of your faith produces perseverance.

o you see trials God's way—that is, to see them as a matter for joy? Through trials, God is going to produce endurance in your life. What God says in James is to "count it all joy," meaning to stop and think the situation through to gain God's perspective, which will in the end bring joy.

Second, we can fall into trials rather quickly because they can come in a wide variety. We can even be in more than one trial at once.

James 1:3 says that God is not trying to destroy us, but is rather testing or proving our faith. He is leading us to trust him. This testing process makes us stronger. It produces patience, perseverance, and endurance. Through these trials, God makes us stronger.

Last, we are to cooperate with the Lord through the trial. Let the Lord do what he wants to do. Don't give up, don't run away, don't be discouraged, but rather simply believe and trust God. You will become a stronger, more well-rounded Christian because of it.

Bob Grenier
Senior Pastor, Calvary Chapel, Visalia, CA

PATIENCE IN ACTION

He committed no sin, and no deceit was found in his mouth.
When they hurled their insults at him, he did not retaliate;
when he suffered, he made no threats. Instead, he
entrusted himself to him who judges justly.

1 PETER 2:22–23, NIV

atience not only requires great faith that God's in control, and that his timing and ways are perfect, but it operates in every aspect of God's love (as defined in 1 Corinthians 13:4–8). For example, impatience is insensitive to the needs of others, and therefore, very capable of being unkind.

We may not intend to be unkind, but if we are impatient, there's a good chance that we could offend someone, speaking when we should remain silent.

Love is kind. . . . Patience is kind. . . . Kindness is patient.

Jorja Stewart
Cofounder, www.musicthatblessesothers.com, Author,
Relation Tips blog (jorjastewart.com)

MOTIVATED BY LOVE

Then He said to them in His teaching, "Beware of the scribes,
who desire to go around in long robes, love greetings in the
marketplaces, the best seats in the synagogues, and the best places at
feasts, who devour widows' houses, and for a pretense make
long prayers. These will receive greater condemnation."

MARK 12:38–40, NKJV

When Jesus hung on the cross, do you think he was worried about looking spiritual? Do you think he died a torturous, humiliating death because he wanted respect? Of course not! If it was respect he wanted, he would have avoided the cross and hung out with the very people who crucified him.

You see, love motivated Jesus. He wasn't playing games, and he wasn't playing church. He was simply thinking about you.

As a believer, why do you go to church? Is it because the pastor or preacher is the latest rage? Or because you want to look godly? Or because of the rich people who also attend? I hope not. Those were the very motivations of the people who plotted to kill Jesus, not worship him.

Today, may you worship and serve the Lord simply because you "love the LORD your God with all your heart, with all your soul, with all your mind, and with all your strength" (Mark 12:30). Don't waste time trying to look spiritual. Simply think about him, and let love be your motivation.

Mike Macintosh
Senior Pastor, Horizon Christian Fellowship, San Diego, CA

THEN . . . THE END WILL COME

*T*he temple destroyed? Not one stone upon another?

"His disciples came to him privately and asked, 'When will all this take place? And will there be any sign ahead of time to signal your return and the end of the world?'" (Matthew 24:3, NLT).

The disciples were scared. Jesus had called the religious leaders "hypocrites, blind guides, and snakes"! He openly rebuked them for trusting in traditions and rituals. Then he pointed to the Temple. "You think that's beautiful? You're awed by that?" Jesus said, "It will be a pile of rubble!"

The temple represented everything to the Jewish people—their God, spirituality, national identity. To understand how the disciples felt when Jesus said this, we have to visualize the tallest buildings in New York, Washington D.C., Los Angeles, Chicago, Dallas, Miami, and Houston all being destroyed in the same day.

If Jesus had stopped with that, it was bad enough. But he didn't. He said, "It's going to get worse." After that he described disasters, wars, famines, false prophets. . . . Then he said, "And the Good News about the kingdom will be preached throughout the whole world, so that all nations will hear it; and then, finally, the end will come" (v. 14, NLT).

It's been almost 2,000 years since Jesus spoke those words. Today, 2,000 languages—340 million people—still do not have one verse of Scripture in their language. By 2025 we anticipate there will be Bible translations in every language so all can hear the Good News. You may ask yourself how God wants you to help spread his word.

Roy Peterson
President and CEO, The Seed Company

I Need People Here
to Help Me Get There

He makes the whole body fit together perfectly.
As each part does its own special work, it helps the other
parts grow, so that the whole body is healthy
and growing and full of love.

EPHESIANS 4:16, NLT

*G*rowth doesn't happen in isolation. Going it alone just doesn't fit with God's plan. God gave his Son to make possible this thing we call the church. It's imperfect. It's made up of sinful human beings. It's a crazy place sometimes, but it's the place God intended for our healing and our growth on into eternity.

My physical family lasts until my physical body is put into its grave. But for eternity, I'm going to be doing life with my spiritual family—other believers in Christ. If you've been struggling to make it on your own, realize that God gave you people to belong to and to believe with, and you need a community in which to live out God's purposes.

Brandon A. Cox
Founding Pastor, Grace Hills Church, Northwest Arkansas, Editor of Pastors.com
and Rick Warren's Pastor's Toolbox *newsletter*

YOU ARE MADE TO WIN

In all these things we are more than conquerors
through him that loved us.

ROMANS 8:37, KJV

*E*veryone likes to win—but not everyone wins in life. Some people lose because they mess up. Other people lose simply because they live with a negative, defeatist mentality.

God doesn't create losers. He said in Romans 8:37 that we are more than conquerors through him who loved us. You don't have to lose in life, but you do have to rid yourself of defeatist thinking before your dreams and goals can become a reality to you.

For example, if you think about how badly your friend beat you at Ping-Pong, I guarantee you'll get whipped again during the second game. If you're worried that you'll never get promoted or have enough to pay the bills, you'll find yourself struggling continually. Negative thinking robs your positive expectation of the future, so it's extremely vital that you follow Paul's direction in 2 Corinthians 10:5 and bring thoughts of defeat and failure into captivity to the obedience of Christ.

Don't hold yourself back with negative thinking. Adopt the winning mentality that God created you to have, and always remember: If you don't quit, you will win.

Mac Hammond
Senior Pastor, Living Word Christian Center, Brooklyn Park, MN

THE PATH TO MATURITY

I don't know about you, but I don't enjoy pain. I will do just about anything to avoid an ache or difficulty. Yet these difficulties can often be the very thing that helps me to grow up. James wrote, "My brethren, count it all joy when you fall into various trials, knowing that the testing of your faith produces patience. But let patience have its perfect work, that you may be perfect and complete, lacking nothing" (James 1:2–4, NKJV).

I used to think that patience was the only result of trials. But look closer at the passage and you see that patience is just the vehicle that gets me to maturity and wholeness. God's goal isn't just to make me patient. God's goal is to grow me up.

The caterpillar has to be fully committed to reach the stage of development we call a butterfly. It can't quit halfway through the cocooning process. The caterpillar's chrysalis is its greatest time of trial. In the chrysalis, most of the caterpillar's parts are digested as the new structures of a butterfly are developed from the imaginal cells. As the new butterfly emerges from the cocoon, the struggle isn't finished. The proboscis has to be assembled, and fluid has to be pumped into the newly formed wings. Yet the caterpillar that endures is the one that experiences the maturity of a butterfly.

I wonder if sometimes I don't short-circuit my own growth by trying to avoid pain. Instead of staying in the trial until maturity, I settle for a half-baked mess. Let patience have its perfect work.

Rich Cathers
Senior Pastor, Calvary Chapel, Fullerton, CA

NO PRETENSE

The people were delighted with all
the wonderful things he was doing.

LUKE 13:17B, NIV84

uke 13:10–17 tells the story of a woman who had suffered severely for eighteen years with a crippled back, whom Jesus instantly healed. The joy and relief she felt are hard to imagine. But not everyone was happy with Jesus for healing this woman. The synagogue ruler was angry that Jesus showed such gross disregard for the religious traditions—healing her on a Sabbath day, during the synagogue service no less!

There has never been another person who loved God more and followed the commandments of God more carefully than Jesus. And yet there is not a hint of religious pretense about him. He didn't follow the commandments of God for show. He didn't add to the commandments of God to prove his devotion. He didn't shackle himself with a bunch of religious restrictions out of some need for affirmation because of personal insecurity.

The common people immediately recognized the difference between the religious-rule-following types and Jesus. People see the difference in our day, too. I hope you will make a commitment today to show the love, grace, and mercy to others like our Savior did to those wanting a second chance.

Jeff Miles
Senior Pastor, Touchstone Christian Fellowship, Sacramento, CA

THE BRIDEGROOM'S VISIT

Let us rejoice and be glad and give him glory!
For the wedding of the Lamb has come, and
his bride has made herself ready.

REVELATION 19:7

In the ancient Hebrew marriage, the future Hebrew bridegroom had to first make a visit to the house of his future bride. And there, in her house, he would state his love and pledge to her his life in a proposal of marriage.

God said that you are the bride and he is the Groom. And 2,000 years ago, in order for the marriage to begin, the Bridegroom visited the bride. God became man and visited this world, this life, our lives. He came into the house of the bride. He came to our house so that we could become his—that we could leave the old house and come away with him to a place of joy.

You see, no matter who you are, where you're at, no matter how messed up your life is, no matter how cold your heart has been, no matter how far you are from God or how far you think you are . . . the Bridegroom has to come to the house of the bride.

The Bridegroom has to make the journey to your house. No matter where she lives, no matter what condition her house is in, he comes to your house, to your life, to your problem, to your need, to your burden. Jesus, your Bridegroom, knows it all! He's right there on the other side of your problem. He stands at the door and knocks. Are you ready to let him in and receive the gift of his great joy?

Jonathan Cahn
Author, The Harbinger, *Senior Pastor and Messianic Rabbi*
the Jerusalem Center / Beth Israel, Wayne, NJ

IT'S ALL ABOUT ME

For where you have envy and selfish
ambition, there you find disorder
and every evil practice.

JAMES 3:16, NIV

*J*ames, under the inspiration of the Holy Spirit, is warning in the above passage that a self-absorbed, me-first kind of attitude is the perfect breeding ground for the wicked spores of every other kind of vile behavior. It makes sense. Whatever sin it might be, it's rooted in self-centeredness, committed in total disregard for God, his Word, or how it will affect anyone else.

When the *unholy* trinity is ruling (me, myself, and I)—when it's all about *me*, what I want, when I want it, with no other considerations beyond my personal gain—disaster is only a heartbeat away. Eventually, James says, there will be chaos and sin-laden disorder, because life was not designed to have its center in me and my will, but in God and his will.

Fortunately, the converse of this principle is true: Where self has been mastered and Jesus is Lord, there you will find peace and every good thing!

Dr. Ross Reinman
Senior Pastor, The Rock, Santa Rosa, CA

DIVINE APPOINTMENTS

Then a man named Jairus, a synagogue leader,
came and fell at Jesus's feet, pleading with him to come
to his house because his only daughter, a girl of about twelve,
was dying. As Jesus was on his way, the crowds almost crushed him.
And a woman was there who had been subject to bleeding
for twelve years, but no one could heal her. She came up
behind him and touched the edge of his cloak,
and immediately her bleeding stopped.

LUKE 8:41–44, NIV

'm task oriented. In this story, I suspect I would have acted more like Peter, concerned that Jesus wasn't going to make his next appointment. Perhaps I would have viewed Jesus's interaction with an important leader and his sick daughter as more important to the cause than a seemingly minor and likely inconsequential interaction with just one of what were probably hundreds of onlookers that day on the dusty road.

But Jesus doesn't pass up this opportunity to make his divine appointment with the chronically ill woman. Despite the delay it would cause him, Jesus senses that a soul can be won, and that a life can be changed. The other stuff can wait.

How many divine appointments are placed into our lives each and every day, only to be crowded out by our busyness. Let us strive to meet our divine appointments with confidence that God has placed people into our lives who need to see the light of Jesus.

Beck A. Taylor
President, Whitworth University, Spokane, WA

WORTHY LIVING

☙ BIBLE READ: EPHESIANS 4:1–3

As a prisoner for the Lord, then,
I urge you to live a life worthy of the
calling you have received.

EPHESIANS 4:1, NIV

Does your behavior connect with your beliefs? Is there any connection between what we confess and the lifestyle we adopt? Will your actions today reflect your calling as a follower of Christ?

Ephesians is the perfect balance between doctrine and duty. The stirring appeal in Ephesians 4:1 brings together the themes of chapters 1–3 and introduces the priority of worthy living found in chapters 4–6.

As followers of Christ we have new standards and expectations for living. Paul insisted that our behavior is to be worthy of our divine calling.

Five key virtues help us better understand what worthy living looks like on a daily basis. Our lives are to be characterized by humility and gentleness, or lowliness and meekness. Long-suffering, forbearance, and love further exemplify Christ-centered living.

These virtues not only reflect our call to worthy living but provide the practical realities to help us exemplify true spiritual unity in the bond of peace.

David S. Dockery
President, Union University, Jackson, TN

GETTING YOUR HOPE BACK

*Hope deferred makes
the heart sick.*

PROVERBS 13:12, NIV

ave you ever had one of those seasons where you seemed to be running out of hope? It can happen to any one of us. The Bible is full of stories of those who began to lose their hope. Luke 24 gives us a great example of this as we see the disciples walking "downcast" and brokenhearted on the road to Emmaus. They were feeling so hopeless that they even began to discuss their faith in the past tense! The very disciples who had talked with Jesus, walked with Jesus, ate with Jesus, and experienced the miraculous with Jesus did not even recognize him.

So how did these downcast disciples get their hope back? Jesus made the Word come alive to them again! In an instant, he changed their heartbreaking experience into a heart-burning experience! "And they said to one another, 'Did not our heart burn within us while He [Jesus] talked with us on the road, and while He opened the Scriptures to us?'" (Luke 24:32, NKJV). For 2,000 years, Jesus has been opening the Scriptures for his people. For 2,000 years he has been transforming his people from heartbreaking experiences into heartburning experiences again.

So if you need to get your hope back, ask the resurrected Jesus to open the Scriptures to you again!

Brian Cashman
Senior Pastor, Valley Metro Church, Sherman Oaks, CA

SEEK FIRST THE KINGDOM

Thus speaks the LORD of hosts, saying:
"This people says, 'The time has not come, the time
that the LORD's house should be built.'" Then the word of
the LORD came by Haggai the prophet, saying,
"Is it time for you yourselves to dwell in your paneled houses,
and this temple to lie in ruins?" Now therefore, thus says
the LORD of hosts: "Consider your ways!"

HAGGAI 1:2–5, NKJV

What an amazing time in Israel's history! God opened the door for them to return to Jerusalem and rebuild the Temple after seventy years of captivity in Babylon. Yet, due to misaligned priorities, the children of Israel decided not to rebuild the Temple because they alleged that "the time has not yet come." Their selfish ambitions and self-centered ways were reflected as they lived in their "paneled houses" while the house of the Lord was in ruin.

How often do we neglect the work of God in favor of our own comforts or personal gain? God instructs us to consider our ways that our lives may be pleasing unto the Lord. May we truly seek first the kingdom of God and his righteousness each and every day.

Eric Cartier
Senior Pastor, Rocky Mountain Calvary Chapel, Colorado Springs, CO

EXTRAORDINARY LOVE

*Greater love has no one than this: to
lay down his life for his friends.*

JOHN 15:13, NIV

A fatally wounded soldier in the Iraqi desert holds his position while being surrounded by enemy fire. This brave soldier fires his weapon over and over at the approaching enemy giving his comrades time to get away. A sacrifice of one for many.

A young woman awakes early every morning to help her four younger siblings get ready for school. The reason? Her mother, a widow is now dying of cancer leaving her the responsibility of taking care of the family. While her friends went off to college, she is at home taking care of her mother, brothers and sisters.

Even though both of these stories are different, they both represent a sacrifice of love. Examples of people considering the lives of others more important than their own. You may never see their acts of kindness mention in public. They may never win an award, a medal, or see their name on a wall of honor. These are the unsung heroes, just ordinary people living extraordinary lives. These are the kind of people who inspire us as Christians to be more than average. These are just common everyday godly people who make our world a little better each day.

Steve M. Woods
Chairman, Board of Directors, WoodsMasteryLearningFoundation.org

PRAY WITHOUT CEASING

Pray without ceasing.

1 THESSALONIANS 5:17, NKJV

*T*hough this verse is only three words, it is a key to living a supernatural life. Two of the greatest benefits to constant prayer are that we get (1) more answered prayers and (2) ongoing fellowship with God.

Except when speaking about disobedient people, the Bible teaches us that God answers prayer. Jesus knew the Father better than anyone, and every time Jesus taught about prayer, he boldly declared that God answers prayer. For example, "Ask and it will be given to you" (Matthew 7:7). So generally speaking, people who pray more are people who experience more of God's blessings.

Simply put, prayer is talking to God. So if we are constantly praying, we are constantly talking to God. From the first chapter of the Bible we learn that God's dream is to have regular fellowship with us. He wants to teach us, guide us, and encourage us. So praying without ceasing keeps the channels of communication open for God to speak to us.

Jerry Dirmann
Senior Pastor, The Rock Church, Anaheim, CA

God's Blessings

*Blessed is the one who does not walk in step with the
wicked or stand in the way that sinners take or sit in the company
of mockers, but whose delight is in the law of the Lord, and
who meditates on his law day and night. That person is like
a tree planted by streams of water, which yields its fruit in season
and whose leaf does not wither—whatever they do prospers.*

PSALM 1:1–3, NIV

God's blessings are great. God loves giving them, and we certainly enjoy receiving them. But one caution frequently underscored throughout the Bible is that we are to be careful that our hearts don't learn to trust in the blessings. When God graciously grants us relationships, riches, or good health we must remember that these blessings ought to bolster our confidence in the Giver and not the gift.

Sadly, our tendency is just the opposite. It seems that we often seek the Lord with growing levels of faith when we are in need or in pain. If only we would learn to deepen our faith while God grants his blessings. While we enjoy God's gifts, may we be quick to remember God's words in Jeremiah 9:23–24: "Let not the wise man boast of his wisdom or the strong man boast of his strength or the rich man boast of his riches, but let him who boasts boast about this: that he understands and knows me, that I am the Lord who exercises kindness" (NIV84).

Who or what will you put your trust in today? I hope you choose the One who is greater than the blessing!

Mike Fabarez
Senior Pastor, Compass Bible Church, Aliso Viejo, CA

RECEIVING GOD'S FORGIVENESS

Blessed are they whose transgressions are
forgiven, whose sins are covered.
Blessed is the man whose sin the Lord
will never count against him.

ROMANS 4:7–8, NIV84

When we hear about God's forgiveness, it can sometimes be difficult to believe that his forgiveness extends to us. We often think that God can forgive others much more easily than he can ourselves. But sin is common to all of us; every single person has made decisions or acted in ways that have grieved the heart of God.

Though God does not overlook our sin, Jesus took our punishment upon himself when he was sacrificed on the cross. His death and resurrection have provided a way for each of us to personally receive God's forgiveness and to live blamelessly before him. When we repent of the wrong we have done and give our lives to God, through Jesus we find peace with him. This passage reminds believers of their true identity—people who are loved by God and who have been completely forgiven by him.

Is Jesus your Lord and Savior? If not, take this moment to ask him to forgive your sins and to come into your life. Your new beginning is just one prayer away.

Scott Chapman
Senior Pastor and President, Christ Together
The Chapel, Northern Chicagoland, IL

COMMUNITY

And they devoted themselves to the apostles'
teaching and the fellowship, to the breaking
of bread and the prayers.

ACTS 2:42, ESV

I recently heard a statistic that the average Facebooker spends 169 minutes in that online community—per visit. It amazes me that we can spend so much time together . . . without actually being together!

When God created the world, he said it was good. The first time the Lord lets on that something isn't good is when he points out that man is alone. God created man to enjoy relationships—and no wonder, as he himself, though singular in being, enjoys fellowship within his own triune nature. We were made in his image, and we were made to be in community.

As outcasts in the first century, the early church needed to be there for one another. They spent time in the Word and prayer together, and they encouraged and met one anothers' needs as they arose. They were the Body of Christ!

Don't get me wrong. Online communities have their place. I tweet as much as the next guy! But when it comes to true fellowship, it's like the old expression, "I guess you had to be there."

Brian Bachochin
Senior Pastor, Calvary Chapel, Franklin, TN

BEARING ONE ANOTHER'S WEAKNESSES

We then who are strong ought
to bear with the scruples of the weak,
and not to please ourselves.

ROMANS 15:1, NKJV

*J*esus is our example because he didn't come for himself, but came to please his Father. "And He who sent Me is with Me. The Father has not left Me alone, for I always do those things that please Him" (John 8:29). We may grow at different rates spiritually, and have different degrees of maturity, but we need to be considerate of where other people are in their walk, bearing with the weaknesses of our brothers and sisters who may not be as mature yet. It is God who exhorts us to have unity as believers, and he will stir within us the patience necessary to support one another. Let us grow together as believers—that we may be of one mind to glorify the God and Father of our Lord Jesus Christ. Thus, having unity encourages us to live as one Body of Christ, not dividing ourselves.

Paul summed up this message perfectly: "Therefore receive one another, just as Christ also received us, to the glory of God" (Romans 15:7). Jesus Christ received us and welcomed us into his fellowship. May we always follow his example.

David Rosales
Senior Pastor, Calvary Chapel, Chino Valley, CA

HOLD ON TO YOUR HOPE

My soul finds rest in God alone;
my salvation comes from him. He alone is my
rock and my salvation; he is my fortress,
I will never be shaken.

PSALM 62:1–2, NIV

*L*ife is full of aches and pains. If we did not have hope that our future would be better than our present, we would surely lose the joy of living in the midst of our daily struggles.

The psalmist wrote, "Why are you cast down, O my soul? And why are you disquieted within me? Hope in God; for I shall yet praise Him, the help of my countenance and my God" (Psalm 42:11, NKJV). "Hope in God." Why? Because that's where our future lies.

How can we have hope today that tomorrow will be better? Because Jesus has promised us that he will be in our tomorrow as well as our today. Therefore, we have hope that he is working all things together for our good.

Hope provides an anchor when the waves of life billow against our soul. In the dark night of depression, pain, loneliness, sickness, and even death, we have an anchor of hope from our Heavenly Father that causes us to rest securely in the harbor of his love and care.

Steve DeNicola
Senior Pastor, Calvary Chapel, Foothill Ranch, CA

Choosing to Do Well

BIBLE READ: LUKE 9

*Guard your heart above all else, for it
determines the course of your life.*

PROVERBS 4:23, NLT

As my student colleagues envision the future, I always return to Luke 9, where Christ asked his disciples, "Who do the people say I am?" (v. 18); and later, "Who do you say I am?" (v. 20); and still later in the same chapter, "What good is it for a man to gain the world, and yet lose or forfeit his very self?" (v. 25, NIV84). There you have it: Are we drawn to mere success, or do we press on for true significance?

How do good people lose their way? Let me relate a personal story very briefly. My father had a heart attack a number of years ago. When I arrived at his bedside in the intensive care ward, I asked how such a thing could happen to a man with an otherwise excellent health history. As it turns out, he had experienced a number of smaller episodes (which he had ignored) that weakened the heart muscle to the point that the heart, finally, did not respond well to a major event. My father survived, and the lesson was not lost on me.

Life is like that, too. When we lose our way, it is often the product of losing track of that which is really important. Doing well and faithfully is a lifetime product of consciously protecting our hearts in every decision we make.

Andrew K. Benton
President and CEO, Pepperdine University, Malibu, CA

A YEAR OF ABUNDANT HARVEST

Jesus said to them, "My food is to do the
will of him who sent me and to accomplish his work.
Do you not say, 'There are yet four months, then comes
the harvest'? Look I tell you, lift up your eyes, and
see that the fields are white for harvest."

JOHN 4:34–36, ESV

Jesus said these words to His disciples after He helped the Samaritan woman to have a relationship with God.

Jesus is inviting you and me to believe that He will use us to help so many people enjoy the benefits of knowing Him as their Savior.

We read in Genesis 26:12 "And Isaac sowed in that land and reaped in the same year a hundredfold. The LORD blessed him." When Isaac planted crops in that land, he did not reap a normal harvest but a supernatural blessing from God. Today God invites you to share His Word with the people around you and expect a harvest not according to your abilities but according to His power and plan.

So many people we meet are separated from God, hurting because they are slaves to sin and Satan. Therefore let us be a blessing to Jesus by sharing the gospel with as many lost people whom God loves. Let us likewise believe that God will bless us in return and that this year will be the year of hundredfold.

Samy Tanagho
Founder and President of Glad News for Muslims Ministry
www.gladnewsministry.com

WHO NEEDS A SHEPHERD?

♛ BIBLE READ: PSALM 23

The LORD is my shepherd,
I shall not want.

PSALM 23:1, NKJV

*T*his wonderful psalm may be the most recognized part of the Bible. We sing it with joy, hold tightly to it in sorrow, and through these simple verses God measures out comfort and courage in every kind of situation. But have you ever considered just who it is that is declaring a deep need for a Shepherd?

Most scholars believe David wrote this psalm, and did so after he was anointed king of Israel. Here he was, the most powerful man in the realm, endowed with the Spirit of God and secure in the promise that God had made to him and his family forever. Here was the conqueror of Goliath and the great commander of Israel's mighty men. If ever there was a man who could take on the challenges of life, it was David. And yet in this simple psalm we see his heart. He realized that down deep he was a sheep in need of a shepherd, and no ordinary shepherd would do. Only the Lord was consistently faithful, and able to provide, protect, guide, and care for him in this life and the next. What a joy to know this Shepherd!

Dr. David W. Hegg
Senior Pastor, Grace Baptist Church, Santa Clarita, CA

FOR HE IS WITH YOU ALWAYS

For He [God] Himself has said,
I will not in any way fail you nor give you
up nor leave you without support.
[I will] not, [I will] not, [I will] not in any degree
leave you helpless nor forsake nor let [you] down
(relax My hold on you)! [Assuredly not!]

HEBREWS 13:5, AMPLIFIED

God has gone to every extent he can to emphasize his presence in our lives. Why, then, do we sometimes feel so alone? People often feel alone in life because they've become desensitized to God's presence. They aren't conscious of the fact that he is with them all the time. The good news is that you can develop the habit of being aware of God's presence.

When you leave your devotional time, do so with the determination that every moment of the day you're going to be aware of God. Choose to commune continually with the Lord on a heart level. That way, when a problem comes up, you come to God first and say, "Okay, Lord, this is your deal. What would you like me to do about it?" Pray in the Holy Ghost about it. He will respond.

It doesn't matter what's going on around you or what challenge you're faced with. If you are aware of God's continual presence in your life, you will not be intimidated by any circumstance you face.

Mac Hammond
Senior Pastor, Living Word Christian Center, Brooklyn Park, MN

FRUITFULNESS

Every branch in me that beareth not fruit
he taketh away: and every branch that beareth fruit,
he purgeth it, that it may bring forth more fruit.

JOHN 15:2, KJV

This promise is valuable to those who desire to bear fruit. Even if it sounds strange when you first hear it, does the fruitful branch need purging with a knife? No doubt this is painful because much of God's work of cleaning is done as a result of much suffering.

Romans 8:18 says, "For I reckon that the sufferings of this present time are not worthy to be compared with the glory that will be revealed in us." The promise of suffering in this verse is not meant for an evil person but for a righteous one. The end result will give satisfying reward equal to the nature and way of suffering.

If we desire to bring more fruit for the Lord, we do not need to be troubled about the suffering we are going through. Because of the word, we will be more profitable and graceful. The Lord who created us in his wisdom to be fruitful will use every way to cause us to reach the highest level of fruitfulness. Is this our joy? No, but we have more and greater rest in the promise of fruitfulness than the promise of riches.

Lord, grant me quickly your gracious promise and cause me to bring forth greater fruit for your kingdom!

Dr. Elias Malki
Founder and President, Middle East Gospel Outreach

CHANGE IS A PROCESS

Do not conform any longer to the pattern of this world,
but be transformed by the renewing of your mind.
Then you will be able to test and approve what God's
will is—his good, pleasing, and perfect will.

ROMANS 12:2, NIV84

In Acts 10 Peter is challenged with a need to change his heart about someone—a whole group of people, really. God sends a vision three times in which Peter recognizes his intolerance toward others. The first time Peter rejects the very idea! The second time Peter tolerates the possibility of embracing these others. By the end of the chapter, when Peter retells the story, it is clear the third time was the charm as he embraces the idea that we all find equality in Christ.

When you sense that God is leading you through a time of change in your thinking or in your life, don't reject it out of hand. Give yourself a break and let the process go on. Change is not an event; it's a process.

Jeff Jernigan
Senior Pastor, Corona Friends Church, Corona, CA

A Model for Speaking Out

But in your hearts revere Christ as Lord.
Always be prepared to give an answer to everyone who
asks you to give the reason for the hope that you have.
But do this with gentleness and respect.

1 PETER 3:15, NIV

The university I attended was replete with "diversity." Communist newspapers, gay dance invitations, and petitions against U.S. government policy abounded. The chaplain, converted to Buddhism, railed against the sins of Christian America.

Few identified themselves as Christian. Professor Leech, an American history scholar, was one. I learned from him that a person can have an impact for Christ in quiet and gentle ways.

One day I read in *Newsweek* a letter to the editor from Leech. He responded to an article questioning Christ's resurrection. He maintained that there was as much evidence to support the resurrection as there was for many other events in history. He stood for Christ in a national magazine, with scholarship and humility.

When I reached his office, we spoke about the Christian witness at the university. He offered me a copy of *Good News for Modern Man* from a stock he kept on the corner of his desk. His humble witness, employing his scholarship, is an example for all who call themselves Christian.

Dr. Lee G. Royce
President, Mississippi College, Clinton, MS

GOD IS WITH YOU

For Israel is not forsaken, nor Judah,
by his God, the Lord of hosts, though their land
was filled with sin against the Holy One of Israel.

*H*ave you ever been through spiritual warfare that seemed insurmountable while looking at your faults and wondered where God stood with you on this matter? Even though God said that he "will never leave you nor forsake you" (Hebrews 13:5) and "will be with you to the end of the age" (Matthew 28:20), we still have doubts that he might abandon us this time.

The Holy Spirit is in us and with us, and we are never left alone. You might be in some sort of internal torment; just know you're the apple of his eye. Though your stomach may churn and menacing things are on the horizon, remember that your Lord is with you. Even though Israel "in a chastising kind of way" had been dealt with, he said, "Israel is not forsaken, . . . by his God." God would utterly destroy the armies of those who had previously taken them captive.

God's mercies are new every morning, even for his children who have sinned against him. The Holy One of Israel is a present help for you right now, and he has grace and mercy for those who have sinned. But one thing is for sure: You are not forsaken! Hold on to that truth. God loves you and is waiting for you to turn away from your sin and come back to him.

John Schaffer
Senior Pastor, First Love Calvary Chapel, Whittier, CA

Amazing Faith

Did you know that amazing faith moves the very heart of God and allows you to see his undeniable faithfulness? Have you ever thought that your faith could move the heart of God?

Now when Jesus had entered Capernaum, a centurion came to Him, pleading with Him, saying, "Lord, my servant is lying at home paralyzed, dreadfully tormented." And Jesus said to him, "I will come and heal him." The centurion said, "Lord, I am not worthy that You should come under my roof. But only speak a word, and my servant will be healed. For I also am a man under authority." . . . When Jesus heard it, he marveled, and said, "I have not found such great faith, not even in Israel." (Matthew 8:5–9, 10, NKJV)

The foundation of the centurion's faith was his understanding of authority. The same is true for us. Many of us call Jesus "Savior," but can we call him "Lord"? That takes great faith, to give up control and allow Jesus to rule your life. But that is exactly what faith is: trusting Jesus with your life, no matter your daily circumstances. When he is the authority in my life, I am able to see him not for the answers he gives but for who he is as my Lord.

Have you ever given Jesus a chance to marvel at your faith?

Just say it out loud: "Jesus, you are the authority in my life today!" Then ask the Spirit of God to guide, direct, and teach you to walk with amazing faith, because you will move the very heart of God and will begin to see his undeniable faithfulness.

Matthew Cork
Senior Pastor, Yorba Linda Friends Church, Yorba Linda, CA

TEMPTATION

Blessed is the man who endures temptation;
for when he has been approved, he will receive the
crown of life which the Lord has promised to those who
love him. Let no man say when he is tempted,
"I am tempted by God," for God can't be tempted
with evil, nor does He Himself tempt anyone.

JAMES 1:12–13, NKJV

*A*re you a different person behind closed doors than you are in public? Keep in mind that as Christians, how we act in private is just as important as how we are perceived in public. If you are watching pornography in secret, God sees you.

When I travel, I have them block the cable television in my room. I learned this from Billy Graham back in 1991. More often, I travel with someone, and then there is accountability. That way I can maintain my integrity.

You can say, "Oh, I'll never be tempted," but you will be tempted. I do not care who you are, you are not Superman. We are all tempted at different times in our lives, but the wise person knows to keep one's eyes on the Lord. Only he can deliver us out of the temptation.

Raul Ries
Senior Pastor, Calvary Chapel Golden Springs, Diamond Bar, CA

STRENGTH ON THE MOVE

*But I trust in you, L*ORD*; I say,*
"You are my God."

As a culture, we prefer to have our ducks in a row before we move forward. That is often not the way God works. In Judges 6, the angel of the Lord appears to Gideon, announcing, "The LORD is with you, you mighty warrior" (v. 12). This was a surprise to Gideon on two counts. One, things were not going well for the children of Israel. Like many of us when things are not going our way, we say, "If the Lord is with us, why then has all this happened to us? Where are the wonderful deeds that our ancestors have told us about?" In other words, "Where are you, God?"

Two, Gideon did not view himself as a "mighty warrior." As he tells the angel, "My clan is the weakest in Manasseh, and I am the least in my family" (v. 15).

The angel of the Lord did not answer his questions. Rather, he gives Gideon a task: "Go in this might of yours and deliver Israel from the hands of Midian" (v. 14). He also gives Gideon a promise: "I will be with you" (v. 18, author's paraphrase). God will make us adequate to do what he calls us to do—not before we need that strength, but as we go.

All he asks is our obedience.

Shirley A. Mullen
President and Professor of History, Houghton College, Houghton, New York

Building Walls

So we rebuilt the wall till all of it reached
half its height, for the people worked
with all their heart.

NEHEMIAH 4:6, NIV

When Nehemiah was allowed to go to Jerusalem and rebuild the wall, God had already brought his people back to the land some ninety years earlier. The problem was they had done nothing to rebuild the wall. The Temple was built, but the wall of God's city was in shambles.

Unfortunately, this is true spiritually about many Christians. God has saved them, redeemed them, and brought them into a right relationship with himself. However, there are things in their lives they keep leaving undone that God wants them to build up.

Just because we are saved does not mean we can put our lives in cruise and abide and glide. No! Instead, our lives should be marked by the continual striving toward godliness and holiness.

Let your love for others be unconditional. Don't abide and glide in your walk with God. Set your mind to build up the walls of your most precious faith!

Ron Hindt
Senior Pastor, Calvary Chapel, Houston, TX

A Gentle Whisper

👑 BIBLE READ: 1 KINGS 18–19

*The LORD is close to the brokenhearted and
saves those who are crushed in spirit.*

PSALM 34:18, NIV

The battle between the Lord God and Baal was over. Elijah the prophet had an exceptional day of victory. But not long afterward the sweet revival victory party turned sour when the wicked Queen Jezebel wanted him dead. Fear overwhelmed Elijah as he ran for his life. He felt defeated, tired, and depressed as he prayed to God that he might die.

As Elijah waited for God, a vast and fierce wind shredded the mountain apart and shattered the rocks, but God was not in the wind. After the wind there was an earthquake that violently shook the ground, but the Lord was not in the tremor. After the earthquake came a blazing fire, but the Lord was not in the fire. In the stillness of the moment after the fire dissipated, a gentle whisper was calling his name.

Have you ever felt like Elijah—defeated, alone, or discouraged? Maybe you were overwhelmed by the situation which made you emotionally or physically run and hide.

Like Elijah, sometimes we expect an exasperated God coming after us in judgment. But the Lord was not there. God in his incredible mercy and grace came as a gentle whisper of healing and encouragement for a broken, discouraged heart. He is waiting for you with open arms.

Steve M. Woods
Chairman, Board of Directors, www.WoodsMasteryFoundation.org

A CALL TO WORK

👑 BIBLE READ: NEHEMIAH 2

For we are God's workmanship,
created in Christ Jesus to do good works,
which God prepared in advance for us to do.

EPHESIANS 2:10, NIV84

*E*very Christian is called to be involved in the work of God, doing their part for his kingdom as God, not man, directs them.

But the particular work God calls a person to is personal and important for that period of time, such as with Nehemiah, whom God called to return to rebuild the walls of the city of Jerusalem after the seventy years of captivity.

Nehemiah reveals that his call to work was characterized by three things:

1. A careful consideration of the task (2:11–16)
2. A clear communication to the people (2:17–18)
3. A confident confrontation of the opposition (2:19–20)

God will call, enable, and work through us to fulfill his purpose and will, if we are willing to give up leading and simply follow his lead! The question is "Are you doing works for God, or are you doing the work of God?"

Xavier Ries
Senior Pastor, Calvary Chapel, Pasadena, CA

YOU ARE WORTH A HIGH PRICE

For God bought you with a high price.

1 CORINTHIANS 6:20, NLT

*T*he world around us reminds us of our faults and our failures. The voice within us, conditioned by the poison of unrealistic expectations and unfair criticism, whispers worthlessness to our hearts. And the enemy is lurking before the throne of God to accuse us.

But God has thundered the ultimate declaration of our worth by commissioning his Son to be the ultimate payment for our sin. Your worth is accounted for by the price Jesus paid for you on the cross . . . and it was immeasurably high.

Brandon A. Cox
*Founding Pastor, Grace Hills Church, Northwest Arkansas, Editor of Pastors.com
and Rick Warren's* Pastor's Toolbox *newsletter*

BELIEVING IN ORDER TO SEE

Every place on which the sole of your foot treads,
I have given it to you.

JOSHUA 1:3, NASB

"I have given it to you." This is a staggering thought—to believe God for the promise before you can see the outcome. Can you see the promise fulfilled? Oswald Sanders has said, "Eyes that look are common. Eyes that see are rare." God will keep his promises he made to you and me. God said in Numbers 23:19, "God is not a man, that he should lie, nor a son of man, that he should change his mind. Does he speak and then not act? Does he promise and not fulfill?" (NIV84).

Hebrews 11:1 says, "Now faith is being sure of what we hope for and certain of what we do not see." This type of faith is life-giving because a faith that believes to see keeps back discouragement. The next time fear and doubt enter your mind, remember this: *fear* imprisons, *faith* liberates; *fear* paralyzes, *faith* empowers; *fear* disheartens, *faith* encourages; *fear* sickens, *faith* heals; *fear* makes useless, *faith* makes serviceable—and most of all, *fear* puts hopelessness at the heart of life, while *faith* rejoices in its God.

Are you willing to trust in an invisible God, even when you don't feel like it? Lord, teach me to see with eyes in my heart that look beyond the natural . . . to believe with faith that will not only liberate me but others through me.

Dan Carroll
Senior Pastor, Water of Life Community Church, Fontana, CA

IN HIS PROTECTION

And all people of the earth shall see
that thou art called by the name of the LORD;
and they shall be afraid of thee.

DEUTERONOMY 28:10, KJV

ased on God's promise there is no reason for us to fear. Our fear reveals a lack of faith in God's name. His glory on us causes those around us to confess that truly we carry the name of the Lord and that we belong to Jehovah, the mighty God!

My prayer is that we receive the full grace that God wants to give us—that we are confident and understand that the evil people hate the saints but at the same time fear them. For example, Haman used to tremble in fear of Mordecai even after he arranged to kill him. Haman's hatred of Mordecai was a true hate full of fear. But Haman could not make it known publicly.

Fear is the character of those who do evil. They are the enemy of the Lord of Hosts. We are in perfect safety, those of us who are called by the name of the eternal God. When a Roman soldier fell into trouble, all he had to say was, "I am a Roman!" as did the apostle Paul. He would immediately find himself under the protection of the great Roman Empire. God is ready to send all the angels of heaven in order to protect even one of his children who are called by his name.

So, let us defend the truth like lions. "Because if God is with us who can be against us?" (Romans 8:31).

Dr. Elias Malki
Founder and President, Middle East Gospel Outreach

RELATIONSHIP AND FELLOWSHIP

But if we walk in the light as He is in the light,
we have fellowship with one another. . . .
If we confess our sins, He is faithful and just to
forgive us our sins and to cleanse us
from all unrighteousness.

1 JOHN 1:7–9, NKJV

It is important to understand the difference between relationship and fellowship. Relationship is how we're connected (mom, son, friend, etc.), but fellowship is the communication and enjoyment we share in these relationships. Many people in relationship do not have fellowship. But a lack of fellowship does not mean a lack of relationship. A disobedient son may have broken the fellowship with his mother, but he's still her son.

We come into relationship with God by confessing Jesus Christ as Lord (Romans 10:9). When we sin, we're still in relationship with God, but fellowship is broken. To restore fellowship, we need to apologetically admit that we did wrong. And God promised that he will then forgive us, which restores our fellowship with him. So confessing Jesus brought relationship, and confessing sin restores fellowship. Take this moment to confess any sin that might be hindering your relationship with God. Like the prodigal son experienced, your heavenly Father is waiting for you to return home.

Jerry Dirmann
Senior Pastor, The Rock Church, Anaheim, CA

A PLACE OF SAFETY

From the ends of the earth, I will cry
to you for help, for my heart is overwhelmed.
Lead me to the towering rock of safety, for you are
my safe refuge, a fortress where my
enemies cannot reach me.

PSALM 61:2–3, NLT

ou know you are in trouble when you feel so far away from God's presence that your address might as well be "the ends of the earth"! David felt the quicksand of doubt, fear, and unbelief underneath his feet. As he grew weaker by the minute, his desperate cry was to be brought to a spiritual position where his feet could feel the Rock of God beneath him.

The moment your feet are safely settled on that Rock, God will keep you in "perfect peace" because your "thoughts are fixed on [Him]" (Isaiah 26:3). Trust is the feeling of security you have when your feet are solidly planted on a Rock that towers high above all your enemies.

That Rock is also a place of safety where you can find secure refuge and shelter (Psalm 61:3–4). As Isaiah phrased it, "But to the poor, O Lord, you are a refuge from the storm. To the needy in distress, you are a shelter from the rain and heat" (Isaiah 25:4).

Climb up on the Rock right now and rest in his perfect peace.

Larry Stockstill
Teaching Pastor, Bethany World Prayer Center, Baton Rouge, LA

APPETITE FOR GOD

Blessed are those who hunger
and thirst after righteousness:
for they shall be filled.

MATTHEW 5:6, KJV

To hunger and thirst after righteousness is to have a heart that is completely yielded to pleasing God. Many of us today are full, but yet we've never been filled. We have this inner craving, this appetite that is always wanting more. Our lives are so busy and our schedules are so packed that our daily walk and our walk with God create tension in our daily lives. We have our to-do list for God, and we check it off like a chore, forgetting that what he desires is that we desire to know him!

To have this appetite to know God requires that you empty yourself of anything that stands in the way of your relationship with him. Many hunger more for the temporary satisfactions of this world, and as our lives get full we are never filled. God promises that if we hunger and thirst after righteousness, we shall be filled.

Ask him today to fill you with the only thing that will satisfy your hunger and thirst: more Jesus Christ.

Matthew Cork
Senior Pastor, Yorba Linda Friends Church, Yorba Linda, CA

Are We All Children of God?

Yet to all who received him,
to those who believed in his name, he gave
the right to become children of God.

JOHN 1:12, NIV84

An atheist once wrote to me, "And if my child continues to deny that I exist, I send him into everlasting torment? Nice chain o' logic there." He accuses the Christian of being illogical, but there's a big disconnect in his own logic. I told him that if his child denies that he exists, I think it would be wise to take him to a good child psychiatrist. If he clothed, fed, and educated him—and even gave him his own room, taught him right from wrong, loved him and nurtured him—and he denied that the atheist existed, the child certainly needs evaluation or he's just plain rebellious to the point of being really weird. Either way, he should make that trip to the psychiatrist.

Alluding to God sending his children to hell is a typical mistake often made by those who profess to be atheists. God never sends his children to hell. All of them will go to heaven. However, children of the devil will go to hell, and that's what the Bible clearly says we are— until our sins are forgiven and we are born into the family of God.

Ray Comfort
Founder and CEO, Living Waters / The Way of the Master

A WORTHLESS WALK WITH GOD

If anyone considers himself religious
and yet does not keep a tight rein on his
tongue, he deceives himself and his
religion is worthless.

We see it all the time: Great achievements, outstanding talents, and noble positions of privilege brought to nothing by just a single character flaw. We read of the triathlon champion found doping, the genius CEO discovered acting inappropriately, or the gifted football star with a cruel streak. All that good nullified by one little thing—what a shame!

This is James's point about the so-called Christian with loose lips. If we're not careful with our words—gossiping or slandering, or maligning others with a sharp, critical spirit—James tells us that the value of our entire Christian life can become "worthless." Let us allow the Holy Spirit to help us keep a tight rein on our tongues, so that nothing will diminish the value of our walk with Christ.

Dr. Ross Reinman
Senior Pastor, The Rock, Santa Rosa, CA

WE NEED TO PRAY

Likewise the Spirit also helps in our weaknesses.
For we do not know what we should pray for as we ought,
but the Spirit himself makes intercession for us
with groanings which cannot be uttered.

ROMANS 8:26, NKJV

*O*ftentimes, when we encounter difficulty we don't pray. Amazingly, many of us act first and pray later or not at all. We get on the phone and share with people that we are being mistreated, but we won't pray. We whine and we complain and we murmur, but we do not pray. The problem is that Satan is stepping up his kingdom, but we continue to fight the enemy on our own strength. We cannot hold a marriage, family, or friendship together without prayer. And because we love the Lord, Satan is working against us in these relationships. The evil one desires to sink our families, divide our children, and even ruin our businesses or careers.

Sadly we are living in a time when we are allowing sin to dominate our minds, and the still small voice of God is becoming fainter and fainter. We need to pray first and more frequently. That to me is maturity—when all of a sudden we find out that something is wrong with our spouses and we don't call people, but we go to God first. What a wonderful thing to understand the purposes of God within our life of prayer.

Steve Mays
Senior Pastor, Calvary Chapel, South Bay, CA

HOW GOD SEES SINNERS

And the Pharisees and scribes complained,
saying, "This man receives sinners
and eats with them."

*I*t just didn't make any sense! How could somebody who claimed to represent God spend so much time around people who were so sinful? That's what the Pharisees and scribes couldn't comprehend about Jesus. He claimed to be the Son of God, but was close to sinners. This seemed so contradictory to the Pharisees and scribes.

But the Pharisees and scribes couldn't see God's perspective of sinners. They saw sinners as lost causes; God saw them as lost sheep. They responded to sinners with judgment; God responded with mercy. They wanted to condemn sinners; God wanted to rescue them. They wanted to leave them as they were; God wanted to change them.

Jesus saw what the religious leaders of his day didn't, and he did what they wouldn't. And we should be thankful he did, because at the end of the day none of us is perfect and all of us are sinners, and it's this same Shepherd's heart that reached out and rescued us.

Bob Coy
Senior Pastor, Calvary Chapel, Fort Lauderdale, FL

GOOD ENOUGH?

For all have sinned and fall short
of the glory of God.

ROMANS 3:23, NKJV

am always amused when I hear someone say, "Well, people are basically good." God's Word says that we are *not* naturally good. Rather, we are transgressors of God's law, filled with iniquity, and born in sin.

No matter what you've done in your life (or haven't done), everyone is in the same position: All sinners are in need of God's mercy and grace. No one can get into heaven based on their own goodness; compared to God's standard of goodness our good works are as filthy rags (Isaiah 64:6). The only way we will ever get into heaven is through the righteousness of Jesus Christ and his sacrifice on the cross making atonement for our sins.

Are you thinking that you are pretty "good," and are you relying on that "goodness" to get you into heaven? Don't be deceived; let your confidence and reliance be solely in Jesus Christ. If you confess that you are a sinner, trusting in Christ to save you from that sin, he will clothe you in his righteousness and you will indeed be a citizen of heaven!

David Rosales
Senior Pastor, Calvary Chapel, Chino Valley, CA

SEEKING HIS GLORY

*Then Nadab and Abihu, the sons of Aaron, each took
his censer and put fire in it, put incense on it, and offered profane
fire before the LORD, which He had not commanded them.
So fire went out from the LORD and devoured them,
and they died before the LORD. And Moses said to Aaron,
"This is what the LORD spoke, saying: 'By those who come near Me
I must be regarded as holy; and before all the people I
must be glorified.'" So Aaron held his peace.*

LEVITICUS 10:1–3, NKJV

What a momentous occasion when Moses finally brought
all of Israel together to offer the first ordained sacrifice
to the Lord. All the preparations were made by Moses and Aaron
as God had demanded. God approved their coming by sending fire
from heaven to consume this offering upon the altar, and the congregation, seeing his glory, fell on their faces. All did except these two
sons of Aaron who, seeking to be seen themselves, put strange fire in
their censers and ran out among the people . . . and the fire from the
Lord sprang out and devoured them immediately.

When we come to the Lord we must see him as *holy and act
accordingly,* and if he allows us to stand before others in his name,
he must be glorified, not us! What an impression this left upon the
gathered congregation that day. May it leave one on us as well.

Jack Abeelen
Senior Pastor, Morning Star Christian Chapel, Whittier, CA

LED WITH A PURPOSE

Then Jesus was led up by the Spirit into the
wilderness to be tempted by the devil.

MATTHEW 4:1, NKJV

If God is calling you to do something for him, expect to be tested. Temptation challenges your convictions and exposes your weaknesses. But it serves an important purpose.

Here in Matthew 4, Jesus is being led up into the wilderness to be tempted by the devil. He was probably dreading the trip. He hadn't eaten in forty days, it was hot, and the terrain was rugged. But it wasn't the devil who led him up into the wilderness; it was the Spirit of God.

Yes, the Holy Spirit led Jesus. Notice that word "led." The Greek word here, *anago*, means "to lead up into a higher place." You see, the Holy Spirit was leading Jesus into a higher place. And in the same way, testings from God lead you into a higher place. Only there can he broaden your perspective and deepen your understanding. Only there can he give you the bigger picture.

So often when negative things happen, we let them bring us down. But God's plan is to take you higher. Remember, he is leading you with a purpose!

Mike Macintosh
Senior Pastor, Horizon Christian Fellowship, San Diego, CA

A WHOLE LIFE

I press on toward the goal to win
the prize for which God has called me
heavenward in Christ Jesus.

PHILIPPIANS 3:14, NIV

have heard it said when someone died at a ripe old age, "He lived a whole life." However, it isn't necessarily true that just because someone lived to an old age, that person lived a whole life. The effect of a person's life is not measured by how long that person lived but how that life was lived. If a person lived a long, unproductive, carnal life as a believer, what did he or she accomplish? Conversely, if a person's life was short but holy, the person lived a whole life. A holy life is a whole life.

Robert Murray McCheyne was a young Scottish preacher in the early 1800s. He died at the age of twenty-nine, and yet his impact continues to be felt. One of his favorite sayings was, "Live so as to be missed." He did just that!

Consider Stephen in the book of Acts. Christianity had just gotten started when he died as the church's first martyr. Yet the impact of his life is still being felt. It was his death that catapulted the gospel from the Jews in Jerusalem to the Gentiles to the ends of the earth.

Again, the effect of one's life is not measured by how long one lives, but how one lives. A whole life is a holy life. God, help us to live so as to be missed!

Ron Hindt
Senior Pastor, Calvary Chapel, Houston, TX

NO FEAR

Therefore, since we are receiving
a kingdom which cannot be shaken, let us
have grace, by which we may serve God acceptably
with reverence and godly fear.

HEBREWS 12:28, NKJV

*T*he world is being shaken. The economy seems to be held together by a thread. Who knows day to day what will happen in the stock market? Jobs are uncertain, and as we have seen, there is the real possibility of unemployment, no matter who you are or what position you hold. Good health can fly away in a moment with the shocking news of cancer, heart disease, or for any number of reasons.

However, in light of an uncertain world there is a kingdom that cannot be shaken. The economy, unemployment, and illness can't shake God's kingdom. God doesn't change. He is the same yesterday, today, and forever. Stand firm with no fear because God will never leave you or forsake you. That is a promise you can count on!

Eric Cartier
Senior Pastor, Rocky Mountain Calvary Chapel, Colorado Springs, CO

JESUS IS MORE

👑 BIBLE READ: JOHN 6:15–25

So Jesus, perceiving that they were intending to come
and take Him by force to make Him king, withdrew
again to the mountain by Himself alone.

JOHN 6:15, NASB

*J*ohn puts this story right after the feeding of the 5,000. The crowd tried to draft Jesus as their king. Certainly, after seeing the miracle of the feeding up close and personal, the disciples were all for it. After all, if Jesus became king, they'd hold the highest offices in his court.

He dashes their expectations by dispersing the crowd and sending the disciples across the lake. Halfway across, a fierce storm begins to knock them about. Think about how disappointed they had to be! They feared for their lives but were doing what Jesus told them to do.

Have you ever been disappointed with God? Have you ever put an expectation on him that he didn't deliver on? Watch what Jesus does: He comes to them in the midst of the storm and proves he is *far more* than they imagined.

He's more than the source of endless fish sandwiches. He's more than the political king of a minor kingdom. He is Master of the elements. Yes, he is God. Jesus is *more* than our petty thoughts of him. Always more.

Lance E. Ralston
Senior Pastor, Calvary Chapel, Oxnard, CA

THE WAY UP IS DOWN

He humbled himself and became obedient
to death—even death on a cross!

PHILIPPIANS 2:8, NRSVB

hat opinion do you have of yourself? Because of the lofty position you hold, at least in your own eyes, what service do you think is degrading and "beneath" you? Washing dishes? Babysitting children? Visiting prisoners?

The apostle Paul, writing from a Roman prison cell, exhorted you and me to have the same attitude of Jesus, "who, being in the very nature God, did not consider equality with God something to be grasped, but made himself nothing, taking the very nature of a servant, being made in human likeness. And being found in appearance as a man, he humbled himself and became obedient to death—even death on a cross!" (Philippians 2:6–8, NIV84). God considers your attitude prideful to think anything—any job, any person, any position, any service, any task, any place—is beneath you and me when Jesus, Lord of glory, Creator of the universe, left heaven's throne and took upon himself the form of a servant. Remember that the way up is down.

Anne Graham Lotz
Founder, AnGel Ministries, www.annegrahamlotz.com

How's Your Balance?

Finally, my brethren, be strong in the Lord and in
the power of His might. Put on the whole armor of God,
that you may be able to stand against the wiles of the devil.

EPHESIANS 6:10–11, NKJV

We hear terms like "Take a stand," "Hold your position," "Don't let them take you down," "Balance your priorities," and a host of other phrases and words to describe our need for balance. Pastor Chuck Smith has said, "Blessed are the flexible, for they shall not be broken." Learning how to balance yourself in the storms of life is often difficult, and we learn quickly that life is a lot about balance—and that success is measured oftentimes by one's ability to stay upright. Right now the U.S. economy is on shaky ground and in a state of instability. In sports, athletes work on balance continually, and a ship is of little value in the sea if it loses its balance and capsizes. Balance is critical to our well-being.

The book of Jude reminds us that even in shaky and unstable times we can still find our balance in Jesus Christ. Jude 1:24–25 says, "Now to Him who is able to keep you from stumbling, and to present you faultless before the presence of His glory with exceeding joy, to God our Savior, who alone is wise, be glory and majesty, dominion and power, both now and forever. Amen." That's a great promise, and a great reminder, too, for us to place our hope and trust in God. He won't let you fall, for when you do, he'll be there to catch you. Amen!

Mike Osthimer
Senior Pastor, Calvary Chapel, Bakersfield, CA

WHAT A WASTE!

When we experience unfortunate circumstances, we often say, "What a waste! Nothing good can come out of this." The good news of the gospel is that tough times do not have to be wasted!

God promises never to waste an experience. Romans 8:28 says, "And we know that in all things God works for the good of those who love him, who have been called according to his purpose" (NIV84). The "for the good" part of that promise is revealed in verse 29—"to be conformed to the likeness of his Son." God uses the most horrible of events to develop amazing character and strength.

God will then use us to help others who are struggling through similar problems. Are you available? That's the essence of the "God of all comfort" described in 2 Corinthians 1:4: "He comforts us in all our trouble with the comfort we ourselves have received from God." He comforts us so that we can, in his name, encourage others. Will you look for his hand and heart in every life experience? If you don't, that would be a real waste!

Scott Miller
Senior Pastor, Graceland Baptist Church, New Albany, IN

Battles May Be Won

BIBLE READ: DANIEL 10–12

For our struggle is not against
flesh and blood, but against the rulers,
against the authorities, against the powers of
this dark world and against the spiritual
forces of evil in the heavenly realms.

EPHESIANS 6:12, NIV

Battles may seemingly be won by the enemy of our souls, but God will win the war. There are battles taking place in the unseen world between evil and good angels that fit into God's overall plan for humanity. But God is in complete control, and we have nothing to fear. Even the apparent win by our enemy is short-lived and is a part of God's plan for us.

God uses evil to accomplish his plans for our lives. Trust his heart and his Word when you don't understand his plan.

Brent Wagner
Senior Pastor, Voyage Calvary Chapel, Fountain Valley, CA

THE FOLLY OF FAVORITISM

My brothers, as believers in our glorious
Lord Jesus Christ, don't show favoritism.

JAMES 2:1, NIV84

*F*avoritism is perhaps the ugliest of all human vices. Let's modernize James's illustration given in James chapter 2: An attractive, well-dressed visitor pulls up to church in a Maserati and struts into the church foyer, with designer jeans and expensive shades greeted by a bunch of oohs and aahs. Mr. Hollywood is fawned over, served coffee, and given the best seat.

The same morning, in walks a man who's obviously less fortunate; his clothes are old and mismatched, his jalopy outside barely runs, and anyone near him realizes he could use a shower! The rich man receives preferential treatment while the poor man is shunned, because it's easier and more gratifying to befriend a wealthy, attractive person than someone who may require of us time and energy, patience and self-denying care. But as ambassadors of Christ, we must represent God accurately by expressing his love to others the way he does, freely and without regard to social status.

Dr. Ross Reinman
Senior Pastor, The Rock, Santa Rosa, CA

LIFE'S UNANSWERED QUESTIONS

BIBLE READ: JOB 28

*The fear of the LORD is the beginning
of wisdom, and knowledge of the
Holy One is understanding.*

PROVERBS 9:10, NIV

What do we do with life's unanswered questions? Job came to realize that not all suffering comes from a sin, nor does doing well automatically bring reward. In order to understand this, we need divine wisdom, which is unavailable to man in its fullest sense. We can know why we suffer only when God chooses to disclose it to us. "The fear of the Lord is the beginning of wisdom."

Leave the unanswered questions to God. Trust and obey him. That is true wisdom.

Brent Wagner
Senior Pastor, Voyage Calvary Chapel, Fountain Valley, CA

Remembering Stones

I will remember the deeds of the LORD;
yes, I will remember your miracles of long ago.
I will consider all your works and meditate
on all your mighty deeds.

PSALM 77:11–12, NIV

In Joshua 4, as the children of Israel are crossing the Jordan, Joshua asks twelve men to pick up a stone from the middle of the river, one for each of the twelve tribes of Israel, and to carry it to the campsite. The stones will remind them of God's powerful activity on their behalf. The stones will also provide an occasion for retelling the story of God's faithfulness for generations to come. As the text says, "When your children ask in time to come, 'What do those stones mean to you?' then you shall tell them that the waters of the Jordan were cut off in front of the Ark of the Covenant of the Lord" (Joshua 4:21–22).

The stones are both a reminder for the present and a witness to the future of God's faithfulness. If we want courage in the present, we must remember what God has done in our past.

We don't build altars these days. But we owe it to ourselves and to our children to collect "remembering stones"—tangible objects that remind us of God's power and his presence and that invite enough attention in the public arena to occasion opportunities to retell these stories to our friends, our neighbors, and our children.

Shirley A. Mullen
President and Professor of History, Houghton College, Houghton, NY

LOVE IS PATIENT

Love is patient, love is kind. It does not envy,
it does not boast, it is not proud.

1 CORINTHIANS 13:4, NIV

*G*od's love endures long and never gives up. It calmly tolerates delay, confusion, and inefficiency.

Jesus's suffering on the cross is the supreme example of patient suffering in action. There is suffering in patience: We're denying ourselves and surrendering to God's will.

In the decision-making process, patience works slowly, calmly, and methodically. Confusion is very stressful, both to the person trying to make a decision and to the people involved in that process. Seeking God's wisdom, and *patiently waiting* for clear answers, always pays off. The reward is supernatural peace about what to do—and guidance on how to go about it.

Jorja Stewart
Cofounder, www.musicthatblessesothers.com
Author, Relation Tips blog (jorjastewart.com)

A LIGHT FOR OUR PATH

Your word is a lamp to my feet and a light to my path.

PSALM 119:105, NKJV

What directs your life? How do you make decisions from day to day? A lot of people simply make their own plans and head out into life in whatever direction they wish to go. However, for the Christian, this is not an option. So how do we follow God's plans for our lives?

Our best source of direction is found in God's Word. His Word is a lamp for our feet and a light for our path. When we try to walk by any other plan in life, this will ultimately lead us into darkness and cause us to stumble. This is just like trying to find the outhouse in the middle of a dark night while camping in the mountains. If you do not bring a flashlight you are setting yourself up to stumble.

Here's the problem: We want the five-year plan or the ten-year package. We want the blueprints of our life to float down from heaven and land on the kitchen table. But God's Word doesn't promise that, and do you know why? Because if God sketched out our entire life plan, then we would check out. We might stop seeking him, looking to him for direction, pursuing him for his presence along our path. God's plans for our lives are such that he wants to be a part of them. In fact, his purpose for our life is so amazing, we were not meant to accomplish it on our own without him.

Bob Botsford
Senior Pastor, Horizon Christian Fellowship North, Rancho Santa Fe, CA

Hard Ground

As the rain and the snow come down from heaven,
and do not return to it without watering the earth and making
it bud and flourish, so that it yields seed for the sower and bread
for the eater, so is my word that goes out from my mouth:
It will not return to me empty, but will accomplish
what I desire and achieve the purpose
for which I sent it.

ISAIAH 55:10–11, NIV

Almost every winter I'm confronted with the prospect of my backyard drains being overwhelmed by a flood of water. This passage talks about how rain and snow water the ground. I am amazed how the same rain that brings new life can also cause destruction. But one of the most important aspects of God creating new life is the ground being ready for the seed to grow.

Are our lives open and receptive to receive the Word of God? Every year in the rainy season I'm wading through ankle-deep water to plug in an electrical pump because the ground isn't able to soak it in. That water is doing absolutely no good. It's the hardness of the ground caused by drought on my backyard that prevents the water from soaking in and instead backs up and creates a flood. Often that is the case with us. God has planted the word of truth in our lives, but our lives are not receptive to his Spirit. Let God break up the hard ground in our lives that prevents the Holy Spirit from doing his good work.

Dr. Carl Moeller
President and Managing Partner, Sequoia Global Resources

MORE THAN CONQUERORS

*No, in all these things we are more than
conquerors through him who loved us.*

ROMANS 8:37–39, NIV

*T*he eighth chapter of Romans is one of the most popular chapters in the New Testament, and for good reasons. First, it contains some profound theological teachings, but perhaps even more important to the Romans was the hope it offered as they began to face persecutions. They had not yet felt the full impact of these persecutions as Christians in other areas had, but soon the rage of Nero would fall upon them. When that happened they needed all the hope that was available to sustain them through those trails.

Paul asserts that not only can we survive or bear the many adverse realities he had been describing but that we can be victorious in the midst of the trials and achieve a great conquest. To be more than conquerors therefore means to experience joy, exuberance (abundance, plenty), and power. Christians can know and experience this in the face of obstacles.

Nothing can separate us from the love of Christ. Through the power of him who loved us, we defeat all those threatening and tragic things. We keep our faith, we remain secure in Christ's love.

In all these troubles we are victorious, and more than conquerors, we will be triumphant.

Eugene Burrage
Senior Pastor, Original Greater Rock M.B. Church, Chicago, IL

Pressing On

Not that I have already attained, or am
already perfected; but I press on, that I may lay
hold of that for which Christ Jesus has also laid hold of me.
Brethren, I do not count myself to have apprehended;
but one thing I do, forgetting those things which are behind
and reaching forward to those things which are ahead,
I press toward the goal for the prize of the
upward call of God in Christ Jesus.

PHILIPPIANS 3:12–14, NKJV

In all of our lives, we have trials, tests, discouragement, and other things that keep us from drawing closer to Jesus. Paul addressed this issue in Philippians 3:12–14: "I press on," leaving those things behind.

In my life, I know there are times I feel that I am taking only one step at a time, and sometimes that seems hard enough. But the important thing is to keep moving forward, each step getting closer to Jesus. Remember, one small step is still a step in the right direction.

Jerry Foster
Senior Pastor, Calvary Chapel, South Lake Tahoe, CA

CHRIST IN THE WORD

These are the Scriptures that
testify about me.

*f*ew of us who love the Word feel that it is possible to do so without finding the Christ in the Word. Yet so it is. You can be diligent in study and yet miss the person of whom the Scriptures speak. Is it not an amazing thought that the Scriptures—meaning in this context the Old Testament Scriptures—speak of *Jesus*? Perhaps we easily discover in Deuteronomy, Genesis, or the psalms rules by which to live. But Jesus? Still, Jesus himself tells us that these Scriptures "testify" about him.

Today as you study the Bible, let the Bible lead you to the Christ of the Bible—not in a shallow, disorganized, allegorical fashion but in a Christ-centered, God-directed trajectory. The Old Testament is like an arrow, the tip of which is Christ. The Old Testament is like a question mark, the answer to which is Christ. The Old Testament is thirst; Christ is living water. Not that we have to wait to read the New Testament before we read about Christ (according to Paul in 1 Corinthians 10:4, even such seemingly abstruse details as "the rock" are Christ himself in the Old Testament). But when we read the Old Testament, if we read it right, we read "Jesus" in mile-high letters.

Josh Moody
Senior Pastor, College Church, Wheaton, IL

HONESTY

An honest answer is like a kiss on the lips.

PROVERBS 24:26, NIV

If you were to ask employees what they value most in an employer, their answer would most likely be . . . honesty. If you were to ask employers what they most value in an employee . . . honesty. In marriages, a spouse's most desired character quality with one another . . . honesty. Honesty creates an environment of trust. It allows you to solve problems together and not be on opposite sides. It enables you to work with people in an environment that is healthy and productive, and you know what is expected of you.

Honesty is an amazing character quality. In Proverbs 24:26, the author writes, "An honest answer is like a kiss on the lips." Picture the kiss on your lips that you love to get. Everybody loves that feeling. It brings up a feeling of sweetness and smoothness. That is what honesty is like.

Proverbs 10:19 says, "When words are many, sin is not absent" (NIV84). How does it relate to the factor of honesty? The more you are a talker and engage with people, the more likely you are to gossip, exaggerate the facts, shade the truth, or say some words that may take you down a dark path. The more I hold my tongue in conversations, the better I sleep at night knowing I didn't say anything that would lead people astray.

When you are honest with people, they feel like they got a kiss on the lips! How is the honesty factor in your life?

Mark Ashton
Senior Pastor, Christ Community Church, Omaha, NE

THE GOD OF THE HOUSE

Jacob built an altar there and named
the place El-bethel (which means "God of Bethel"),
because God had appeared to him there when
he was fleeing from his brother, Esau.

GENESIS 35:7, NLT

The first time Jacob spent time at this particular spot of ground, he named it Beth-el, which means "house of God." He had a religious experience with his Creator, but it seemed to leave him largely unchanged. The second time he passes through with his family in tow and renames the place El-beth-el, which means "God of the house of God." His second experience was with the living God, who is too big to be defined by a place.

Don't merely seek the religious building, ritual, or rule to be followed. Seek the God who lives above and beyond all that we see—the God of the house.

Brandon A. Cox
Founding Pastor, Grace Hills Church, Northwest Arkansas, Editor of Pastors.com
and Rick Warren's Pastor's Toolbox *newsletter*

ON THE OTHER SIDE
OF CALVARY

For when God made a promise to Abraham,
because He could swear by no one greater, He swore by
Himself, saying, "Surely blessing I will bless you,
and multiplying I will multiply you." And so, after he
had patiently endured, he obtained the promise.

HEBREWS 6:13–15, NKJV

When I read this verse, the last part strikes me as odd. Abraham patiently endured? What about his blunder in Egypt? What about Hagar? What about Ishmael? Abraham demonstrated a huge lapse of faith by not trusting God, taking matters into his own hands and creating a mess of things. Life is full of moments of failure, mistakes, and lapses of faith. However, God's grace is sufficient for our sin.

The book of Hebrews was written *after* Calvary. It is on the other side of Calvary where all our sins, and shame, and lack of patience are completely taken care of. On the other side of Calvary, God's perspective of Abraham was that he patiently endured to obtain the promise. Remember that! When you have a momentary lapse in your faith and react in the flesh, remember that the blood of Jesus Christ shed at Calvary's cross covers *all* your sins and shame. If you do, then God's testimony of your life will be that you, like Abraham, patiently endured to obtain the promise!

Rob Salvato
Senior Pastor, Calvary Chapel Vista, Vista, CA

ESTEEM THE LORD

Then Jesus said to his disciples, "If anyone desires
to come after Me, let him deny himself, and
take up his cross, and follow Me."

MATTHEW 16:24, NKJV

We all have frailties and insecurities, but Jesus says, "If anyone desires to come after Me, let him deny himself." It's not self-esteem the Lord requires; it's self-denial.

The apostle Paul was quick to admit that when it came to self-denial, he was the worst. "If anyone else thinks he may have confidence in the flesh," he wrote, "I more so" (Philippians 3:4). That's coming from a man who was stoned, imprisoned, and persecuted for his unyielding faith in Jesus. And he struggled not to esteem himself.

You see, our insecurities are not caused by a lack of self-esteem. We esteem ourselves naturally—but the higher the pedestal we build for ourselves, the less stable our footing becomes and the farther we fall. Our frailties are caused by our lack of self-denial to the One by whom all things were created, and in whom is all power, wisdom, and strength (Revelation 5:12).

Don't fall for the myth that says you need more self-esteem. We can't follow God if our eyes are fixed on ourselves. Esteem the Lord in your life.

Mike Macintosh
Senior Pastor, Horizon Christian Fellowship, San Diego, CA

PRAYING FOR THE PERSECUTED

Blessed are you when people insult you,
persecute you, and falsely say all kinds of evil
against you because of Me.

MATTHEW 5:11, NASB

*J*esus says that his followers will encounter opposition and
that the persecuted will be blessed. American believers may
occasionally be shunned or overlooked for a promotion, but few of
us have experienced significant persecution. Honestly, most of the
persecution we face is because we are obnoxious and irritating, not
because we are reflecting Jesus!

Remember in prayer those who are persecuted around the world.
Their examples of faithfulness inspire us to deeper Christian commitment. They remind us of the courage of first-century Christ-
followers who have just been beaten: "The apostles left the Sanhedrin,
rejoicing because they had been counted worthy of suffering disgrace for the Name. Day after day, in the temple courts and from
house to house, they never stopped teaching and proclaiming the
good news that Jesus is the Christ" (Acts 5:41–42, NIV84).

Lord, please give your persecuted children around the world the
courage to persevere. Allow them to know in a powerful way that you
are walking with them through the valley of the shadow of death. Use
their examples to inspire the church, and may your kingdom grow in
numbers and influence.

Scott Miller
Senior Pastor, Graceland Baptist Church, New Albany, IN

BATTLEFIELD OF LIFE

BIBLE READ: EPHESIANS 6:10–19

Therefore take up the whole
armor of God.

EPHESIANS 6:13, NKJV

As Christians we have the necessary spiritual armor for the battlefields of life. This armor gets scratched, dented, and worn during the battles we fight against the enemy. Yet we are able to withstand the powers of darkness in the strength of the Lord.

But be encouraged, because we are fighting battles with full knowledge that the victory is ours in Christ Jesus. Jesus defeated Satan on the cross. He is the Victorious One. He has overcome Satan and all the powers of darkness, and we are overcomers in Jesus. As Jesus states in John 16:33, "In the world you will have tribulation; but be of good cheer, I have overcome the world."

Keep fighting, not looking at the battle-scarred armor, but looking unto Jesus. Remember, "If God is for us, who can be against us?" (Romans 8:31). Therefore, endure tough assignments by relying on him. Do not miss the opportunities that can bring glory to his name. Remember, God's strength is perfected in our weakness.

Tom DeSantis
Senior Pastor, Calvary Chapel, Santa Clarita, CA

JOY

You will show me the path of life;
in Your presence is fullness of joy;
at Your right hand are pleasures forevermore.

PSALM 16:11, NKJV

The greatest visible statement of our relationship with Jesus is a joyful life. Joy is the overflow of a happy person who has discovered the Jesus-filled life. C. S. Lewis, the renowned Oxford professor, in writing to Sheldon Vanauken said, "It is a Christian duty, as you know, for everyone to be as happy as you can." God indeed wants us to find happiness in this life, and this happiness is found only in him. It is one of the kingdom secrets: God wants us to be full of joy. The discovery of true joy is found in the presence of the Joy-Giver, Jesus. So today, go after joy! Bathe in the presence of Jesus in all you do—whether at work, checking off the honey-do list, or changing diapers. Renew your mind with the thought that Jesus is with you. Embrace him. Worship him. Find his joy today.

My prayer: Jesus, I desperately need your joy today. I want my life to overflow with joy. In all that I do today, remind me that you are with me, walking with me, and loving me. Empower me to embrace your presence and joy.

Steve Holt
Founder, Word & Spirit Network, Founder and Lead Pastor,
Mountain Springs Church, Colorado Springs, CO

THE TREASURES OF
TRUE WISDOM

Blessed are those who find wisdom,
those who gain understanding, for she is
more profitable than silver and yields
better returns than gold.

PROVERBS 3:13–14, NIV

*T*he book of Proverbs tells us that wisdom is actually like a treasure. It is incredibly valuable and it needs to be discovered. Wisdom is so much more than knowledge. It's defined as "the ability to use knowledge in the right way." Because we have so many choices in life today, discovering God's wisdom should be a top priority. It is such a liberating topic that the entire book of Proverbs was dedicated to it!

James 1 reminds us that God has even more wisdom available to all who ask, if we would only ask for it in faith: "If any of you lacks wisdom, let him ask of God, who gives to all liberally and without reproach, and it will be given to him. But when you ask, you must believe and not doubt" (James 1:5–6, NASB/NIV). So don't let the world shape you. Let God's wisdom shape you through his Word.

Brian Cashman
Senior Pastor, Valley Metro Church, Sherman Oaks, CA

TIME AND ETERNITY

♛ BIBLE READ: ECCLESIASTES 3:1–11

There is a time for everything, and a season
for every activity under heaven.

ECCLESIASTES 3:1, NIV84

hat is time? This perplexing question seems to be at the heart of the well-known poem in Ecclesiastes 3. This beautiful chapter presents a picture of time, "a time to every activity under the heaven" (Ecclesiastes 3:1).

It is only as we look back with some distance in between some of the key events in our lives—as we reflect upon major local, national, and world events that have occurred in our lifetime—that we recognize with greater clarity that God has a purpose in all things. At the moment of the event, we can never fully understand what God is doing, for the secret things belong to the Lord our God (Deuteronomy 29:29).

In order to prevent us from becoming cynical or pessimistic about time and the events in our lives, Solomon urges us to recognize that life needs a different perspective because God has put eternity in our hearts. We are reminded that God has set a time and place for everything. The challenge for God's people is to determine the right time for the actions, words, and responses.

Father, help us to live with a sense of contentment as we trust you for the grace needed for this day and all the seasons of life.

David S. Dockery
President, Union University, Jackson, TN

QUENCH NOT

Do not quench the Spirit.

1 THESSALONIANS 5:19, NASB

"Quench" can mean to satisfy thirst. Or it can mean to extinguish fire. Interesting, isn't it? One arrangement of six letters with two extremely different definitions.

God quenches our thirst. We quench God's Spirit.

I stand in Sunday morning church, my arms dangling at my sides, my mind wandering. The melody is too slow. I don't know the words. The PowerPoint blips off-cue, and I miss the chorus that I was just beginning to own. I roll my eyes. I sigh. I quench the Holy Spirit.

In those moments when I raise my bucket to slosh its contents on the context around me, I can instead hold up and hesitate. Raising it higher, I can hand it over to the Spirit, who quite ably pours it over my own being, quenching me with what I need in the moment, so that I then do not quench him.

Our thirst for hope, help, and happiness is uniquely quenched when we drink deeply from the well of our relationship with God. His presence alone truly slakes a parched spirit. Conversely, Paul cautions the Thessalonians against extinguishing—putting out or quenching—the Spirit's fire in 1 Thessalonians 5:19 ("Quench not the Spirit," KJV). Perhaps he means that we should be careful not to pour water on the wrong thing.

Quench. Quench not. I choose one so that I do not choose the other.

Elisa Morgan
Author, Speaker, Publisher, www.fullfill.org, President Emerita, MOPS International

THE GOSPEL

For the wages of sin is death, but the gift of God
is eternal life in Christ Jesus our Lord.

ROMANS 6:23, NASB

*T*he Bible tells us that "the wages of sin is death." Jesus came to solve both problems: sin and death! Sin was paid for at the cross on that dark Friday afternoon. Death was conquered at the empty tomb early on Sunday morning. The point of the gospel is to have the payment of the cross applied to your sin as you genuinely repent of your sin and wholeheartedly place your trust in Jesus Christ as the complete solution to the debt your sins have racked up against a holy God.

Don't fall to history's most frequent religious error: thinking that being good, sincere, or better than the next person will somehow be a sin-canceling credit. We need to see our lives, including whatever perceived credits we might think we have, exchanged completely for the life, death, and resurrection of Christ.

Be sure your hope is in Jesus and not yourself. Turn from sin and trust him today.

Mike Fabarez
Senior Pastor, Compass Bible Church, Aliso Viejo, CA

EATING AND BELIEVING

I tell you the truth, he who believes has everlasting life.
I am the bread of life. Your forefathers ate the manna in the
desert, yet they died. But here is the bread that comes down
from heaven, which a man may eat and not die.
I am the living bread that came down from heaven.
If anyone eats of this bread, he will live forever.
This bread is my flesh, which I will
give for the life of the world.

JOHN 6:47–51, NIV84

*J*esus uses the word "eat" as a very powerful metaphor for believing in him, and it helps to fill out what it really means to believe in Jesus.

When we eat something, we are taking it into us. We are inviting the thing eaten to become a part of us. We are recognizing the thing eaten as valuable and important for our survival. When we eat something, we are giving the food access to us on the most personal level possible in the physical realm.

To believe in Jesus means that we take him into us. We invite him to become a part of us; we recognize him as vitally important for our spiritual nourishment and survival; we draw our life source from him; we give him unlimited access to everything about us in the most personal way possible.

Jeff Miles
Senior Pastor, Touchstone Christian Fellowship, Sacramento, CA

To Gain Wisdom

The fear of the LORD is the beginning of wisdom,
and knowledge of the Holy One
is understanding.

PROVERBS 9:10, NASB

Wisdom is a gift that is bestowed upon us through the grace of God. Having this wisdom challenges us to dig deep into our inner beings and explore uncharted areas of our lives. It allows us to live out many of our dreams by having the necessary faith to press on, regardless of the obstacles that lie ahead. Many of us may have a number of challenges confronting us. While we are working on these life events, we should remember that patience produces wisdom through God. It is in this state of waiting on God that we gain wisdom through our faith and trust in our mighty God. When we align ourselves in God's will for our every decision, we find God's wisdom for everyday living.

Dr. Le'on M. Willis I
Reverend, Wesley United Methodist Church, Chicago, IL

THE BUG PRINCIPLE

*H*ave you ever noticed that in the summer when you go outside and turn on a bright white light, bugs come from everywhere? I am not sure why, but it seems that the bigger and the brighter the light, the more bugs it attracts. I guess we could call that the "bug principle"; bright lights bring many bugs! If you want to have a light shining in the darkness, you are also going to have bugs.

In 1 Corinthians 16 Paul is closing out his letter to the church. And in verses 8 and 9 he makes an interesting statement: "But I will stay in Ephesus until Pentecost, for a wide door for effective service has opened to me, and there are many adversaries" (NASB). Reading this, it strikes me: This is the spiritual version of the bug principle.

When you turn on the light of God's gospel and proclaim it and live it and seek to take it to the ends of the earth, there will be opposition, adversaries, challengers, and foes. So we should not be surprised that the more we shine God's light of truth, the more we share the hope of the gospel, the more the enemy will attack and oppose (see Ephesians 6:10–12).

So if you find yourself in a place where you are seeking to live out and to share the gospel, don't be surprised when you are opposed and attacked and face challenges from every side. It is part of the plan of the enemy to discourage you and distract you. Instead, stand firm. Put on your armor. Turn on the light. And watch God work!

Mike Bickley
Senior Pastor, Olathe Bible Church, Olathe, KS

THE BEGINNING

In the beginning God created the
heavens and the earth.

GENESIS 1:1, NASB

The Bible begins by saying that there was a beginning, and that (of course) there was a Cause that preexisted the beginning. Everything material must have a cause, because anything that is material cannot produce itself. The atheists' "Nothing created everything" doesn't work, because for it to possess the ability to create itself, it must preexist itself; to make itself, it would have to have existed before its existence. So if it preexisted, it wasn't the beginning.

Atheistic evolution doesn't have a beginning. Those who think it does refer to the big bang, but that wasn't the beginning, because you have to have preexisting materials for a big bang. You have to have gases, and even if atheists reduce the materials that caused the beginning down to a tiny dot, it still wasn't the beginning, because the dot existed. What caused their dot? They don't know. Genesis 1:1 tells us the Cause of all things.

Ray Comfort
Founder and CEO, Living Waters / The Way of the Master

MEMORY LANE

Remember His wonderful deeds
which He has done; His marvels and
judgments from His mouth.

1 CHRONICLES 16:12, NASB

few years ago I decided to take a trip down memory lane and visit the house where I grew up. After walking through the familiar kitchen and dining room, I made my way upstairs to my old bedroom. I looked down at the space where my little bed once stood. This is where I had knelt down as a kid to give my heart to Jesus Christ. This is the spot where my life truly began.

It occurred to me as I stood there that the Christian life is as much about remembering God's work in the past as it is about seeing his work in the present. Sometimes we forget that while faith calls us to move forward, it also calls us to look backward.

So today, travel back in your mind to that bedside or that dorm room or that church where God first called you out of darkness and into his marvelous light. Return to those places where faith was built and remember what God did there. Then rejoice in the fact that the same God who led you in the past is still leading you in the present.

Dr. Stephen Davey
Senior Pastor, Colonial Baptist Church, Cary, NC

WHEN GOD SWEARS BY HIS OWN NAME

The LORD had said to Abram, "Leave your native country, your relatives, and your father's family, and go to the land that I will show you. . . . All the families on earth will be blessed through you."

GENESIS 12:1, 3, NLT

In Genesis 12, God chose Abram and sent him to Canaan with a promise. In chapter 15 he made that promise into a covenant. Later, he required the blood of Abram and his descendants through circumcision. When Abram was ninety-nine years old and God gave him the new name of "Abraham," God promised him that he and his elderly wife, Sarah, would have a son.

God began to fulfill his promise through Isaac's birth. Then, after a dramatic demonstration of Abraham's trust in him, God told Abraham, "I swear by my own name that I will certainly bless you. . . . And through your descendants all the nations of the earth will be blessed" (Genesis 22:16–18).

Many generations later, God's Son sat with his disciples and told them, "For this is my blood, which confirms the covenant between God and his people. It is poured out as a sacrifice to forgive the sins of many" (Matthew 26:28). All the peoples of the earth need to hear!

God swore by his own name. He keeps his word because of who he is. And here's the miracle: He's keeping it in you!

Roy Peterson
President and CEO, The Seed Company

Our Great God

O magnify the LORD with me, and
let us exalt His name together.

PSALM 34:3, NASB

*O*ur lives exist to magnify God. The word "magnify" can be used in two different senses. It can mean that we use a microscope or a magnifying glass to make something appear greater in size than what it really is. Or it can mean that we use a telescope to make something appear as great as it truly is. When David urges us to magnify the Lord, he wants us to see God as strong and powerful as he really is.

We have a tendency, however, to turn a microscope to our problems, making them bigger than they really are. How many of us have had sleepless nights of worry, making our problems greater and our God smaller? Instead of magnifying your problems, turn a telescope toward God and see how great his love and power are. Suddenly God seems able to deal with life's challenging circumstances. And then watch how your life becomes a telescope, showing a watching world just how great God really is.

Terry Sanderson
Senior Pastor, Calvary Church, St. Peters, MO

On the Lookout

For the eyes of the Lord range throughout
the earth to strengthen those whose
hearts are fully committed to him.

2 CHRONICLES 16:9, NIV

Asa started his career as the king of Judah with great success. He loved God, loved God's people, and cherished the opportunity that he had been afforded. By all accounts, he lived his life right before the Lord . . . and God blessed him! But somewhere down the road, King Asa lost his way. What started with great strength in 2 Chronicles 14 ended in disarray in chapter 16. King Asa's life became a reminder of the importance of starting *and* finishing well.

Near the end, God sent a seer named Hanani to speak to King Asa. Hanani's words still resound loudly across the pages of history . . . even into our ears today. He told the king, "The eyes of the Lord range throughout the earth to strengthen those whose hearts are fully committed to him."

God is looking to support, encourage, embolden, and fortify the lives of those who are *fully* committed to him. He is constantly on the lookout for such people. As his eyes range throughout the earth on the search, what will happen when they fall on you? Are you committed to him? Is yours the type of life he can bless? If not, what needs to be surrendered to the Lord, that he would find you to be fully committed to him?

Brent Eldridge
Lead Pastor, First Baptist Church of Lakewood, Long Beach, CA

THE CHRONICLE OF TWO GARDENS

👑 BIBLE READ: GENESIS 3:8–21; MATTHEW 26:36–39

And walk in the way of love,
just as Christ loved us and gave himself
up for us as a fragrant offering
and sacrifice to God.

EPHESIANS 5:2, NIV

The Garden of Eden and the Garden of Gethsemane—these are two landmarks in human history where man's guilt met God's grace. The once-pristine beauty of Eden was tarnished and stained by disobedience. In that place, God confronted and covered sin at a great cost. The innocent were slain for the guilty. The consequences of man's sinfulness sent tremors through all creation, lasting to this very moment in time.

Many centuries later, the Lord Jesus—God in human flesh—would drink the cup of God's wrath for the sins of mankind once and for all. Gethsemane (the olive press) would be the place where the Savior would submit to the will of the Father and love this fallen, broken world extravagantly. Here in these two gardens the fragrance is formed from the intermingling stench of man's sin and the sweetness of God's grace. How beautiful is God's amazing grace!

Danny Sinquefield
Senior Pastor, Faith Baptist Church, Bartlett, TN

THOSE WHO TRUST

Those who trust in the LORD are like Mount Zion,
which cannot be moved, but abides forever.

*M*ount Rushmore is an engineering marvel. Cut into the side of the mountain are faces set in stone—faces that will never change. Likewise, God is working through each trial in your life. Trials work like that of a hammer strike on Mount Rushmore—with each strike a little more removed and a little more revealed. God is carefully removing fear, pride, and unbelief through trials, while he reveals his faithfulness and love. God does not approach your life in a haphazard fashion. But like an artist, he carefully protects and preserves his work in the process.

Your life is a glorious project under construction in the hands of the God who created you. Each day is a new opportunity for God to reveal a little more of himself to you and through you. Look forward to each new trial with anticipation, as God completes his rock-solid work in you.

Aaron Newman
Senior Pastor, Calvary Chapel, Paso Robles, CA

HIS POWER

But you shall receive power when
the Holy Spirit has come upon you; and you
shall be witnesses to me in Jerusalem, and
in all Judea and Samaria, and
to the end of the earth.

ACTS 1:8, NKJV

*M*any times we try to fulfill the call of God without the power of God. For the disciples, the power of the Holy Spirit came before they were called to be witnesses. Too many times I rely on my own strength, resources, or wisdom to live a godly life, instead of relying on the power of the Holy Spirit. God is more than willing to give us his power through his Spirit if we simply stop, ask, and wait.

Eric Cartier
Senior Pastor, Rocky Mountain Calvary Chapel, Colorado Springs, CO

YOUR OWN FAITH

Your faith has healed you.

MATTHEW 9:22, NIV

e cannot live off someone else's faith. The seven sons of Sceva discovered this when they tried to take their practice of casting out demons to the next level by copying the techniques of the apostle Paul. "In the name of the Jesus whom Paul preaches, I command you to come out" (Acts 19:13). The only problem was they did not know Jesus themselves; they were simply mimicking the methods of Paul. Sadly for them, the demon talked back: "Jesus I know, and Paul I know about, but who are you?" (v. 15).

Do your problems ever talk back to you? You might declare, "In the name of the Jesus whom Billy Graham preaches, be healed!" If nothing happens or things get worse, it might be the result of trying to live off someone else's faith. Your personal problems know Jesus, and probably have heard of Billy Graham, but who are you? Where is your faith? Do you have faith that causes your name to be known in hell?

Dr. Jim Reeve
Senior Pastor, Faith Community Church, West Covina, CA

REAL STABILITY

If you are not firm in faith, you will not be firm at all.

ISAIAH 7:9, ESV

In this section of Isaiah, Judah (the Southern Kingdom) finds itself being pressured to join an alliance with Syria and Israel (the Northern Kingdom). Even though King Ahaz of Judah feels tremendous pressure and his kingdom is facing conquest, he turns to Assyria for help. But God sends Isaiah to tell Ahaz not to make the alliance. He should turn to God rather than turn to Assyria. God promises victory and even says he will give the king a sign. But the king refuses to trust in the Lord and instead goes with the biggest war machine he can find: Assyria. It turns out that what King Ahaz looked to for security and stability would be the very nation that God would use to chastise Judah.

And that is what happens with so many of God's people every day. We long for stability and security in the midst of our turmoil. But instead of looking to God first, we go after other sources of wisdom, power, and help.

The starting point for all security and stability is by being firm in our faith in God. It starts with reverencing and deciding to obey God no matter what. If you want to repair your marriage, your starting point is not with your spouse but with the Lord. If your life is falling apart, if there is not enough money at the end of the month, look to God first. Remember, if we compromise in our faith in God, then we will not be firm at all. He alone is the place to turn for stability and security.

Mike Bickley
Senior Pastor, Olathe Bible Church, Olathe, KS

RETREAT INTO FORGIVENESS

Whoever claims to love God yet
hates a brother or sister is a liar. For whoever
does not love their brother and sister, whom
they have seen, cannot love God,
whom they have not seen.

1 JOHN 4:20, NIV

As the retreat ended, the leader said, "Write down your sins, and as a symbol of Christ's forgiveness, throw those papers into the fire." I had nothing to write. All my sins had been forgiven. I walked away thinking, *This exercise does not apply to me.*

Suddenly I was overcome by an extraordinary sense of sinfulness. A clear message came. I had violated Jesus's teaching. I had harbored hatred in my heart, with guilt like that of a murderer (Matthew 5:21–22). I was angry with my father for the terrible pain he had inflicted and for his anti-Christian life. The Lord showed me that I wanted to kill my father.

Just as God forgave me and my father, I knew I must forgive my father. Through forgiveness, my relationship would be healed. My attitude had blocked God's love.

I told my father that nothing would hinder our relationship. I forgave him for all he had done to our family. I said that I loved him and wanted him to become a Christian. He was speechless. I was set free. Ask God today to reveal to you any relationship that may need healing and forgiveness.

Dr. Lee G. Royce
President, Mississippi College, Clinton, MS

GOD'S PURPOSES IN PRAYER

Devote yourselves to prayer, being watchful and thankful.

COLOSSIANS 4:2, NIV84

When I was a small boy, my dad would often ask me to rake leaves with him in the fall. At the time, I thought his reason for asking revolved around my leaf-raking prowess, but truthfully I did a lot more playing, rolling around, and jumping than raking and bagging. It wasn't until years later I realized his purpose in including me was to connect relationally around a common task.

Over the years I've come to understand that God's purposes in prayer have similar motives. That is, God loves an opportunity to hang out with us. In the process, he also allows his life to begin to shape our own. I have discovered at least four clear-cut purposes of prayer that have transformed my interaction with God:

- *Connecting us to God's presence.* God enjoys hanging out with his kids, and wants them to learn to love being with him as well.
- *Connecting us to God's perspective.* God wants to expand our vision and infuse an eternal perspective into the way we think.
- *Connecting us to God's passions.* God wants us to learn to love what he loves and inspire us to give more of our lives to the things he cares about.
- *Connecting us to God's power.* God wants to make his power available to us, and to heal, deliver, and transform us in ways that can only be explained by him.

As we devote ourselves to prayer, we will experience more of God's life within us than we ever thought possible.

Scott Chapman
Senior Pastor and President, Christ Together
The Chapel, Northern Chicagoland, IL

FULLY COMMITTED

Love the LORD your God with all your heart
and with all your soul and with all your
mind and with all your strength.

MARK 12:30, NIV

*T*he command to love God with the totality of our being is one of the most important directives in all of Scripture. A full devotion to God in the emotional (heart), spiritual (soul), and mental (mind) aspects of our being is something we talk about in church on a weekly basis.

But how about the last part of that command? That "loving God with all your strength" part? Clearly that's a reference to our physical selves. How often does your church emphasize the proper care of one's body, since it is the temple of the Holy Spirit (1 Corinthians 6:19)? Weekly? Monthly? Once a year? Is there some reason we emphasize other aspects of our commitment to Christ apart from what we do with, and to, our bodies?

Jesus did not separate how we love God emotionally, spiritually, and mentally from how we love him physically. To do so would be nothing short of idolatry. As we commit our total selves to God, let's be sure we take proper care of our bodies so that we might serve him with all of our strength.

Dear God, I commit every area of my life to you, including my physical body. Give me the grace to treat this temple of God with the dignity it deserves.

Steve Willis
Lead Pastor, First Baptist Church, Kenova, WV

WHAT REALLY MATTERS

👑 BIBLE READ: ECCLESIASTES 12:13–14

Now all has been heard;
here is the conclusion of the matter;
fear God and keep his commandments,
for this is the whole duty of man.

ECCLESIASTES 12:13, NIV84

o you ever go through the events of a day or even a week and wonder if anything matters? Ecclesiastes affirms that life truly is absolute futility apart from God. These final words in this magnificent book lead us not only to the conclusion of the book but to wise counsel for all seasons of life: "Fear God and keep his commandments." This is "the conclusion of the whole matter," a summary of the beginning, middle, and end of life as we know it on Earth.

To fear God and keep his commandments is not a recipe for legalism; rather, it is an invitation to live faithfully before God, offering adoration and worship to him. Here we learn that this is our "whole duty."

We come before God to revere him and to adore him, to live faithfully before him and with others. Life's meaning is wrapped up in the worship of God and in a life lived obediently before him. What really matters in life is to come before the one true God in worship and obedience.

David S. Dockery
President, Union University, Jackson, TN

A New Perspective

aul reminds us that a new perspective, a new way of looking at things, is at the heart of transformation. "Do not be conformed to this world, but be transformed by the renewal of your mind" (Romans 12:2, ESV). "Renewal" as used here doesn't mean renovated but rather to be made completely different from before. It is the same word used in Titus 3:5 describing the renewal of the Holy Spirit we experienced when we first trusted in Christ. That's what transformation does: it offers a complete metamorphosis.

Is there something in your life that needs transforming? Pray that God would give you a new perspective, one that leads to that metamorphosis you are seeking.

Jeff Jernigan
Senior Pastor, Corona Friends Church, Corona, CA

Eternal Dividends

All honor and glory to God forever and ever.
He is the eternal King, the unseen one who
never dies; he alone is God. Amen.

1 TIMOTHY 1:17, NLT

Since God is the eternal One, how should we respond to him?

- *By worshiping him.* "To the only God our Savior, through Jesus Christ our Lord, be glory, majesty, dominion, and authority, before all time and now and forever. Amen" (Jude 1:25, NASB).
- *By serving him.* Everything exists for him: "For by Him all things were created, both in the heavens and on earth, visible and invisible, whether thrones or dominions or rulers or authorities—all things have been created through Him and for Him" (Colossians 1:16, NASB). Whatever we do in word or deed, do all for the glory of God.
- *By declaring him.* There are a lot of things in this world that try to usurp God's rightful place: people, philosophies, policies, false religions. We declare the truth about the true and the living God.

You can help spread the word about God around the world through prayer, your personal witness, and giving. The investment of your resources into the work of the kingdom of God will bring about eternal dividends. You will accrue eternal interest. What an opportunity!

Mark Martin
Senior Pastor, Calvary Community Church, Phoenix, AZ

THREE THINGS TO "BE" AND WHY

*My dear brothers and sisters, take note of this: Everyone should
be quick to listen, slow to speak, and slow to become angry, because
human anger does not produce the righteousness that God desires.
Therefore, get rid of all moral filth and the evil that is so prevalent and
humbly accept the word planted in you, which can save you.*

JAMES 1:19–21, NIV

When trouble comes we are often tempted to react in anger. But that action will not bring about what God intends in the situation. Thus we are given three important bits of instruction about how to act, how to "be":

- *Be swift to hear,* which means be a ready listener. Jesus said, "Whoever has ears to hear, let him hear" (Mark 4:9). So, be ready to listen instead of acting upon your anger.
- *Be slow to speak.* Take time before you speak. Don't be so quick to speak. Be thoughtful and let the Lord minister to you. Don't be in such a hurry to say what's on your mind.
- *Be slow to wrath,* which means be slow to take offense and to get angry. Don't let it get to you so quickly. And don't respond so quickly in anger.

The reason for these three "bes" is simple. The wrath and anger of man do not accomplish the right things of God. Finally, we are told to abandon sin and wickedness, and to embrace into our lives God's Word, which is the guidebook for our life. It will save our souls, and it will set us apart and lead us to God.

Bob Grenier
Senior Pastor, Calvary Chapel, Visalia, CA

THE VOICE FROM HEAVEN

Whether you turn to the right or to the left, your ears will hear
a voice behind you, saying, "This is the way; walk in it."

ISAIAH 30:21, NIV

Hearing the voice of God in the hustle and bustle of the twenty-first century can be compared to creating art. For example, drawing on your first canvas, in the beginning, your image may be hard to recognize as something tangible with only a blank canvas to stare at. However, as you practice and pursue your craft perhaps you'll find your images, and the art will become much easier to create.

The same principle is true when it comes to hearing the voice of God from heaven. God always does his part to help you!

"This is the way; walk in it." You see, he is the one who made your heart to be a depository for his Word, his Voice. Hearing from heaven is the most important thing in your whole life.

In the early days of my Christian life, I learned to pray and listen for him. One day as I was quietly reading my Bible and meditating on his Word, I heard him say, "I'm with you!" Tears started running down my face as I recognized my Savior's voice. I was so moved that I quietly whispered, "And I'm so grateful." Today, I depend on hearing from heaven when it comes to my family and the people I meet through the ministry.

Learn to seek his wisdom, to listen to his instructions regarding the everyday matters of life. That way, when the big problems come, you'll be ready. You will have confidence in his presence and his voice as you learn to hear from him.

Paige Junaeus
Founder, Paige Junaeus Ministries, www.turn2paige.com

Hanging by a Thread

"I know the Lord has given you this land. . . . For we have heard
how the Lord made a dry path for you through the Red Sea. . . .
For the Lord your God is the supreme God of the heavens above
and the earth below. . . ." And she sent them on their way
leaving the scarlet rope hanging from the window.

JOSHUA 2:9, 10, 11, 21, NLT

Rahab the prostitute . . . was shown to be right
with God by her actions when she hid those messengers
and sent them safely away by a different road.

JAMES 2:25, NLT

Rahab's door was opened to strangers, and she probably didn't ask too many questions when she took the Israelite spies in. Despite her reputation, the harlot Rahab had qualities others didn't see—but God did. She reverenced him, and she was smart. "For the Lord your God is the supreme God," she said. "Now swear to me by the Lord that you will be kind to me and my family since I have helped you" (Joshua 2:12). The men agreed.

Rahab had a greater purpose—and value—than met the eye. God chose the least likely person in Jericho to advance his plan. By faith, Rahab dangled a scarlet cord from her window, saved her entire family, and will forever be in the Messiah's lineage (Matthew 1:5). Keep in mind, God has likewise chosen us despite our imperfections and flaws. What a wonderful privilege that he can use even me!

Roy Peterson
President and CEO, The Seed Company

A Prayer Away

*Jesus said, "Come!" So Peter got out of the boat
and walked on the water, and he came toward Jesus.*

MATTHEW 14:29, NIV

*N*othing is impossible for God when our focus is on Jesus. If
you remember the story, Peter was walking on water with
Jesus during a violent sea storm on a dark, lonely night. When Peter
perceived and felt the strong winds, he lost his focus on Jesus and
began to sink.

Have you ever redirected your attention off Jesus? A broken dream
. . . you begin to sink. Maybe you are turning thirty, forty, or fifty with
thoughts of regret, feeling remorse . . . you begin to sink. Another
job promotion gone, another bill to pay when your bank account is
almost depleted. Time moves forward, another day, another week,
another month goes by. A promise of God that seems so far away
begins to dim . . . and you sink deeper into the sea of despair, fear,
and disbelief.

Like Peter, Jesus wants you to walk toward him above the sea of
doubt, no matter how hard the winds of life have blown, no matter
how impossible your circumstances seem at this time. Call out to
Jesus, for he cares and is always near. He is just one prayer away.

Steve M. Woods
Chairman, Board of Directors, www.WoodsMasteryFoundation.org

THE WHOLE WORLD

*G*od is the greatest missionary in the universe! He seeks to reveal his glory more than anyone ever has or ever will. He's been raising up missionaries all throughout history. We tend to think about mission work as a New Testament concept, but consider one of the most important missionary stories of all time.

The soon-to-be-king David was facing off in one of the most epic battles in history. He was face-to-face with a literal giant, a champion warrior! The great Goliath stood between little David and the "man after God's heart" he would become. Just before he engaged his foe, David shouted, "This day the LORD will deliver you into my hands, and I'll strike you down and cut off your head. This very day I will give the carcasses of the Philistine army to the birds and the wild animals, and the whole world will know that there is a God in Israel" (1 Samuel 17:46, NIV).

Did you catch that? The *whole world* would know that there is a God in Israel! Even on the battlefield, a missionary story unfolds. And for 3,000 years, the story of the little kid who beat the giant is legendary. Everyone has heard it, and everyone knows that only God could accomplish something so incredible.

God is constantly at work to reveal his glory. He can do it anywhere with anyone who seeks to display his might. May God reveal his glory through you today . . . that the *whole world* would know who God is and how much he has given to bring us back to him!

Brent Eldridge
Lead Pastor, First Baptist Church of Lakewood, Long Beach, CA

QUIET PLACES BEFORE GOD

*But Jesus often withdrew to lonely
places and prayed.*

LUKE 5:16, NIV

*J*esus often withdrew from his busy ministry to be alone with his heavenly Father. In fact, the time you spend in God's presence is the most important part of your day. During your quiet time before God, he will work on your heart and mind. God desires to change you to be more like Jesus and will always work on your behalf.

Remember that the most important changes that can happen in your life only God can do through His Spirit. Ask God to help you enjoy His presence throughout the day. Surrender your life to him, obey him, and wait for him.

Your heavenly Father loves you so very much. God desires to spend time with you, bless you, and give you new gifts each day. I encourage you to take time out of your busy day to meet with God alone and listen for his voice. Your heavenly Father will always make time for you.

Samy Tanagho
Founder and President of Glad News for Muslims Ministry
www.gladnewsministry.com

A FEW SMALL THINGS

What can I do to help you? Elisha asked.
"Tell me, what do you have in the house?"

2 KINGS 4:2, NLT

God's miracles always start with the question: What do you have? The little boy with five loaves and two fish provided the only resource for Jesus to bless and feed the 5,000. The widow who fed Elijah during the famine possessed only a small meal and a little oil as a resource. The common thread in both of these miracles is that faith was mixed with a few small things offered to God.

If you have a need, you must first put something into God's hand for him to work with and multiply back to you. We call this "seed sowing," or placing into the soil of faith some object that we "lose" in order that God may multiply it into a harvest.

Don't wait for God to supply your need; use what you have! God asked Moses, "What do you have there in your hand?" (Exodus 4:2, author's paraphrase), and the rod became the means of Israel's deliverance from Egypt. Give your resources to God, and watch him multiply them for your deliverance!

Larry Stockstill
Teaching Pastor, Bethany World Prayer Center, Baton Rouge, LA

THEY WILL FOLLOW

👑 BIBLE READ: 1 SAMUEL 17:48–52

As the Philistine moved closer to attack him,
David ran quickly toward the battle line to meet him.
Reaching into his bag and taking out a stone, he slung it and
struck the Philistine on the forehead. The stone sank into
his forehead, and he fell face down on the ground.

1 SAMUEL 17:48–49, NIV

*F*or forty days the armies of Israel ran from the battle line when Goliath would taunt them. They did not think they were big enough or strong enough to do battle with this giant. A shepherd boy shows up and takes on the giant, and all of a sudden the armies have all of the courage in the world. What happened? The courage of one fueled the courage of others.

We typically feel that if we take on a big challenge and fail, then we will let everyone down. The truth is that our willingness to step out and take on a challenge inspires others to do something they may not have done before. A great spiritual lesson is that our lives are put here for the benefit of others, not just ourselves. An army and nation rallied because a young man stepped up.

Who is waiting on you to step out and step up?

Mike Linch
Senior Pastor, NorthStar Church, Kennesaw, GA

THE PEACE OF GOD

And the peace of God, which surpasses all
understanding, will guard your hearts
and minds through Christ Jesus.

PHILIPPIANS 4:7, NASB

Think of your own life—the things you are facing. If you are going through trials and tribulations, are you seeking man's advice or God's? In Philippians, the apostle Paul is teaching us to guard our hearts and minds by seeking the counsel of God, not the counsel of man. It is God who gives peace and understanding, not the world.

You do not have to worry about anything. Whenever there is stress or disorder, you know Satan or the flesh is at the center. It cannot be of the Lord, because God is a God of order. Whenever you and I are striving or stressing, guess what? It is not God, because God has given us his peace. In Matthew 11:30, Jesus says, "For My yoke is easy and My burden is light."

The problem is me, not God. I take too much upon myself. I trust too much in myself, instead of trusting the Lord. Every day, we must look to the Lord for peace, strength, and wisdom. Only he can provide these things in our lives.

Raul Ries
Senior Pastor, Calvary Chapel Golden Springs, Diamond Bar, CA

LIVING TO MAKE JESUS FAMOUS

Therefore, if anyone is in Christ, the new creation has come:
The old has gone, the new is here!

2 CORINTHIANS 5:17, NIV

*T*he thought of living in the power of transformation has been rolling around my head the last few days. It seems that the mystical side of our relationship with God is often not lived out in the light of our current reality. I believe that God's transformation of my soul should become evident to all who know me in practical ways.

The process started with a decision. Decisions or choices change the direction of our lives. In 2 Corinthians 5, the apostle Paul takes us on a journey to the truth of Jesus Christ being the answer we are looking for . . . the decision that changes everything is about Jesus.

Let me go a bit deeper: You make a choice, then live it out. When you choose to give your life to Christ, you enter into a relationship that is started by God through Jesus's death and resurrection; you are drawn to God by his wooing, sealed by God through the Holy Spirit, and empowered by God with the indwelling power of the Holy Spirit. This is the gospel: God is for you!

When we come to Christ, it starts the process of transformation that brings changes from the inside out. God wants us to know him and then live like him in the world. As we allow Jesus to become more at home in our hearts and live him out through our behaviors, our lives get better and God gets bigger. We must make a choice to live out what we know so that Jesus receives all the glory, honor, and praise.

Scott Weatherford
Lead Pastor, First Alliance Church, Calgary, AB, Canada

09

WHY NOT LOVE LEAH?

When the Lord saw that Leah
was unloved, he opened her womb;
but Rachel was barren.

GENESIS 29:31, NKJV

*T*he lives of Jacob, Rachel, and Leah in Genesis 29 are a lesson for us all. Jacob was in awe of Rachel's physical beauty and in the dark about Leah's devotion and divine importance. We must wonder how Jacob would have treated Leah if he'd known that God was going to bring the seed of the Messiah through her, not Rachel. The unloved one—the one he married in the dark, the one so devoted to him—was the one greatly blessed by God.

Gideon was a nobody, and the angel of the Lord called him "a mighty man of valor." Joseph was unloved by his brothers but ordained by God to rule over them. Jesus said the greatest commandment is to love God "with all your heart, with all your soul, and with all your mind" and "love your neighbor as yourself" (Matthew 22:37, 39).

Could it be, when we pass by the odd or the different to associate with the nice and attractive, that the Lord places us into a dark place in our life to associate with those who have a seed of faith in them, waiting to be loved into the kingdom of God?

Garry Ansdell
Senior Pastor, Hosanna Christian Fellowship, Bellflower, CA

WITHIN REACH

👑 BIBLE READ: MARK 5:25–34

"You see the people crowding against you," his disciples answered, "and yet you can ask, 'Who touched me?'" But Jesus kept looking around to see who had done it. Then the woman, knowing what had happened to her, came and fell at his feet and, trembling with fear, told him the whole truth. He said to her, "Daughter, your faith has healed you. Go in peace and be freed from your suffering."

MARK 5:31–34, NIV

Can you imagine the scenario? A woman, after twelve years of doctors, is supposed to stay on the outskirts of the social milieu, but nothing can stop her from this day. As Christ passed through crowds the Bible says the masses "followed and crushed" him. But one woman reached out to make contact in faith. Just the humblest of faith; just the hem of his garment. You can't get any lower than that. But there is also no higher power than what happens when need touches the heart of a need-meeting God.

Today, we touch through the heart of God through our prayers—the discipline of silence, the intimacy of his presence, time in his Word. Faith is a blank check he fills out as we seek him. "According to your faith be it [done] unto you" (Matthew 9:29, KJV). His power is there for you, if you dare to be the one to reach beyond the "pressing crowds" and touch with your faith. He is within reach, longing to help and heal (Acts 17:27). Choose today to reach out to God with every ounce of your "heart, soul, mind, and strength" (Luke 10:27).

Shawn Mitchell
Senior Pastor, New Venture Christian Fellowship, Oceanside, CA

311

A PRIVILEGE TO SUFFER

For it has been granted to you on behalf of
Christ not only to believe in him, but also to suffer for him.

PHILIPPIANS 1:29, NIV

A pastor friend of mine in Colombia told me of a horrible story of persecution. Two of his congregation members had been killed because they refused to turn their children over to the drug traffickers to help in the harvest, working in their cocaine fields. We wept together as two pastors grieving for the loss of life—so tragic and so unnecessary, and in such violent ways.

I asked him how he could minister in such difficult and trying circumstances. He replied, "Carl, we take very seriously what the apostle Paul said in this verse. We consider suffering for the Lord Jesus a privilege. Even though it is hard, we see he is enough in the midst of our suffering."

Can you imagine that? What faith that is! What perspective and what courage!

If this pastor can minister in such difficult persecution, can we trust Christ to be enough in the midst of *our* circumstances? Can we live with the spiritual courage of the persecuted?

Dr. Carl Moeller
President and Managing Partner, Sequoia Global Resources

WHAT A DIFFERENCE
JESUS MAKES!

But you remain the same, and
your years will never end.

PSALM 102:27, NIV

istening to the news each day and watching what is taking place in our country, it's easy to understand why the idea of change resonates within the souls of most people.

All this talk about change is interesting in light of the promises that God makes to us. One of the most incredible promises in the Bible is found in Malachi 3:6: "For I am the Lord, I do not change" (NKJV). Isn't it wonderful, in a world full of a need for change, that our God promises us that he will never change? His love and mercy are everlasting!

God does not change; he promises those who come to him that he will change them. He will give a heart of flesh for a heart of stone; Jesus promises life and that we may have it more abundantly. This is not just a remodeling of our exterior personality but a true change of character and of who we are within the depths of our soul.

Once a life has been truly given to him, that person will never again be the same!

Steve DeNicola
Senior Pastor, Calvary Chapel, Foothill Ranch, CA

THE ARK'S ARCHITECT

By faith Noah, being divinely warned . . . prepared an ark.

HEBREWS 11:7, NKJV

id you ever notice how Noah's faith was behind his immortal exploits? He heard the warning of God, accepted it as true, and then set out to do something about it. Activity accompanied Noah's faith, which goes for any and all true trust in God.

Faith isn't a spectator. It doesn't remove itself from responsibility. It's the fuel that leads a person to gather the materials, pick up the hammer, and summon the strength to build the ark. Without genuine faith, God's warning would have been ignored; the ark would have never been built, and mankind would have perished. But with faith came the actions that God wanted and humanity needed. Faith was the ark's real architect.

God isn't going to tell us to build an ark. But he will warn us about certain situations that will arise in our lives. The big question is, "Do we have the faith to heed his warning and act accordingly?" It's a question we need to ask ourselves, and it's a question that our actions will ultimately answer for us.

Bob Coy
Senior Pastor, Calvary Chapel, Fort Lauderdale, FL

A WONDERFUL LIFE

BIBLE READ: GENESIS 29:30—30:1–24; 49:29–31

For the LORD is good and his love
endures forever; his faithfulness continues
through all generations.

PSALM 100:5, NIV

eah lived her whole life in the shadow of the pretty younger sister, Rachel. When Leah met Jacob, she was crushed to find out that he loved Rachel, and only through the subterfuge of her father, Laban, was she married to him. The picture we often have of Leah is a sad one. Yet through the births of her six sons, we see what was indeed a wonderful and blessed life—a life that testifies to her growing understanding of God.

Her first son she names Reuben, meaning "behold a son" or "God sees." She names her second son Simeon, meaning "God hears." Leah names her third son Levi, meaning "joined" or "attached." Leah's fourth son is named Judah, meaning "praised." She names her fifth son Issachar, meaning "rewarded," and her sixth son Zebulun, meaning "honored."

Leah is a name often associated with being unloved and without honor. The truth is that Leah had a wonderful life, richly blessed. So let Leah be an encouragement, that even in the midst of feeling alone and unloved, you can experience a wonderful life knowing that God sees, God hears, God joins, God is praised, God rewards, and God honors.

David Wesley Whitlock
President, Oklahoma Baptist University, Shawnee, OK

A LOT GOT OUT

*And it came to pass, when God destroyed the cities of
the plain, that God remembered Abraham, and
sent Lot out of the midst of the overthrow.*

GENESIS 19:29, NKJV

*S*in happened in Sodom and Gomorrah, but Lot got out! Sin is the advertised special of today: everywhere for all to see and choose. Lot's righteous soul was tormented from day to day by seeing and hearing their lawless deeds (2 Peter 2:8), but God delivered Lot.

Like Lot we, too, are waiting for God to take us home. When will the rapture happen? Who knows the day or hour? We do know that when Jesus comes for his bride, no matter how bad the world has treated her, even like the battered bride of Solomon (Song of Solomon 5:7), our Beloved will catch us away.

"For the Lord himself will descend from heaven with a shout, with the voice of an archangel, and with the trumpet of God. And the dead in Christ will rise first. Then we who are alive and remain shall be caught up together with them in the clouds to meet the Lord in the air. Thus we shall always be with the Lord" (1 Thessalonians 4:16–17). Are you ready?

Garry Ansdell
Senior Pastor, Hosanna Christian Fellowship, Bellflower, CA

According to Your Faith

We live by faith, not by sight.

2 CORINTHIANS 5:7, NIV

After Jesus healed, he would frequently note, "Your faith has healed you," or "According to your faith let it be done to you" (Matthew 9:22, 29). The healing touch was not then simply a matter of Jesus arbitrarily choosing to touch someone while ignoring another—a sort of divine game of "eeny meeny miny moe"—it was rather a divine response to faith.

I like to call faith the "currency of the kingdom." If you travel to another nation, you will want to exchange your U.S. dollars for the foreign currency of that country. It might be pounds, euros, rubles, shekels, or pesos, but if you do not have the right currency, you cannot transact business. No pesos, no sombrero.

In the kingdom of God, faith is like money at the mall; it gets the job done. Neither dollars nor pounds, rubles nor shekels, pesos nor euros can exact the transaction you need for God's miracle touch. This kingdom transaction must be done *by faith*. By *your* faith.

Dr. Jim Reeve
Senior Pastor, Faith Community Church, West Covina, CA

THANKSGIVING

Give thanks in all circumstances; for
this is God's will for you in Christ Jesus.

1 THESSALONIANS 5:18, NIV

ecause we live in a world that isn't great at saying "Thank you," we tend to think that gratitude is an extra-credit Christian virtue. Like our temptation to send a thank-you note in response to someone's thank-you note, we might secretly believe that God should be grateful for our thanksgiving.

The Bible, of course, reveals a different perspective. Jesus showed us that gratitude is the minimum expectation of those who are enriched by God's gifts. When ten lepers are healed of their malady, Christ doesn't praise the one who returns to say "thank you"; he disappointedly asks, "Where are the other nine?" (Luke 17:17). The Bible tells us that it is "fitting" and appropriate for his people to praise God (Psalm 147:1). Certainly we, of all people, should recognize the "gracious hand of our God [upon] us" (Ezra 8:18). We should habitually respond with heartfelt thanksgiving, not just on special days and special occasions, but every day and in every circumstance (1 Thessalonians 5:18). May God enable us to always fulfill our fundamental duty to express our joyful thanksgiving to our gracious and generous Redeemer!

Mike Fabarez
Senior Pastor, Compass Bible Church, Aliso Viejo, CA

REDEFINING SUCCESS

*What good will it be for a man if he gains
the whole world, yet forfeits his soul?*

MATTHEW 16:26, NIV84

ur culture says that whoever gathers the most expensive toys and achieves the greatest fame is the winner on the scoreboard. God's scoreboard is different. Our system is rendered obsolete in the reverse mathematics of the kingdom of God. Jesus defines winners as those who "deny themselves and take up their cross" (Matthew 16:24), which means to follow him and abandon self. It's not about gathering, but about releasing. It's not about increasing self, but about decreasing self and living vibrantly for Christ.

How easily we are lured into "worldly success" and influenced by the shimmering glitter of the fading gems that mesmerize the masses. Have you found yourself measuring your success with the wrong measure? Have you jumped on the treadmill of temporal success only to lose at what really counts? Is your soul showing the wear and tear of looking at the wrong scoreboard?

To be successful in the eyes of the world yet poor in the sight of God is truly the ultimate irrevocable tragedy. Let the words of Jesus turn our eyes to the heavenly scoreboard today.

Mark Jobe
Senior Pastor, New Life Community Church, Chicago, IL

GOD'S BATTLE

All those gathered here will know that
it is not by sword or spear that the LORD saves;
for the battle is the LORD's, and he will
give all of you into our hands.

1 SAMUEL 17:47, NIV

avid went to meet Goliath with power and might! He didn't meekly come to his "giant" task, but he came boldly with victory on his heart and mind.

David knew that victory was not in his strength or ability, or his ability to reason or think, or even in his wide array of weaponry, but that victory would be found in the awesomeness of his Almighty God.

David acted on faith.

How will you and I respond today? Do we, like David, recognize that there is no giant in our life that is too big for God? Is there something today that, if you were honest, you might say, "I have held on to this trouble. It seems like a Goliath, and I don't know what to do about it"? Quit trying in your own might. The battle is the Lord's, and he has bigger swords than you and I.

Let him fight for you today!

Ron Edmondson
Senior Pastor, Immanuel Baptist Church, Lexington, KY, RonEdmondson.com

FILLING EACH ROOM

By wisdom a house is built,
and by understanding it is established;
by knowledge the rooms are filled with all
precious and pleasant riches.

When purchasing a house it's about location, when building a house it's about the materials, and when it comes to making it a home it's about the furnishings.

We read of three important ingredients for life: wisdom, understanding, and knowledge. Proverbs 2:6 tells us, "The LORD gives wisdom; from his mouth come knowledge and understanding." Wisdom is the foundation for life, just as a foundation is vital to a house. The wisdom we need for life is found in God's Word. Understanding is like a building code. The Bible teaches us how to correctly interpret the seasons of life. Understanding enables you to weather life's storms, with Scripture as a foundation anchor. Knowledge is to fill our lives like furnishings fill a home—beautifully displayed, thoroughly enjoyed, and useful to all. The furnishings are not to be well-preserved heirlooms, but familiar and used daily. These materials from God will withstand the storms of life. All other materials will fail, but God's Word will endure forever.

Aaron Newman
Senior Pastor, Calvary Chapel, Paso Robles, CA

DON'T BE A COPY:
BE BRAND-NEW!

Don't copy the behavior and customs of this world,
but let God transform you into a new person by changing
the way you think. Then you will learn to know God's
will for you, which is good and pleasing and perfect.

ROMANS 12:2, NLT

ormal people live for themselves, go with the flow of culture, and tend to be religious in the sense that we try to keep some rules and rituals alive to make us feel that we're keeping God's disappointment at bay. But that's not how God wants his children to live. He wants us to be distinct and recognizable against the backdrop of the world.

Believers have a personal relationship with Jesus, a unique set of values grounded in eternal truth, and a perspective conditioned by the promise of ultimate victory and conquest. The brand-new life God wants us to live out is a challenge to the culture around us, but it's the only way to really live.

Brandon A. Cox
Founding Pastor, Grace Hills Church, Northwest Arkansas, Editor of Pastors.com
and Rick Warren's Pastor's Toolbox *newsletter*

STEPS OF OBEDIENCE

Do not merely listen to the word, and so deceive yourselves. Do what it says.

JAMES 1:22, NIV

As a new Christian I wanted to know God's plan for my life. I prayed about ministry, relationships, and direction. What I wasn't praying about was the pound of marijuana I had purchased shortly before my decision to follow Jesus. I knew I needed to get rid of it, so I did. I buried it deep in a corner of my closet. As I asked Jesus to bless me and lead me into his will, what I heard in my heart was, "Get rid of the pot, Mike."

"Okay, Jesus, but where do you want me to serve?"

"Get rid of the pot, Mike."

"Yes, Lord, I will. But what about college? Should I go into business or ministry?"

"Get rid of the pot, Mike."

What are you hearing from God or reading in his Word that you're praying past? Do you have something buried in a corner of your closet? Do you need to get rid of the pot or the porn or the anger or something else? Don't waste another day deceiving yourself. Take your next right step.

Mike Meeks
Senior Pastor, Eastlake Community Church, Chula Vista, CA

CONSULT THE PLAYBOOK

Your word is a lamp to my feet
and a light for my path.

PSALM 119:105, NIV84

The most important piece of equipment any coach or team has is the playbook. Playbooks outline all the plays designed to exploit the weaknesses of the other team while leveraging the greatest strengths of its team members.

Life can be a lot like a game of football—full of ups and downs. It would make sense, then, that we would need a playbook, too. The Word of God is our playbook. In it he has revealed everything we need to know to live an abundant and profitable life. It provides clear guidance, protection from the enemy, and strength for the road ahead.

I have built my life on the precepts and principles found in God's Word rather than my own preferences or the opinions of others. Accordingly, God has never let me down. His Word has been the perfect playbook for my life.

As you journey through life, always consult the playbook that will lead you to victory every step of the way!

Dr. Tom Mullins
Founding Pastor, Christ Fellowship, Palm Beach Garden, FL

WHAT KIND OF
A CHRISTIAN ARE YOU?

*Be diligent to present yourself approved to God, a worker who
does not need to be ashamed, rightly dividing the word of truth.*

2 TIMOTHY 2:15, NKJV

What kind of Christians are we today? If we're unwilling to answer that question, there are three that are willing to answer that question: Satan, the world, and Jesus Christ. Satan knows what kind of Christians we are. He has us in one of the following categories: (1) He's no problem, (2) he might become a problem, and (3) he's a major problem.

The world is also able to tell us what type of Christians we are. We can wear T-shirts with Christian messages on them or speak about the things of the Lord. We can wear special bracelets and talk about what Jesus would do. But the world is looking for answers and hoping that we might have the answers. So they're going to test us, try us, and even come after us. The world can tell if we are Christians or not.

And finally, Jesus knows what type of Christians we are. He desires that we become a channel, not just a vessel. He desires that we walk daily filled with his power and anointing so that our sweet fellowship and adoration for the Lord will be an appealing fragrance to the people around us. But oftentimes, he sees that the things of this world have become more important than our daily devotional life with him.

Steve Mays
Senior Pastor, Calvary Chapel, South Bay, CA

THE LURE OF THE FOOTPATH

And he told them many things in parables, saying:
"Listen! A sower went out to sow.
And as he sowed, some seeds fell on the path,
and the birds came and ate them up."

MATTHEW 13:3–4, NRSVB

We can all relate to the footpath, because we all once walked its alluring twists and turns, unaware of the hopelessness it offered, and ignorant of the life-giving soil only yards away in the Sower's fields. Perhaps we are tempted to go back from time to time.

It's on the footpaths of life, not in the quiet fields, where all the action is—or so it seems! Perhaps Jesus meant for the footpath to symbolize the busy world, hustling and bustling, lights and glamour, important things to do, people to impress. Oh, that place entices me from time to time. The footpath can be a real distraction.

When driving along the cornfields that populate our landscape, I've noticed that at the fields near the busy road, the stalks don't grow quite as high, and the corn isn't as healthy. Perhaps it's because the road's dust and rocks get kicked up, suffocating the crop. It's a reminder not to get too close to the footpaths of the world, and to seek safety in the fields of life, close to the Sower.

Beck A. Taylor
President, Whitworth University, Spokane, WA

EXPECT OPPOSITION FOR YOUR FAITH

All this I have told you so that you will not fall away.
They will put you out of the synagogue; in fact, the time is coming
when anyone who kills you will think they are offering a
service to God. They will do such things because
they have not known the Father or me.

JOHN 16:1–3, NIV

Sometimes being warned in advance can help us prepare for the worst. In this passage, Jesus was telling his disciples about what was to come, so that they would not lose their faith in him. If the first thing Jesus said to them was that following him would get them killed, I wonder how many of the disciples would've stayed with him! But Jesus saves this for the end of his time with the disciples. When we read this passage, we are compelled to remember those who have literally given their lives for Jesus as martyrs in the persecuted church.

But it's not just those who are giving their physical lives for Jesus. It reminds all of us to expect opposition for our commitment to following Christ. Misunderstanding and even opposition will go hand in hand with our witness for our Lord. Living for Jesus is going to require a commitment greater than many of us have ever experienced. Are we up to it?

Dr. Carl Moeller
President and Managing Partner, Sequoia Global Resources

MEDITATE
DAY AND NIGHT

This Book of the Law shall not depart from
your mouth, but you shall meditate in it day and night,
that you may observe to do according to all that is written
in it. For then you will make your way prosperous,
and then you will have good success.

JOSHUA 1:8, NKJV

In this powerful verse, God reveals a secret to bringing his blessings to anyone's life: meditating on God's Word—the Bible. We all know that reading the Bible and hearing good Bible teaching are important, but meditating on God's Word is powerful because it starts with reading, and then includes speaking, hearing, and pondering. As you mutter a passage over and over, you also hear the Word over and over. And Romans 10:17 tells us that "faith comes by hearing and hearing by the word of God." So as we keep repeating God's Word, we believe it more and more. May you begin living your life each day with the Word in your heart and experiencing God's blessings.

Jerry Dirmann
Senior Pastor, The Rock Church, Anaheim, CA

GOD KNEW YOU

Before I formed you in the womb I knew you;
before you were born I sanctified you;
I ordained you a prophet to the nations.

JEREMIAH 1:5, NKJV

*T*his verse has impacted me greatly over the years. The truth that God knew us before we were in the womb is mind-blowing. God sees our lives in totality. His knowledge is complete from beginning to end. It is astounding to think that the God who knows us also intervenes in our lives and sets us apart for him.

God had a specific purpose for Jeremiah's life even before he was born. The same is true for you and me. We're not just taking up space, waiting to expire. God created us for a reason. May we strive to walk in the purposes for which we were created.

Eric Cartier
Senior Pastor, Rocky Mountain Calvary Chapel, Colorado Springs, CO

THE FIRST COMMAND

Hear, O Israel:
The Lord our God, the Lord is one.

DEUTERONOMY 6:4, NKJV

*W*hat is the first and central command of the Bible? Did you answer this, "Love the Lord your God with all your heart, soul, mind, and strength" (Mark 12:30)? If you did, the answer would be incorrect. God said, 'Hear O Israel, the Lord our God, the Lord is one." Then he said, "You shall love the Lord your God . . ." (Deuteronomy 6:5). Any Jewish person who has ever gone to synagogue a couple of times knows exactly what Messiah said. It is the Shema, which is said by virtually every Jew, in every synagogue, every week throughout the world. "*Sh'ma Yisrael* [Hear O Israel], *Adonai Elohaynu* [the Lord our God], *Adonai Echad* [the Lord is One]." And then it continues, "Love the Lord your God. . . ."

So what was the first thing Messiah said when asked what was most important? Jesus said one word: *Sh'ma*. The word "hear" means *listen*, pay close attention. You see, before we can do great things for God, or anything that's going to last, we have to learn to stop and listen. For when you listen, you will truly learn to know him. And when you really know him, you will grow to love him. When you grow to love him, then you will really love others. Are you ready to stop, listen, and make time today for the most important relationship in your life? Listen to him and begin to learn to really know him. God actually has something to say to you.

Jonathan Cahn
Author, The Harbinger, *Senior Pastor and Messianic Rabbi*
the Jerusalem Center / Beth Israel, Wayne, NJ

FORGIVE AND FORGET

Love prospers when a fault is forgiven, but
dwelling on it separates close friends.

arriage counselors would agree that one of the biggest
problems spouses have is keeping a record of their spouses'
mistakes and then dragging them up in the middle of a conversation, even though they've "forgiven" the other person. In fact, even
outside of marriage, this is something people often do. We say, "I
forgive," but we don't forget.

When someone asks for your forgiveness or you "have fought"
against someone for what they've done, forgiveness and forgetting are
essential. Freedom and liberty from bondage go hand in hand with
the matter of our being willing to forgive—and forget—the wrong
that others have done to us or what we perceive they have done.

People have this idea that forgetting means you get Holy Ghost
amnesia, but that's not true. When you forget, you put it out of mind.
You choose not to allow memories of others' mistakes to occupy
your thought life. If you don't forget, your relationship will always be
affected by your mindfulness.

Don't allow unforgiveness to fester in your heart. Forgive and forget other people's mistakes and allow forgiveness to be in your life.

Lord, help me to forgive those who have wronged me, and put it
out of my mind once I've chosen to forgive. In Jesus's name, Amen.

Mac Hammond
Senior Pastor, Living Word Christian Center, Brooklyn Park, MN

THE RIGHT GOALS

The heart of man plans his way, but the LORD establishes his steps.

PROVERBS 16:9, ESV

I like goal-minded people. They have a sense of purpose about them. They seem to know where they're going. Others shun the idea of setting goals and tend to meander through life, bumping off of one obstacle after another. The old saying is quite true: "If you aim at nothing, you'll surely hit it."

Sometimes the idea of setting goals can sound a bit proud to a Christian. It sounds as if we are going to tell God what is going to happen in our life, and God had better get on board with the plan. But setting goals doesn't have to be this way. For the Christian, healthy goal setting is about learning God's ideas and boundaries. It's about allowing God's heart to shape the direction of our lives. The more we know about God's way of thinking, the more our "goals" can adapt to his goals for us.

Some people have five-year plans and ten-year plans for their lives. They know where they want to be and what they want to be doing by a certain date. A common goal for many is retirement, when we can quit work and do . . . whatever retired people do. Though I commend those working toward retirement, I'd like to suggest a goal that goes beyond retirement. Paul wrote, "I press on toward the goal for the prize of the upward call of God in Christ Jesus" (Philippians 3:14).

Do you have any goals in life? What part does God play in the plans you have? Aim for the day that Jesus returns.

Rich Cathers
Senior Pastor, Calvary Chapel, Fullerton, CA

MIRROR, MIRROR IN MY LAP

Anyone who listens to the word but
does not do what it says is like a man who
looks at his face in a mirror and, after looking at
himself, goes away and immediately
forgets what he looks like.

JAMES 1:23–24, NIV

*J*ames compares the Bible to a mirror—in this case, for our souls. God's Word reflects the state of a person's heart the way a mirror reflects one's face. Mirrors don't lie; they simply reveal what's there: a wrinkle, a blemish, a spot that got missed by the razor. Mirrors alert us to an embarrassing smudge or, more important, a cancerous growth. Similarly, a good, hard look into the Word of God can reveal inner spiritual malignancies and character smudges. If we don't act, James says we're like the guy who sees the dried toothpaste dribble in the corner of his mouth but goes into the business meeting without wiping it off. What good was it to know it was there and do nothing about it? When the Word reveals truth to our souls, we must put the truth into practice, or the knowledge we have is in vain.

Dr. Ross Reinman
Senior Pastor, The Rock, Santa Rosa, CA

GOD'S PEACE

Peace I leave with you; my peace I give you.
I do not give to you as the world gives.
Do not let your hearts be troubled and do not be afraid.

JOHN 14:27, NIV

ow do we find peace in a world that seems to be turned upside-down? Daily on the news we hear stories of random violence, terrorist threats, rumors of wars, senseless killings, natural and manmade disasters, and many other fearful stories. Jesus knew that these troubling, frightening things would take place and that's why he left us a message of comfort and hope. Apostle Paul said, "It's learning to be content in all your circumstances no matter what happens to you or around you, knowing that God can give you the strength to endure." (Read Philippians 4:11–13)

The peace of God is received through the Holy Spirit by prayer, faith, and trusting in God's promises in his word. Peace is not always an emotional feeling but an inner confidence, faith, and hope that everything is under God's complete care.

Remember to go to God first with your daily concerns for yourself, family, or friends. God will answer your prayers according to his perfect plan for your life. Inner peace will come as you learn to let go in faith while trusting God in all your circumstances.

Steve M. Woods
Chairman, Board of Directors, WoodsMasteryLearningFoundation.org

FEAR OF MAN

The LORD is with me; I will not be afraid.
What can man do to me?

PSALM 118:6, NIV84

God's Word says that the "fear of man will prove to be a snare, but whoever trusts in the LORD is kept safe" (Proverbs 29: 25). Unfortunately, the fear of others is a trap that often catches us in its grip. While the temptation to surrender to fear may be hard to resist, the Bible tells us that a life constrained by the fear of what people will think of you or may do to you is a life destined for compromise and defeat (see 1 Peter 3:14).

Instead, the Bible consistently calls the righteous to be "as bold as a lion" (Proverbs 28:1). Vanquishing the terror of man can only be attained by having a proper and healthy fear of God. Jesus shared that if we had an appropriate fear of God, we would not dread what people could do to us, even if they were to seize all that we own (see Matthew 10:28). Remember, God is our ultimate authority. He is the One to whom we will answer. In the long run, pleasing him is all that really matters. Therefore, set your sights on living for the attention of our God. Then you will avoid the snare and encumbrance that comes with the fear of man.

Mike Fabarez
Senior Pastor, Compass Bible Church, Aliso Viejo, CA

LEARNING TO FORGIVE

*O*ne of the great stumbling blocks for all believers is the issue of forgiveness. Do you know how to forgive and why you should forgive? Jesus made a very simple command: "Whenever you stand praying, if you have anything against anyone, forgive him, that your Father in heaven may also forgive you your trespasses. But if you do not forgive, neither will your Father in heaven forgive your trespasses" (Mark 11:25–26, NKJV).

Forgiveness is a choice that you make every day with each offense made against you. Jesus is simply asking you to do what he's already done for you. He freely forgives anyone and anything by his grace. It is not an issue of "I cannot forgive"; it is really that "I will not forgive."

Therefore, give up your excuses, realize your own need for his forgiveness, and then ask God for a willing heart to forgive others. Make the choice to extend God's grace to those who have betrayed you, hurt you, and persecuted you. As you do, you will become the sons and daughters of your Father in heaven (Matthew 5:9).

Steve Carr
Senior Pastor, Calvary Chapel, Arroyo Grande, CA

A PLACE OF GRACE

Now these are the words of the letter which
Jeremiah the prophet sent from Jerusalem to the rest
of the elders of the exile, the priests, the prophets, and all
the people whom Nebuchadnezzar had taken into
exile from Jerusalem to Babylon.

JEREMIAH 29:1, NASB

he Jews of the exile were there for their disobedience to God and their failure to walk in the law of Moses. But Jeremiah didn't write to condemn them or to remind them of their failure. He wrote to point them to the grace of God.

God wanted them to see this place of failure as a place where grace would be shown to them and God's work advanced within them. Even as Samson's blindness purified his vision, even as Jacob's limp straightened out his walk, even as Christ's sorrow deepened his joy— so their brokenness would result in their wholeness.

You may be in a place of brokenness and failure, but this is where God's grace and power are most clearly seen. You are not in a place of condemnation but a place of grace.

Tim Brown
Senior Pastor, Calvary Chapel, Fremont, CA

GUARANTEED HAPPINESS

I have fought the good fight,
I have finished the race, I have kept the faith.

2 TIMOTHY 4:7, NIV84

*T*he apostle Paul's use of the race as a metaphor for how we focus our lives always inspires me. From Hebrews 12:1 we find Paul encouraging us to "run with perseverance," followed by Galatians 5:7 and 8, where we learn that there are those who will, indeed, impair our progress. In Philippians 3:12, our brother Paul calls us to "press on" to claim our prize in Christ. Finally, in 2 Timothy 4:7, we are reminded that someday we will "finish the race" and hopefully we will have been faithful.

The Christian life can be hectic and challenging as we proceed toward the promise of heaven. I have also found that the race itself is joy, which—when combined with the very thought of heaven at the end—is indescribable joy. George Santayana once said, "Knowledge of what is possible is the beginning of happiness." I like that. Regardless of where we are in the race, we can and should be happy.

By ourselves the race may seem impossible, but in Matthew 19:26 we are promised that "with God all things are possible." And that is guaranteed happiness.

Andrew K. Benton
President and CEO, Pepperdine University, Malibu, CA

THE VALLEY OF
THE SHADOW OF DEATH

BIBLE READ: PSALM 23

*Even though I walk through the valley of the
shadow of death, I fear no evil, for
You are with me; Your rod and
Your staff, they comfort me.*

PSALM 23:4, NKJV

The valley can be scary! The Great Shepherd leads me through the valley of the shadow of death. I have learned that shadows can be scary, but they can't hurt me. The good news is that Jesus leads me through the valley to the other side, a mountain peak. It's from the mountain peak that I can see my path that brought me through the valley of the shadow of death. From the mountain peak, the fear of the valley loses its grip. To reach the mountain peak I must first go through the valley.

Trust the Great Shepherd to lead you through the valley of everyday life to the other side, a mountain peak.

Brent Wagner
Senior Pastor, Voyage Calvary Chapel, Fountain Valley, CA

GOD IN THE NIGHTTIME

Let us cross over to the other side.

When facing difficult times in your life, have you ever thought, *Lord, don't you care?* The disciples experienced this during a storm that threatened to overtake their boat. They were anxious, fearful, and desperate during the storm, yet the Lord was at rest. How often have you asked that same question? So often we don't understand why God is silent, seemingly ignoring our cries for help.

Trials and tribulations bring us closer to the Lord; it's in the nighttime of our life that we are able to truly understand the Lord's presence and to overcome the things that diminish our faith.

Jesus had told them they were going to cross over to the other side, but they did not believe that. In the same way, are there trials in your life that rock your faith and tempt you to doubt God's love and promises to you? In the dark places of your life, when you cry out to the Lord, remember his Word—his promise of salvation, guidance, provision, and eternal life.

The Lord does care about you. Have faith and believe in him!

David Rosales
Senior Pastor, Calvary Chapel, Chino Valley, CA

CUSTOMER SERVICE

Respect those who work hard among you . . . Hold them
in the highest regard in love because of their work.

1 THESSALONIANS 5:12–13, NIV84

*H*ave you noticed that customer service is not what it used to be? We all have dreadful stories of incompetent waitresses or contractors or grocery clerks who have driven us crazy. Not to mention the seasonal sales people who seem to do their best to make Christmas shopping more of a nightmare than a joyous time. What is a consumer to do?

While we can't fix the problems, we can strive to be more understanding. Many people simply don't like their jobs and are not properly trained by employers. The turnover in some service industries is as high as 45 percent. In spite of this, Christians are called to be respectful consumers. In God's eyes our time is not more important than anyone else's. All honest labor is to be commended because our jobs are a means of using our gifts to serve others. God's love would not be rude or self-seeking, and it is not easily angered (I Corinthians 13:5).

When faced with bungling service, we may feel like helpless victims, but we're not! We have options. We can complain, write letters to the management, or just walk away, and at times that may be appropriate. Or we can strive to be Christ-centers, check our attitudes and model His mercy in the marketplace. It's a tough job, but when we succeed, we are much happier consumers and much better Christians. . . . especially in December.

Pat Verbal
Manager of Curriculum Development, Christian Institute
on Disability, Joni and Friends, Agoura Hills, CA

PRESSING ON IN CHRIST

I press toward the mark for the prize of the
high calling of God in Christ Jesus.

PHILIPPIANS 3:14, KJV

The apostle Paul's accomplishments in Christ were already worth mentioning when he waved us onward and said, "Come on, there's a lot more ahead ... and it's all good." Paul insisted that the sufferings he had experienced in his ministry were no longer worth considering when compared to the glory that lay ahead.

Paul's former career offered self-satisfaction, status, influence, and security. But God had something better for him in Christ. Paul came to recognize that his family connections, his clean moral record, and his religious zeal could not earn God's favor.

"I press toward the mark." This is the image of a runner straining every muscle and ligament in an all-out effort, focused on the finish line for the prize that is the high calling of God in Christ Jesus. "Press" means we are pushing, squeezing, forcing to get the mark, not letting anything in the past slow us down. We exert all our strength of body, mind, and spirit to move toward our goal to become more like Jesus.

Paul did not claim to have laid hold of his reward. He had not crossed the finish line thus far in the Christian race, but he was committed to going all out in order to reach it. Our lives need to follow this model. Pressing on in the Christian life is hard, but remember the goal is worth the climb.

Eugene Burrage
Senior Pastor, Original Greater Rock M.B. Church, Chicago, IL

GOD STANDS BY ME

And as a great dissension was developing,
the commander was afraid Paul would be torn to
pieces by them and ordered the troops to go down and take
him away from them by force, and bring him into the barracks.
But on the night immediately following, the Lord stood
at his side and said, "Take courage; for as you have
solemnly witnessed to my cause at Jerusalem,
so you must witness at Rome also."

ACTS 23:10–11, NASB

Even the apostle Paul had times of discouragement and loneliness. In sharing the gospel with his own people, we read in
Acts 23:10 how they sought to tear him to pieces! How's that for gratitude? Many times we, too, feel like we're all alone, rejected. Yet in the
very next verse we read, "The Lord stood by him" (v. 11, NKJV). The
next time you feel like you're going to pieces, remember the Prince
of Peace who stands by you.

Joe Coleman
Senior Pastor, Calvary Chapel, Palm Desert, CA

By His Grace

*For all have sinned and fall short of the glory of God,
and are justified freely by his grace through the
redemption that came by Christ Jesus.*

ROMANS 3:23–24, NIV84

*A*ll humans have a conscience that speaks to us in everything we do. It is this small voice within us that screens everything that we say or do by putting it into a catalog of good or evil. Many of us continue to ignore this system that is so dear to us until we have reached the end of our rope. At this point in our journey we welcome God into our lives. When God is invited into our lives the spiritual economics in us change drastically. This change comes free of charge by the redemption that was paid by Jesus. It is maintained by you through the help of God. When we give our lives to God, all things that we need are met. By loving God we are able to love others as Christ loved us, even our enemies.

Dr. Le'on M. Willis I
Reverend, Wesley United Methodist Church, Chicago, IL

PRAYER: THREE KINDS

Be earnest and unwearied and steadfast in
your prayer [life], being [both] alert and intent
in [your praying] with thanksgiving.

COLOSSIANS 4:2, AMPLIFIED

*T*here are three primary settings for biblical prayer that should have priority in our lives. The first is a focused type of scheduled prayer (Matthew 6:6). This is the kind in which, like Daniel's three times a day or Jesus's predawn appointments, we plan to meet with God for a significant session of "pouring out our hearts before the Lord" (Psalm 62:8).

The second setting for prayer is a team effort. This is when we meet with other Christians in groups to help one another direct our thoughts, intercessions, and thanksgivings to God (Acts 12:12). Praying with others allows us to share one another's burdens (Galatians 6:2) and prompts us to express requests and concerns to God that would have never otherwise crossed our minds.

A third setting for prayer can take place in your life right now. It is the kind Paul called "praying continually" (1 Thessalonians 5:17, NIV). These are the comments and requests that should punctuate our lives as we reach out to our omnipresent God amid all the events and activities of our day (see Nehemiah 2:4–5). Let's make all three a priority as we seek to deepen our relationship and communication with the living God.

Mike Fabarez
Senior Pastor, Compass Bible Church, Aliso Viejo, CA

SO SAY WE ALL

This is the confidence we have in approaching God:
that if we ask anything according to his will, he hears us.
And if we know that he hears us—whatever we ask—
we know that we have what we asked of him.

1 JOHN 5:14–15, NIV

In tough economic times, many members of our church family were out of work for long periods of time. Each unemployed church member prayed fervently, "God, I need a job. Please give me a job soon!" But not much seemed to happen.

And then it dawned on us during a study of the Lord's Prayer that Jesus never taught us to pray, "Give me today my daily bread" (see Matthew 6:11). Instead, we were to pray as a group for God to provide not just for ourselves individually but for all of us. Therefore, many members in our church started praying, "God, many in our church family need jobs. Please give us jobs soon."

An amazing thing happened. Believers began to report more job interviews and more job offers. Coincidence? We didn't think so, and we began to apply this to other prayer requests: Lord, heal us from cancer. . . . Lord, save our troubled marriages. . . . Lord, open the eyes of our friends and loved ones who don't know of your love. Give it a try and see what happens.

Rick Stedman
Senior Pastor, Adventure Christian Church, Roseville, CA

CAN YOU HEAR THE TAPPING?

Greater love has no one than this:
to lay down one's life for one's friends.

A Pearl Harbor survivor tells the heart-wrenching story of the sinking of the battleship *Arizona* after the attack by Japanese warplanes. Some avoid death by moving into lower-deck areas where oxygen and supplies are available. Numerous heroic attempts are made to save these trapped individuals. An eyewitness describes hearing the *tap, tap, tap* of desperate sailors attempting to be rescued. Eventually the tapping becomes more sporadic and then ceases altogether. This veteran sailor breaks down and weeps uncontrollably as he describes the emotional frustration of being so close to his comrades yet being unable to rescue them.

Paul expresses similar frustration and passion over the plight of his fellow countrymen. "I have great sorrow and unceasing anguish in my heart. For I could wish that I myself were cursed and cut off from Christ for the sake of my brothers, those of my own race" (Romans 9:2–3, NIV84). Paul is willing to trade eternal places with the lost. Do you have such a passion for the lost around you? Can you hear the tapping? Passionately point them to Jesus. One day the tapping will cease.

Scott Miller
Senior Pastor, Graceland Baptist Church, New Albany, IN

IT'S ABOUT THE HEART

Create in me a clean heart, O God.
Renew a loyal spirit within me.

PSALM 51:10, NLT

*T*he greatest victories available to God's people still lie ahead for most believers. This is primarily because we see circumstantial deliverances or changes in our chemistry while God is concerned with the heart. Until my heart is clean and my spirit renewed, even the best of actions will be supported by poor motives and intentions. But when our hearts are open before the Almighty, he can do stunning things through us!

It's ultimately about this big question: *How is your heart today?*

Brandon A. Cox
Founding Pastor, Grace Hills Church, Northwest Arkansas, Editor of Pastors.com and Rick Warren's Pastor's Toolbox *newsletter*

CONFESSION

Then the LORD God called to the man, and said to him,
"Where are you?" He said, "I heard the sound of
You in the garden, and I was afraid because
I was naked; so I hid myself."

GENESIS 3:9–10, NASB

*A*dam had eaten the forbidden fruit. He knew he did it, he knew that God knew that he did it, but he still tried to hide that he did it and tried to make it look like someone else did it. Why wouldn't he confess his sin?

To confess sin means accepting responsibility, and we don't want to face the responsibility of the consequences of our sinful choices. If I accept responsibility, then I have to change something—the way I think/feel/behave/speak/relate—and change is hard work.

To confess sin means that I have a Judge over me and that I am accountable. The lack of confession gives the illusion of the absence of accountability and the presence of independence.

To confess sin means that I live in relationship and community with others—God and people. Relationship puts boundaries around me, and confession is an admission of those limitations. To confess sin means that I am not a radically independent person.

Why are we slow to confess our sin? Because confession of sin will cost us something—but the lack of it will cost us more. May you be quick to confess your sin and embrace Christ. He's waiting for you.

Tim Brown
Senior Pastor, Calvary Chapel, Fremont, CA

Better Together

Two are better than one, because they
have a good return for their labor.

ECCLESIASTES 4:9, NASB

*J*esus knew that people needed him. In fact, Jesus commissioned his disciples to go into every town and seek to bring Christ's love to anyone and everyone.

Jesus said, "The harvest is plentiful, but the workers are few" (Luke 10:2). Did you catch that? He said there is more work to be done than there are people to do it. But if you read the verses closely, you'll find that Jesus sent his disciples out "two by two." Does that strike you as being strange? Think about it: If the harvest was truly more plentiful than the workers who were available, don't you think it would have made more sense for Jesus to send each disciple out individually? They could have covered twice as much ground. They could have reached twice as many people! If the workers were "few," why send them out in pairs?

The answer to that question is also one of the greatest truths about Christian fellowship. God does not intend for any of us to walk through this world alone. Jesus knew that as his ambassadors, we are better together. Don't neglect those special people whom God has put by your side. They are his gift to you, and you are his gift to them. We were meant to care for and encourage each other!

Brent Eldridge
Lead Pastor, First Baptist Church of Lakewood, Long Beach, CA

I'M HOME

BIBLE READ: PSALM 84

*Because you are his sons, God sent the
Spirit of his Son into our hearts, the Spirit who calls
out, "Abba, Father." So you are no longer a slave,
but God's child; and since you are his child,
God has made you also an heir.*

GALATIANS 4:6–7, NIV

For the believer, heaven is a reward, not a punishment. In Psalm 84 we learn that as children of God, we are pilgrims on this earth who have a holy homesickness for heaven. Whereas a vagabond is without a home and a fugitive is running from home, we as pilgrims are headed for home! Our souls thirst and our hearts cry out for the Living God, looking forward to the day when we can say, "Dad, I'm home!"

Joe Coleman
Senior Pastor, Calvary Chapel, Palm Desert, CA

351

God the Spirit, Protector
of God's Blessings

Having also believed, you were sealed in
him with the Holy Spirit of promise.

EPHESIANS 1:13, NASB

*I*n the ancient world, important letters often carried the seal
of the author. These seals protected the contents from unau-
thorized eyes, while also declaring that the message inside was serious business.

At the end of a long list of spiritual blessings enjoyed by the Christ-
follower, the apostle Paul seems to hear his readers voicing an obvious question: "But Paul, how can we be sure that these blessings will
really be ours? What keeps them from being lost?" Paul's answer is
very simple: Those who are "in Christ" (Ephesians 1:13, NIV) have
been sealed with the greatest seal ever, the Holy Spirit. His indwelling presence in the life of the believer is not only the source of gifted-
ness, guidance, knowledge, conviction, and courage. He also is there
to make sure that all God has for us becomes a reality.

Simply put, God the Spirit protects in us what God the Father
has granted to us through what God the Son has done for us. While
we are called to persevere in holiness, the fact is that God is the one
persevering in us, to make us more and more like Jesus Christ, the
Savior of our souls.

Dr. David W. Hegg
Senior Pastor, Grace Baptist Church, Santa Clarita, CA

HE IS WILLING

A man with leprosy came to him and
begged him on his knees, "If you are willing,
you can make me clean." Jesus was filled with compassion.
He reached out his hand and touched the man.
"I am willing," he said. "Be clean!" Immediately the
leprosy left him and he was cleansed.

MARK 1:40–42, NIV84

This man with leprosy has no doubt about Jesus's *ability* to heal him, but he wonders if Jesus is *willing* to heal him. He has been shunned and treated as an outcast by others his whole life. Will Jesus treat him the same way and refuse to help him?

We, too, find it easier to believe in God's ability than in his willingness. It is not hard to believe that an all-powerful God can help us, but we have a much harder time believing that God is willing to help us. Does God really care about me? Does God really love me? Will God help me?

God's answer to you and me is the same answer Jesus gave to this man with leprosy: "I am willing."

Jeff Miles
Senior Pastor, Touchstone Christian Fellowship, Sacramento, CA

ALZHEIMER'S AND ADVENT

They will call him Emmanuel, which means,
"God is with us."

MATTHEW 1:23, NLT

his is Mom's last night in her home of the past forty-six years. Tomorrow morning she will be lovingly escorted to the East McComb Nursing Home, where the last chapter of her life will begin. None of us knows how long or short that chapter will be. Dad is eighty-six, in relatively good health, and tired. He has cared for her as long as he could. Tonight he will sleep with her. Tomorrow night he will sleep by himself, alone for the first time in sixty years.

His questions have been fair. Why? Why her? Why now? Why this? Mom has spent her life in service to God and the church—pianist, church treasurer, Sunday school teacher, maker of Kool-Aid for sixty years' worth of Vacation Bible Schools. Dad's prayers, which have moved mountains across decades, did not budge this one. Alzheimer's came . . . and kept on coming.

Advent celebrates the coming of God—first in Jesus as an infant, finally in Jesus as the one who makes all things right. But in between these two comings there are millions being touched by the love of God. Can God come to one whose grasp of history is fading, to one who cannot recall the Bible stories that have shaped her? Can God visit someone who has Alzheimer's? And will she know that God came? I know God came to the East McComb Nursing Home. I hope Mom recognizes God. I choose to believe both.

Dan Boone
President, Trevecca Nazarene University, Nashville, TN

FROM ABRAM TO ABRAHAM

No longer shall your name be called Abram,
but your name shall be Abraham; for I have made
you a father of many nations. I will make you exceedingly
fruitful; and I will make nations of you, and
kings shall come from you.

GENESIS 17:5–6, NKJV

I was blown away by these verses. Abraham—his name was originally Abram when God called him. Then God changed his name from Abram, which in Hebrew means "exalted father," to Abraham, which means "a great multitude."

Abraham was Abram for many years, and he thought he had accomplished much in his life. But when his name was changed, he realized he had done nothing compared to what God would do with Abraham. When God changed Abram's name to Abraham, he showed Abraham, through prophecy, how he was going to touch hundreds, thousands, millions, and billions of people.

When you get older, you start thinking a bit differently. You start looking more toward eternity, but you also look back at everything God has done in your life and what he is doing. As you serve the Lord, you realize, "I have accomplished all these things in life." Keep in mind, it was never you; it was what God was doing through you. Therefore, always be open to God's Holy Spirit. God wants to continue to use you until he takes you home.

Raul Ries
Senior Pastor, Calvary Chapel Golden Springs, Diamond Bar, CA

WHAT ABOUT HIM?

When Peter saw him, he asked,
"Lord, what about him?" Jesus answered,
"If I want him to remain alive until I return,
what is that to you? You must follow me."

JOHN 21:21–22, NIV

pparently, finger-pointing is an international problem. In Donetsk, Ukraine, a man asked me, "Why, since you live in such a wicked nation and have so many needs in America, would you come over here to preach to us?" Although he does ask a legitimate question, this gentleman is avoiding the real issue: his own spiritual need.

Peter does the same thing in John 21. Jesus casts a strong vision for Peter's future and then challenges him with a message Peter has heard before: "Follow me!" Then Peter points his finger. Verses 20a and 21 say, "Peter turned and saw that the disciple whom Jesus loved was following them. When Peter saw him [John], he asked, 'Lord, what about him?'" In essence, Jesus responds, "Don't worry about him, Peter. Just focus on your own relationship with me."

When we point fingers at others, we are missing the point. I have so much work to do in my personal relationship with Jesus that I really shouldn't ask, "What about him?" I should heed Jesus's individual, powerful challenge: "Don't worry about him. You follow me."

Scott Miller
Senior Pastor, Graceland Baptist Church, New Albany, IN

OPEN OUR EYES

Do not fear, for those who are with us are
more than those who are with them. Then Elisha prayed
and said, "O Lord, I pray, open his eyes that he may see."
And the Lord opened the servant's eyes and he saw;
and behold, the mountain was full of horses and
chariots of fire all around Elisha.

2 KINGS 6:16–17, NASB

The king of Syria wanted to take Elisha the prophet into custody and sent his army to capture him. They came to Dothan, the city where Elisha was staying, and surrounded the city. When Elisha's servant woke up, he looked outside and saw his doom and cried out, "Alas, my master! What shall we do?" This is when Elisha spoke what has been recorded above. The eyes of the servant were open to see the power and provision of God. He still had his problem—the army of Syria was still surrounding them—but in one very real way his problem was solved; he had seen the power of God. Though the problem was still there, it became infinitely smaller in light of what the servant saw.

Every day we are surrounded by one problem or another. It is easy to think that this is the end of the road. But if our eyes are open to see God's power and provision in Christ Jesus, we will get all our problems in perspective. How important it is to read the Bible, to pray, to worship—to have our eyes open to see the Lord. We are trying to solve our problems, and God is trying to open our eyes. May the Lord open all our eyes to see all of him.

Tim Brown
Senior Pastor, Calvary Chapel, Fremont, CA

TRUST GOES BEYOND ANSWERS

Trust in the LORD with all your heart
and lean not on your own understanding;
in all your ways submit to him, and
he will make your paths straight.

PROVERBS 3:5–6, NIV

rust goes beyond answers. Sometimes questions cause us to avoid trust. It's not true that if all our questions were answered it would be easier to trust. Actually, it's easier to trust when we know the person to whom trust is given. God doesn't answer all our questions concerning life's events, but we can learn to trust him more now because of who he is rather than waiting to find answers to our questions. God is worthy of your trust because of his nature and character—in other words, because of who he is and what he has done.

So when the clouds come and the wind begins to blow, remember that God chose you first. You are his responsibility for all eternity. Therefore, trust the heart of your Father, especially when you think he does not understand.

Brent Wagner
Senior Pastor, Voyage Calvary Chapel, Fountain Valley, CA

358

PRAYING TO DIE AND LIVE

Turn away my eyes from looking at worthless things,
and revive me in Your way.

*T*he psalmist here prays a prayer that touches my heart. He asks the Lord to let him die to certain things in his life while coming alive to others. First, to "turn away my eyes from worthless things" (*shav* in Hebrew: that which is empty, vain, false, lying, or worthless). Who would spend two minutes of their time with worthless things that were of no profit? Only sin's deception would have us staring at the *shav* for way too long while believing they would satisfy and bring contentment. Turn my eyes from that foolishness, cries the psalmist. Solomon in Ecclesiastes discovered time and again how unsatisfying the *shav* really was (see Ecclesiastes 4:4, 6, 13; 5:10, 12; 6:7, 9).

On the other hand the psalmist asks the Lord to revive him in the ways of the Lord. Quicken me, Lord, make me alive again, recover me to again follow after your ways—a prayer of the spiritually mature who senses the battle between the flesh and the spirit but places greater emphasis upon the eternal over the temporal. The flesh always wants more and is never satisfied. The spirit hungers for the things of God. So make me dead to the stuff that dies with the using; make me alive to the ways of your Spirit, and make me more sensitive to keeping my eyes on the eternal. Quite a prayer . . . may it be yours today!

Jack Abeelen
Senior Pastor, Morning Star Christian Chapel, Whittier, CA

Stop Worrying

Casting all your care upon him;
for he careth for you.

1 PETER 5:7, KJV

A common malady among human beings is the tendency to worry about one's health, job, family, finances, relationships, etc. The fact of the matter is that you don't have to live with stress, worry, or any kind of thought process that produces mental agitation.

Paul says in Philippians 4:6 (Amplified), "Do not fret or have any anxiety about anything, but in every circumstance and in everything, by prayer and petition [definite requests], with thanksgiving, continue to make your wants known to God."

One of the biggest causes of agitated thinking is self-pity and self-concern. *How will I pay the bills? Why did this happen to me? What about my needs?* When you begin thinking about how bad it is for you, it only leads down the path to oppression and despair. You cannot allow self-pity to go unchecked in your life.

Instead of letting yourself take center stage, bring your worries to God and choose to focus on him. As you do, his peace that passes all understanding will surround you. God will walk you through each situation you face.

Mac Hammond
Senior Pastor, Living Word Christian Center, Brooklyn Park, MN

THE WORD OF GOD

Your word is a lamp for my feet,
a light on my path.

PSALM 119:105, NIV

God gave his Word to humanity—as a lamp to their path and a light to their feet. If you want guidance through this dark world, then love, trust, and read the Bible daily. If you want to stay in darkness, don't love it, don't trust it, and don't read it. It's your life. What you do with it is up to you.

I have been reading the Scriptures every day, without failure, for nearly forty years, and I have never found a mistake in the Word of God. The mistakes that people think they find are their own mistakes.

So it doesn't concern me as to why or how the New Testament historically came together. It has proven itself to be God's Word. He inspired it, he has preserved it, and it's supernaturally axiomatic. But if the Bible was banned and completely removed from the Earth, it would have no bearing on my salvation at all, because the Bible is just the instruction book of the reality of salvation. It instructs on how to find everlasting life. That life is alone in Jesus Christ, and nothing can separate me from him. Not even death.

Ray Comfort
Founder and CEO, Living Waters / The Way of the Master

Drawing Close

*Let us draw near to God with a sincere heart and
with the full assurance that faith brings.*

HEBREWS 10:22A, NIV

When I was a young father and my son was just six months old, I would spend time with him just staring at him and spoon-feeding him carrot puree. Those were meaningful times between him and me! But now that he is nine years old, spending time with him looks quite different—kicking a soccer ball out in the yard, sitting and answering as many "Why is the sky blue?" questions as I can handle, and laughing about the noises of various bodily functions. The form changes over time, but the goal is the same: a close relationship with my son.

God wants us to have a close relationship with him. It says in Hebrews 10:22, "Let us draw near to God with a sincere heart and with the full assurance of faith." Over time, the way in which we do that might change, but the goal is always the same: a close relationship with God. To effectively live out your identity as a Christ-follower, you will need to actively cultivate a life of intimacy with God. For there to be real intimacy with God, there must be real trust, radical transparency, and regular time together. Take this moment now to draw close to God and spend that time with him.

John V. Hansen
Lead Pastor, Centerpoint Church, Murrieta, CA

WHAT STIRS YOU?

Love the LORD your God with all your heart and
with all your soul and with all your strength.

DEUTERONOMY 6:5, NIV

I have often wondered what would make a young boy go up against someone who is so much larger and trained in battle than he is. Did David not see the odds were stacked against him, and things really did not look favorable? However, when great things happen in this world, the odds never really look good. Why do some people rise to the challenge of attempting something that seems impossible? I think the story of David sheds some light on this. Look at what Scripture captures: "David asked the men standing near him, 'What will be done for the man who kills this Philistine and removes this disgrace from Israel? Who is this uncircumcised Philistine that he should defy the armies of the living God?'" (1 Samuel 17:26).

Goliath flipped a switch inside David that he had to do something about. He crossed the line, and David, in spite of all of the obstacles, had to respond. A few years ago Bill Hybels wrote a great book, *Holy Discontent*. Hybels surmised that nothing great ever happens until we have had enough of something and we have to do something about it! David had enough, and Goliath paid the price.

What stirs you up? What causes you to lay awake at night? I hope that whatever that giant is that stirs you will cause you to do great things!

Mike Linch
Senior Pastor, NorthStar Church, Kennesaw, GA

363

RADICAL LOVE

"Love your neighbor and hate your enemy."
But I tell you, love your enemies and pray for those
who persecute you, that you may be children
of your Father in heaven. . . .

MATTHEW 5:43–45, NIV

*J*esus's revolutionary and radical message was that we can only find true peace, wholeness, and forgiveness when we embrace a love-based relationship with God, others, and even our enemies.

I don't know about you, but I find it sometimes difficult to love family, friends, and others who get on my nerves day after day. These are the times that we need to confess our weakness to our Lord and Savior to find the strength to treat others the way that we want to be treated.

Jesus said, "If you are kind only to your friends, how are you different from anyone else? Even pagans do that" (Matthew 5:47, NLT). Let's be honest: Are you consistently loving to those who bother you the most? Are you able to show unconditional love to the agitators in your life?

Remember Jesus meant what he said when he proclaimed, "Whatever you did for one of the least of these brothers and sisters of mine, you did it for me" (Matthew 25:40). When you think about it, are not our enemies one of the least of these?

Love boldly, love unconditionally . . . radical love!

Steve M. Woods
Chairman, Board of Directors
www.WoodsMasteryLearningFoundation.org

A LIFE WELL SPENT

*Do not store up for yourselves treasures on earth, where
moth and rust destroy, and where thieves break in and steal.
But store up for yourselves treasures in heaven, where
neither moth nor rust destroys, and where
thieves do not break in or steal.*

MATTHEW 6:19–20, NKJV

London is renowned for its famous burial site at Westminster Abbey. Anybody who was anybody in England was buried there. But of all the ornate tombs and monuments I found housed in that building, none of them moved me like the tomb I found in a parking lot behind the Cathedral of St. Giles. There was no memorial or limestone statue—just a strip of yellow paint on parking space 23.

It was the tomb of John Knox—the brave Scottish preacher who had led the Reformation in Scotland. While Charles Darwin's bones are lauded over every year by anxious tourists inside the Abbey, John Knox's bones are driven over out in a parking lot.

But Knox doesn't care. He heeded Christ's words in Matthew 6:19–20 to store up treasures in heaven, and now he is experiencing an eternal memorial for a life well spent.

Will you do the same? A life of godliness may not earn you a "well done" from thousands of admirers . . . but it will earn you a "well done" from the only admirer who really matters.

God.

Dr. Stephen Davey
Senior Pastor, Colonial Baptist Church, Cary, NC

Permissions

The Scriptures in *Wisdom for Everyday Living* were taken from the following sources:

Quotations marked (ASV) are taken from the American Standard Version. (Public Domain.)

Quotations marked (AMPLIFIED) are taken from the Amplified® Bible, Copyright © 1954, 1958, 1962, 1964, 1965, 1987 by The Lockman Foundation. Used by permission. (www.Lockman.org).

Quotations marked (CEB) are taken from the Common English Bible © 2011 Common English Bible.

Quotations marked (ESV) are taken from The Holy Bible, English Standard Version® (ESV®), Copyright © 2001 by Crossway, a publishing ministry of Good News Publishers. All rights reserved. ESV Text Edition: 2007.

Quotations marked (HCSB) are taken from the Holman Christian Standard Bible®, Copyright © 1999, 2000, 2002, 2003 by Holman Bible Publishers. Used by permission. Holman Christian Standard Bible®, Holman CSB®, and HCSB® are federally registered trademarks of Holman Bible Publishers.

Quotations marked (KJV) are taken from The King James Version of the Bible (Public Domain.)

THE MESSAGE. Copyright © by Eugene H. Peterson 1993, 2002. Used by permission of NavPress Publishing Group.

Quotations marked (NKJV) are taken from the New King James Version,® Copyright © 1982 by Thomas Nelson, Inc. Used by permission. All rights reserved.

Quotations marked (NASB) are taken from the New American Standard Bible®, Copyright © 1960, 1962, 1963, 1968, 1971, 1972, 1973,1975, 1977, 1995 by The Lockman Foundation. Used by permission. (www.Lockman.org.)

Quotations designated (NET) are from the NET Bible,® Copyright ©1996–2006 by Biblical Studies Press, L.L.C. http://netbible.com All rights reserved. Scripture quoted by permission.

Quotations marked (NIV) are taken from The Holy Bible, New International Version®, NIV,® Copyright © 1973, 1978, 1984, 2011 by Biblica, Inc.™ Used by permission. All rights reserved worldwide. www.zondervan.com.

Quotations marked (NIV84) are taken from The New International Version 84. The Holy Bible, New International Version®, NIV,® Copyright © 1973, 1978, 1984, 2011 by Biblica, Inc.™ Used by permission. All rights reserved worldwide. www.zondervan.com.

Quotations marked (NLT) are taken from The Holy Bible, New Living Translation, Copyright 1996, 2004, 2007 by Tyndale House Foundation. Used by permission of Tyndale House Publishers, Inc., Carol Stream, Illinois 60188. All rights reserved.

Quotations marked (RSVB) are taken from The Revised Standard Version of the Bible, Copyright © 1946, 1952, and 1971 National Council of the Churches of Christ in the United States of America. Used by permission. All rights reserved.

Quotations marked (NRSVB) are taken from The New Revised Standard Version Bible, Copyright © 1989 National Council of the Churches of Christ in the United States of America. Used by permission. All rights reserved.

Scripture quotations marked (PHILLIPS) are taken from The New Testament in Modern English, Copyright ©1958, 1959, 1960 J. B. Phillips and 1947, 1952, 1955, 1957 The Macmillan Company, New York. Used by permission. All rights reserved.

About the Author

$\mathcal{S}$teve M. Woods is the Chairman of Woods Mastery Learning Foundation, Inc. His vision is to support students and schools that promote Christian family values. Woods has a master's degree in Business Administration from the University of Phoenix and a bachelor's degree in Christian Education from Biola University. Steve has shared his passion for God with hundreds of young people during his fifteen years in youth ministries. Woods is a gifted author, evangelist, and speaker. Visit: woodsmasterylearningfoundation.org.

About the Charity

$\mathcal{T}$he Woods Mastery Learning Foundation's mission is to support Christian schools, colleges, and universities by providing scholarships and grants to Christian students and schools in need of assistance. We believe a solid Christian education is essential for the promotion of Christian/Judean values that our country was founded on by our forefathers. Visit: woodsmasterylearningfoundation.org.